ROUTLEDGE LIBRARY EDITIONS: 19TH CENTURY RELIGION

Volume 7

THE AFRICAN AMERICAN CHURCH IN BIRMINGHAM, ALABAMA, 1815–1963

THE AFRICAN AMERICAN CHURCH IN BIRMINGHAM, ALABAMA, 1815–1963

A Shelter in the Storm

WILSON FALLIN, JR.

LONDON AND NEW YORK

First published in 1997 by Garland Publishing, Inc.

This edition first published in 2018
by Routledge
2 Park Square, Milton Park, Abingdon, Oxon OX14 4RN

and by Routledge
711 Third Avenue, New York, NY 10017

Routledge is an imprint of the Taylor & Francis Group, an informa business

© 1997 Wilson Fallin, Jr.

All rights reserved. No part of this book may be reprinted or reproduced or utilised in any form or by any electronic, mechanical, or other means, now known or hereafter invented, including photocopying and recording, or in any information storage or retrieval system, without permission in writing from the publishers.

Trademark notice: Product or corporate names may be trademarks or registered trademarks, and are used only for identification and explanation without intent to infringe.

British Library Cataloguing in Publication Data
A catalogue record for this book is available from the British Library

ISBN: 978-1-138-06800-1 (Set)
ISBN: 978-1-315-10089-0 (Set) (ebk)
ISBN: 978-1-138-07056-1 (Volume 7) (hbk)
ISBN: 978-1-138-07067-7 (Volume 7) (pbk)
ISBN: 978-1-315-11497-2 (Volume 7) (ebk)

Publisher's Note
The publisher has gone to great lengths to ensure the quality of this reprint but points out that some imperfections in the original copies may be apparent.

Disclaimer
The publisher has made every effort to trace copyright holders and would welcome correspondence from those they have been unable to trace.

THE AFRICAN AMERICAN CHURCH IN BIRMINGHAM, ALABAMA, 1815–1963

A Shelter in the Storm

WILSON FALLIN, JR.

Copyright © 1997 Wilson Fallin, Jr.
All rights reserved

Library of Congress Cataloging-in-Publication Data

Fallin, Wilson, 1942–
    The African American church in Birmingham, Alabama, 1815–1963 : a shelter in the storm / Wilson Fallin, Jr.
        p.   cm. — (Studies in African American history and culture)
    Originally presented as the author's thesis (doctoral)—University of Alabama, 1995.
    Includes bibliographical references and index.
    ISBN 0-8153-2883-4 (alk. paper)
    1. Afro-American churches—Alabama—Birmingham. 2. Afro-Americans—Alabama—Birmingham—Religion. 3. Birmingham (Ala.)—Church history. I. Title. II. Series.
BR563.N4F27 1997
277.61'78108'08996073—dc21   97-10603

Manufactured in the United States of America

I dedicate this book to my dear wife, Barbara, my children, and my parents. Without their patience and love it would not have been possible.

Contents

Preface		ix
Introduction		xi
Chapter I	Slavery, Religion, and African American Churches	3
Chapter II	Migration and the Formation of African American Churches in the New South City of Birmingham	19
Chapter III	Expansion and African American Church Life	37
Chapter IV	Leadership, Institution Building and the African American Church in Birmingham	55
Chapter V	The African American Church Between the World Wars: Continuity and Preservation	77
Chapter VI	The African American Church Between the World Wars: Communism and New Religious Responses	101
Chapter VII	Rising Militancy and the African American Church From World War II to the Civil Rights Movement	123
Chapter VIII	The African American Church and the Civil Rights Movement	141
Conclusion		163
Notes		165
Bibliography		195
Index		213

Preface

In 1963, the Civil Rights movement reached a climax in Birmingham, Alabama. Several journalists covering the events focused on the importance of the African American church for providing the spiritual culture, charismatic leadership, and organization that made the movement possible. However, well before the civil rights movement, the church was the cornerstone institution in the African American community in Birmingham, providing not only worship but also social, economic, political, and educational needs. So important was the church that it is difficult to imagine the African American community without it. This book is a study of the African American church in Birmingham beginning with the days of slavery in pioneer Jones Valley through the civil rights movement in the city.

This study would not have been possible without the support, assistance, and encouragement of many persons. First and foremost, I must acknowledge the role of my major professor, Robert J. Norrell, who suggested the topic and directed it. His criticism, prodding, and encouragement were indispensable in getting me to the end of this long project.

I am also indebted to Justin Fuller, my friend and mentor. It was professor Fuller who inspired me to engage in graduate studies and who constantly encouraged me. As the former chair of the department of social sciences at the University of Montevallo, he provided me with the flexible teaching schedule that allowed adequate time for research. My other colleagues in the history department were most encouraging. Professor Ruth Truss took time from her busy schedule to read portions of the manuscript and made helpful suggestions.

A number of persons assisted me in the research, most of which was done in the Southern History Section and the Department of Archives at the Birmingham Public Library. Several staff persons, including Anne Knight, Yvonne Crumpler, Diane Gregg, Francine Cooper, Elizabeth Wilauer, and Delores Jones, assisted me in many ways as did archivists Marvin Y. Whiting, Don Veasey, Jim Murray, and Jim Baggett. On my many visits, Dr. Whiting listened to my ideas and directed me to the proper sources.

The love and support of my family made this project possible and bearable. Special thanks to my wife, Barbara, children, and parents for their support and encouragement. There are others who are not named here but none are forgotten. Thank you all.

Introduction

Historians agree that the African American church has played a vital role in African American life in the United States. Primarily a religious institution but much more because of the restrictions imposed on African Americans, the African American church provided many functions. A refuge in a hostile world, a promoter of business, a sponsor of education, a dispenser of benevolence, the church has also been the major preserver of African American culture. In the 1950s and 1960s the African American church and its pastors led the civil rights movement that destroyed legal segregation in the United States.

Through the years, a few scholars from various disciplines have attempted general studies of the African American church. Among sociologists, W.E.B. DuBois and his Atlanta University students examined the church in 1903, Benjamin Mays and Joseph Nicholson in 1933, and E. Franklin Frazier in 1955. Among historians, the pioneer work was by Carter G. Woodson in 1921. More recently C. Eric Lincoln and Lawrence H. Mamiya in 1990 wrote a general study. Woodson's book lacked the benefit of modern scholarship and the recent study by Lincoln and Mamiya tended to be more thematic than a historical analysis. Other studies have been denominational histories, monographs on particular subjects, or biographies of significant personalities. A comprehensive historical study of the African American church remains unwritten.

One major reason for the lack of a comprehensive study has been the lack of local historical studies. Local studies are essential, providing the building blocks for a comprehensive history. Except for a few articles, the most ambitious attempt has been David Tucker's book, *Black Pastors and Leaders: Memphis, 1819-1972*. Tucker's book, however, focuses primarily on leadership and does not discuss other aspects of the African American church in Memphis.

This study attempts to fill a gap in the historiography of the African American church by analyzing the role and place of the African American church in one city, Birmingham, Alabama. It traces the roles and functions of the church from the arrival of African Americans as slaves in the early 1800s to 1963, the year that the civil rights movement reached a peak in the city.

African American religion and the church in Birmingham began with the coming of the first African American slaves to the area of Jones Valley,which today includes the city of Birmingham. These slaves developed a Christianity which was a merger of African and evangelical elements that gave them hope and security. After slavery these ex-slaves established the first African American churches in the area. When the city of Birmingham was founded, African Americans migrated in large numbers seeking economic opportunities. They found jobs, but they also encountered a caste system that segregated and oppressed them. Thus, as African Americans moved into Birmingham, they formed churches that served as a shelter in the midst of this racist storm. The African American church had been the source of comfort and strength in the rural South where they had lived. African Americans sought to satisfy the same needs through their churches in Birmingham.

The churches formed in Birmingham served many needs for these African American migrants. It was a spiritual community where they garnered hope, self-esteem, and worth. Through the churches African Americans organized secular institutions to meet their temporal needs. Pastors provided protest and leadership almost from the beginning of the African American immigration into the city. This protest role accelerated after World War II, reaching a peak in 1956 when a group of pastors, led by the Reverend Fred Shuttlesworth, formed the Alabama Christian Movement for Human Rights with the purpose of destroying segregation through direct action and legal means. This movement invited Martin Luther King, Jr., to the city in 1963, and King led massive demonstrations that culminated in greater rights for African Americans in Birmingham and the nation.

Several themes are dominant and appear throughout this study. African Americans in Birmingham developed and maintained a unique version of Christianity that sustained them in a hostile and racist society. This uniqueness had its origins in the religion of the slaves who migrated into the area in the early 1800s. Refusing to accept the religion of their masters, slaves in Jones Valley developed a Christianity that was a merger of African and evangelical elements. African American religion was highly emotional with much dancing, shouting, singing, and chanting preaching. Slaves emphasized Old Testament characters such as Moses and Joshua, whom God had used to deliver the Israelites from slavery. As God had delivered the Israelites, he would in time deliver them. Former sharecroppers from the rural South moved to Birmingham in large numbers with a similar religious orientation. This unique Christianity was the center and basis of their spiritual life. It gave hope and meaning in a city whose white population sought to restrict and dehumanize them. It was this unique Christianity, boosted by the emergence of gospel music, that sustained African Americans in the depression years of the 1930s when unemployment rates among them soared to 75 percent. During the 1950s and 1960s their religion motivated and sustained the Birmingham civil rights movement.

The church as the central institution in the African American community of Birmingham is clearly evident in this study. The rigid segregation that developed in the city relegated blacks to a separate and unequal status and denied them access to political and other secular institutions. The church provided not only spiritual solace but also a social environment in which African Americans could assemble and could cooperate to improve their lives. In the community, the church was the meeting place and social center. Through the church, African Americans built institutions such as schools, banks, insurance companies, and welfare organizations. African Americans in the city showed their loyalty to their churches by supporting them and, in many instances, building large and commodious buildings for worship.

This study also highlights the role of women, a role that has often been neglected in African American church history. This study shows their significance in the life of Birmingham's African American churches. Women made up the majority of the membership of all churches. In addition, women founded churches, and were the chief fundraisers, youth workers, and missionary leaders. The civil rights movement utilized women in roles similar to their roles in the church. Although the role of women was circumscribed in most mainline African American churches, there is no evidence that women openly objected to their traditional roles. The move of some women in the 1920s and 1930s to Pentecostal and Holiness churches where they became ministers and pastors seems to reflect that at least a small group of women wanted leadership positions beyond those allowed by tradition. These women appear to have moved to these churches without trying to pressure the mainline churches. In any case, it is clear that without women there would have been no African American churches in Birmingham.

The leadership of pastors is another major theme of this study. From the beginning of African American migration to Birmingham, pastors assumed a leadership role. They had a natural constituency through their church membership, were close to the people, and had an economic independence that most African Americans did not have. Their leadership was symbiotic in that they often represented the thinking of their congregations and took their cues from them. With the emergence of militancy which grew during World War II, pastors in Birmingham began to call for the immediate end of segregation. And this new militancy of pastors led to the formation of the civil rights movement in Birmingham.

What emerges in this study is the church as the backbone of the African American community in Birmingham. Truly African American in origin, it provided the spiritual cohesiveness and the secular institutions that sustained African Americans in the city. It is not surprising that the church would be the institution that would provide leadership through its pastors to destroy legal segregation in Birmingham.

The African American Church in Birmingham, Alabama, 1815–1963

I

Slavery, Religion, and African American Churches in Pioneer Jones Valley

Religion was important for the African American slaves who moved into the pioneer community of Jones Valley in the early 1800s. Attending camp meetings, the churches of their masters, or worshiping in their own settings, slaves in Jones Valley developed a unique Christianity that was a merger of traditional African and white evangelical religion. It provided them with hope, understanding, and security. Slave masters encouraged and sometimes forced slaves to become members of their churches. These churches disciplined slaves but allowed them no voice in the business of the church or the opportunity to worship in their own way. Wanting independence and the freedom to worship as they pleased, African American slaves after emancipation left the churches of their masters and formed their own churches with African American ministers serving as pastors. These churches became significant institutions for the freedmen of Jefferson County in the small agricultural communities where they lived.

African Americans first came to what includes today the city of Birmingham as slaves when the area was known as Jones Valley. They were brought by their slave masters who migrated from Tennessee, Georgia, and South Carolina. Many of these white settlers became familiar with Jones Valley because they fought with Andrew Jackson in the Creek War of 1813. After the war they moved with their families and slaves to the area that became Jefferson County in 1819, the same year that Alabama became a state.[1]

Most slaves in Jones Valley lived and worked on farms where there were only a few slaves. The relatively poor soil of the area was not conducive for large scale cotton plantations like those in the Alabama Black Belt that required large numbers of slaves. In 1860 only eight farmers in Jones Valley owned more than forty slaves. The largest slaveholder was Williamson Hawkins who owned 106 slaves and farmed on 2,000 acres five miles west of what is today downtown Birmingham. The few slaves that came to Jones Valley, only 2,649 by 1860, primarily worked side by side with their slave masters on small farms.[2]

These early settlers saw religion as essential to building a strong community for themselves and their slaves. Almost immediately after erecting houses in the valley, they formed churches. The churches were often rustic log cabins, and services were simple and emotional. Baptists, Methodists, and Cumberland Presbyterians formed the largest number of churches. In 1860 there were seventeen Baptist churches, fifteen Methodist churches, and four Cumberland Presbyterian churches in the county.[3]

Evangelism resulting from camp meetings and protracted revivals was the major reason for the success of these three denominations. Lasting for several days, camp meetings and revivals recruited members through conversion experiences. The services were very emotional; preaching and singing was done with wild excitement. The people jerked, danced, and sang. Some churches in Jones Valley, such as Bethlehem Methodist located in the western section of the county, and First Methodist Church of Tarrant, previously known as the Bethel Methodist Church, located in the southern section of Jefferson County, became leading centers for camp meetings. For weeks during the layby time, usually in late July and August after the cultivation of the crops but before harvest time, people came in wagons with their families and slaves with services held in brush arbors. The people usually lived in tents around the brush arbor where services took place.[4]

To distinguish their evangelistic meetings from the camp meetings of the Methodists, Baptists called their meetings protracted revivals. These meetings, usually held in churches, lasted for two or three weeks with a visiting minister preaching throughout the duration of the revival. Some Baptist churches, however, held camp meetings in the early days of the valley. The Canaan Baptist Church located in the western section of the county in the Jonesboro community was a center for camp meetings. One Baptist pastor and historian left an account of a camp meeting which occurred near the Canaan Baptist Church in 1831. He reported that in October twelve to fifteen families came in wagons, ox carts, by horseback, and on foot to participate in the meeting. The people built a brush arbor, spread their tents, and began preaching, praying, and singing. This revival started an evangelistic awakening in Jones Valley to such an extent that within twelve months nearly five hundred people received baptism in three or four churches, both whites and slaves.[5]

Observers of camp meetings noted the tremendous emotional outbursts that came from the slaves present at these meetings. Charles A. Johnson, in his study of camp meetings, reported that slave masters were encouraged to bring their slaves because of the belief that religion would make their servants obedient. African American participation was largely unplanned and spontaneous. Breaking away from whites, African Americans held their services on the same camp grounds. Praying, dancing, singing, and shouting were common features of these worship services. When an African American preacher was present, he would deliver a "hell fire" sermon designed to convict his hearers and lead to conversions and religious frenzy.[6]

Besides worshiping at camp meetings and protracted revivals, slave masters in Jones Valley made other provisions for the religion of their slaves that followed the pattern for slaves in Alabama. The rule seems to have been in Alabama and throughout the South that separate missions began where there were large numbers of African Americans. According to the minutes of the Annual Conference of the Methodist Church, South, of 1870, the Reverend W. H. Riley founded a Methodist mission called the Elyton Iron Works Colored Mission by 1865. Separate missions, such as the Elyton Iron Works Colored Mission, began as early as 1827 by Charles Capers, a Southern Methodist evangelist to slaves. In 1844, after the formation of the Methodist Church, South, separate missions increased. The Methodist Church, South, established these missions first on plantations, but as African Americans moved to cities and larger communities, the church founded African American missions in these areas so that by 1857 there were at least 76 African American Methodist missions in Alabama.[7]

At least two plantation slave churches existed in Jones Valley. One of these was what is called today the Mt. Joy Baptist Church of Trussville, that traces its beginnings to 1857. Prior to that time, the African American slaves in the area were members of the white Baptist church where they sat in the rear of the church during the morning worship service. They could not participate in the worship or vote on church matters. In the afternoon, the pastor would preach to them in the church. In 1857 a group of slave members received permission to leave the church and hold services in a separate building. These slaves held services in a log cabin on a plantation owned by Sam Latham. Because most of the members were Sam Latham's slaves and the church was on his plantation, the slaves called it "Latham's Baptist Church." The slaves worshiped on the Latham plantation, located three miles from Trussville, until after the Civil War.[8]

In the Oak Grove community of Jones Valley, Hewitt Ladd provided accommodations for his slaves to worship. Ladd operated on the theory that religion made better servants. His accommodations consisted of a building with seats and a pulpit. Other slaves from the community would often come and worship with his slaves. Ladd observed in these sessions that slaves would worship "in their accustomed way," which meant that he noted the difference between the religion of the African American slaves and whites in the area.[9]

Although religion was emotional for almost all southern Christians, there were unique features to slave religion that Ladd and other observers of slaves in Jones Valley recognized. One observer of pioneer Jones Valley recalled that slaves in worship would get happy and shout and mourn all night. At baptism services many slaves became so emotional they would jump in the creek and would have to be saved from drowning. Another observer recalled that on some occasions slaves would assemble at a tree and worship in a way characterized by emotionalism, with one of the self-styled slave preachers in the community leading them in the worship. Trees were important places for slave worship because according to traditional African religion the spirits of the deceased resided in them. White slave owners, such as William Mims, viewed slaves, and their religion especially, as simply superstitious.[10]

Evidence for the uniqueness of slave religion has also come from historians, slave masters, and travelers throughout the South. The historian Eugene Genovese, after examining private letters and memoirs of southern plantation owners, found that many whites "never doubted that their slave's Christianity contained a big dose of African belief." In his travels through the South, Frederick Olmstead, a northern journalist, found a strange religion practiced by slaves and the general recognition of it by whites. In New Orleans he observed among African Americans what was for him at the time the strangest worship service that he had ever seen. The worship consisted of running, dancing, screaming, and shouting. He reported that a South Carolina rice planter complained to him that his slaves petitioned to have the seats removed from the chapel where they worshiped because when they prayed they needed room for dancing and leaping.[11]

African American teachers and missionaries who came into the South immediately after emancipation noted the peculiar nature of

African American slave religion, with some being appalled by what they saw. Charlotte Forten, a teacher from Philadelphia, called the religious gatherings on the Sea Islands of South Carolina "barbarous." William Wells Brown, a former slave and abolitionist, noted the bizarre emotionalism that characterized many churches. For him this was a cause of the moral and social degradation of the freedman. Daniel Payne, bishop of the AME Church, described what he saw as ignorant and intemperate. For him and other Northerners such actions were a result of the debilitating effects of slavery and needed to be discarded.[12]

In explaining the uniqueness of African American religion, scholars have suggested that it was a synthesis of evangelical Protestant Christianity and African traditional religion. From evangelical Christianity the slaves accepted the God of the Bible, Jesus as savior, and the emotional conversion experience that was an integral part of camp meetings. From their African past they retained spirit possession, the ring dance and shout, and ritual sacrifice. Combining elements of both African and American evangelical religion, the slave's religion was different. African American slaves tended to form rings where they would shout and dance. The ring symbolized the eternal cycle of birth, death, and reincarnation that were a part of traditional African ceremonies. The hand clapping, foot-tapping, rhythmic preaching, and the antiphonal singing and dancing of the slaves showed vestiges of their African past. In the camp meetings and their own religious services, slaves synthesized the African custom of spirit possession with the Christian doctrine of the Holy Spirit. The result was an unbridled emotionalism that seemed strange and mysterious to most whites and northern blacks.[13]

The experience of conversion shows the merger of African and evangelical elements and how slaves welded Christian ideas with African religious traditions. The evangelical Christian doctrine of conversion, in which sinners entered into a state of the recognition of their sinfulness and sought atonement, reminded many slaves of African initiation rites, including initiation into the service of the spirits. Similarly, growing ill and loss of appetite which many seekers experienced was a clear warning from the spirits to change their ways or a call from a god to undergo initiation into their service. Many African American slaves described their experience of conversion in terms of the evangelical Christian and West African world view of death and rebirth. For others, there was more emphasis on the traditional African notion of spirit possession. For these slaves the act of conversion began with the feeling of being estranged from the spirit world. God or his surrogate, commonly an angel, then spoke to the seeker in a manner similar to the way the gods of the spirit world spoke to their African ancestors. The seeker entered the spirit world where he became a new person, both physically and spiritually. The response was dramatic and emotional, with the new convert lapsing into trance-like behavior, uncontrollable and body wrenching contortions, singing and dancing. These emotional features were an integral part of African religion.[14]

Slave religion also differed from white Christianity in its broader Biblical and theological emphases. While for southern whites and African Americans religion was a personal relationship between the believer and Christ that resulted in salvation and a new life, the African American slave's desire for freedom also caused them to identify with the slavery of the Israelites. Just as Moses had delivered his people, God would in due course deliver them. The exodus was told repeatedly in both sermons and songs and was expressive of the theme of deliverance and liberation that was important in African American slave religion. There was a close relationship between Moses and Christ. Slaves often collapsed the two into a single, powerful figure who could destroy the shackles of slavery. In other cases, Moses was the deliverer who prefigured Christ, the perfect deliverer.[15]

The spirituals were one of the most explicit expressions of the uniqueness of African American slave religion. Making no distinction between the sacred and the secular, the African American slaves in these songs expressed their desire for freedom and the assurance that God would deliver him. There was the constant identity with the children of Israel and their deliverance. "My Lord Delivered Daniel," "Go Down Moses into Egypt Land, Tell Old Pharaoh to let My People Go," and "Steal Away" were but a few spirituals that expressed the themes of deliverance and liberation. In addition, the spirituals showed the impact of traditional African survivals. Slaves often sang the spirituals in a call and response manner, some shouted them, and still others danced them. All of these reflected modes found in traditional African religions.[16]

The slave's religion provided them with a sense of community and group solidarity. Going to camp meetings, attending their master's church, or worshiping in plantation church settings slaves met each other and discussed common concerns. Although able to obtain passes to visit other slaves from time to time, religious settings provided an opportunity to meet regularly. A part of the religious meetings were social activities such as picnics and dinners on the grounds, that were also engaged in by the slaves. Worshiping in their own settings not only provided slaves with an opportunity to socialize but also to exercise responsibility and develop leadership. In these worship services slaves also garnered support from each other and gained strength to endure slavery.[17]

Religion was most of all the means by which African American understood their own experience as slaves. Although some antebellum journals and writings in Jones Valley pictured slavery in paternalistic terms, it was also a cataclysmic experience. Kidnapped from their homeland, brought to an alien environment, and forced into servitude, slaves survived through the comfort of their religion. Primarily through the singing of spirituals and the preaching of slave exhorters, they conceived their servile state as merely a temporary state through which they would receive greater reward. If like Daniel and the three Hebrew boys they remained faithful, God would vindicate and reward them with even greater blessings than their masters. For the slaves, God was no respecter of persons but was just and merciful. In addition to liberation, such themes as equality, worth, and ultimate victory were prevalent themes in slave religion.[18]

Although there were a few plantation churches where slaves were relatively free to exercise their unique form of worship, most African Americans in Jones Valley worshiped in white churches where their style of worship and activities were circumscribed. A few pioneer Baptist Churches of Jones Valley have included bits and pieces of information in their compiled church histories concerning slaves as members in their churches. For example, the Canaan Baptist Church had 37 slave members in 1837. African American slaves worshiped in the balcony and were subject to the same discipline as whites, which meant they received public reprimands or exclusion from membership because of moral offenses. An African American slave named Dinah was a founding member of the Ruhama Baptist Church in 1818. Ruhama disciplined its slave members for stealing, adultery, drunkenness, and irregular church attendance. By 1868 there were 37 African American members of the Ruhama Church. The Mt. Hebron Baptist Church of Leeds voted in 1828 to construct an annex for its African American members. The church disciplined both slaves and white members, with one slave being excluded from the church in 1836 for attempting to run away from his master. The first African American slaves became members of the Salem Baptist Church in 1843, where their owners were members. Whites worshiped in the front and slaves in the back, separated by a rail. The Cahawba Baptist Church of Trussville accepted slaves into their church's membership during the antebellum period. By 1860 there were approximately 200 slaves owned by Cahawba Baptist Church members with John Truss, owner of 31 slaves, the largest slave owner in the Cahawba Baptist membership.[19]

Methodist churches in Jones Valley were similar to the Baptists in their treatment of slaves. In 1811 a slave preacher named Adam assisted James Tarrant in the construction of the Bethlehem Methodist Church, located in western Jefferson County, one of the oldest Methodist churches in the area. Adam became a member of the Bethlehem Church and on some occasions was allowed to preach to the congregation. The Pleasant Hill Methodist Church also had slaves as members. The church made provisions for them by providing seats in the back of the sanctuary and subjecting them to the same discipline as white members. By 1832 the Jones Valley Circuit of the Methodist Church had 780 white and 116 slave members.[20]

Besides Baptist and Methodist churches, at least one other church in Jones Valley left records of their slave members, the St. John Episcopal Church. Founded in 1850 in Elyton, the church had no regular pastor during the antebellum period and had to depend upon bishops and visiting ministers to hold worship services. Church records reveal that in 1856 John, the slave of Sam Earlie, and Frank, the slave of W. Tankersly, were members. As late as 1871, St. John listed African Americans on the church's membership roll. This pattern appears to have continued until the white members of St. John organized the St. Mark Episcopal Church for its African Americans members in 1891.[21]

Under the leveling influence of evangelical revivalism, and because of their unusual preaching ability and moral life, a few slave preachers preached to both slaves and whites. In addition to Adam of the Bethlehem Methodist Church, another such slave preacher was a man named Job. Job was brought from Africa to Charleston, South Carolina, in 1806 and sold to Edward Davis. While in South Carolina, Job learned to read and write, became a Christian, and in 1818 received his license to preach. Moving to Jones Valley with his slave owner in 1822, he became a member of the Bethel Baptist Church, located ten miles from Canaan[21] Baptist Church in Jonesboro. He left this church with twenty other members and became one of the founding members of the Roupe's Valley Baptist Church in Tuscaloosa County. Later Job's master moved to Pickens County, in the western part of the state. There Job became a member of the Pilgrim Rest Baptist Church. He died on November 17, 1835.[22]

Job is most remembered as a partner with white Baptist pioneer Hosea Holcombe. Job and Holcombe traveled as a team and preached together at revivals and camp meetings. Both whites and African Americans highly respected Job and considered him to be a preacher with great power. Holcombe in commenting upon the life and work of Job said, "Few better preachers were to be found in Alabama in those days than Job. He lived the Christian and died the saint. He was generally loved and respected by all who knew him." One of the leading Methodists in the county, Bayliss E. Grace, recalled that Job was pious, devout, eloquent, and "those who came to scoff, remained to pray."[23]

Despite the generous treatment of Job by whites, generally the churches in Jones Valley treated slaves as subordinates. The pattern that emerges reveals white churches accepting African American slaves as members and allowing them to worship in the same buildings. These churches disciplined African Americans along with their white members. African Americans, however, never had any responsible voice in church matters. One study of white Baptists and slavery in Alabama found no evidence of any white churches having an African American deacon, moderator, or correspondent. Nor was an African American a delegate to a denominational meeting or state convention. While many white slave owners showed concern for the spiritual welfare of their slaves, there was no attempt to place slaves in positions of equality in the churches in Jones Valley during the slavery period.[24]

The Civil War and Reconstruction disrupted life in Jones Valley and severed the traditional relationship between masters and slaves. Because of the small number of slaves, Jefferson County was not strongly for secession. Many in the county felt that slavery was a poor reason for disunion. When the Civil War began, however, most citizens of the county were loyal to the South. Many of the county's young men went immediately to Shelby County or Tuscaloosa to join an Alabama regiment. On May 10, 1862, William Jemison Mims formed Company G of the Forty-third Alabama Infantry. Only women, children, and older men were left in Jones Valley. The county suffered during the Civil War years. Women were forced to take over the responsibility of operating small farms and plantations. Famine and drought added to the suffering, especially the drought of 1862 that reduced the corn crop and reduced the supply of farm animals. Hundreds of families had no meat and many families of soldiers were left destitute. Few men remained with the skill to make repairs, and there were no spare parts for farm machinery.[25]

The most devastating event in the county during the Civil War was the Union Army's invasion in April 1865. Under the direction of General James Wilson, Union troops came through Elyton and Jones Valley on their way to Selma, Montgomery, and Tuscaloosa. Although Jones Valley was not the main target, the few days spent in the area caused considerable damage and destruction. Wilson's troops burned Lamson's Flower Mill on their way into Elyton, and the Oxmoor and Irondale furnaces as they were leaving. On his return to Elyton after burning the University of Alabama, Brigadier General John Croxton burned the Mt. Pinson Iron Works and a nitre works. Although the army was given orders by Wilson not to pillage and confiscate private property, such actions took place at Elyton. The Union army confiscated the best horses, food, and whatever they wanted. They also pillaged plantations and small farms owned by such prominent citizens as William Mims and James Greene. In some instances, Union troops burned houses. In addition to the Wilson's raids, there was significant loss of life among Jones Valley soldiers in the Confederate Army. Of the 100 men who left Mt. Pinson in 1861 to serve in the Confederate Army, only nine were still alive after the war. The war produced poverty and sadness in Jefferson County.[26]

Reconstruction, which immediately followed the Civil War in Jones Valley, was similar to the general pattern of the rest of Alabama without the extreme violence and turmoil of Black Belt Alabama. For the first time African Americans voted in the county. In 1867 there were 1,366 whites and 430 African Americans registered to vote. Largely because of African American voting, Republican officials ruled the county. Whites saw African Americans as inferior and under the influence of alien and irresponsible white politicians who were against the white people of the South. Most whites in Jones Valley believed some form of control was necessary. The Ku Klux Klan became active in the county as a means of controlling African Americans and defiant whites. The most common means used by the Klan to keep African Americans in line were threats and beatings. According to Judge William Mudd of Elyton, the usual reasons for whipping African Americans were "bad conduct," "stealing cotton," and "being impudent," and "once for voting for the radical ticket."[27]

The immediate reaction to their new freedom by many African Americans was to move from place to place. Several who saw the Union soldiers as liberators and providers followed Wilson's troops to Montgomery and Selma. Some went to places like Tuscaloosa and Talladega seeking better education, medical care, and economic opportunity. Some of those who wandered to other cities soon returned to Jones Valley. Most remained in the county where they became tenants and, although they were physically free, they were still dependent on their former slave masters.[28]

For those African Americans who remained in Jones Valley, one of their first major acts of freedom was to leave the white churches and establish their own. Forming their own churches, like moving from place to place, was for the ex-slaves acting on the reality of their new freedom. They could now worship as they desired without being circumscribed or looked down on by whites. They could listen to and react to their own preachers in their own way: singing, dancing, and shouting. Their own churches gave them some measure of control over their own lives and an opportunity to develop pride and self-respect. With the old communal bonds that had existed in slavery being dissolved, these churches also provided the ex-slave with a caring community.[29]

The formation of African American churches followed several patterns in Alabama and throughout the South. In some cases, they left on their own immediately after the Civil War. Excited about their new freedom and confident of the future, these African Americans did not hesitate to strike out on their own and start churches. Their ministers formed some churches by their own initiative. In still others cases, they remained in white churches for a few years, usually with white encouragement. When it became clear to whites that the old arrangements were not possible, and to African Americans that whites had no desire to give them equality in the churches, one or both parties requested a separation. There was one case of near violence in Alabama. This occurred in Selma at the St. Phillips Street Baptist Church, now the First Baptist Church, when a group of African Americans who had worshiped in the church as slaves attempted to seize the building. The pastor, Rev. J. B. Hawthorne, gathered a few whites who armed themselves and soon ended the threat.[30]

Churches formed by African Americans in Jones Valley followed several of these patterns. Two churches formed in the western section of the county began when African Americans requested separation and received aid from whites. Shortly after the end of the Civil War, the newly freed African Americans in the white Canaan Baptist Church of Old Jonesboro requested their own church. Some white members of the

Canaan Church assisted them in building a frame building in the Jonesboro community. A white minister preached there a short time until they found an African American minister. These former slaves worshiped in Old Jonesboro until 1890 and then decided to purchase land and move their place of worship to the new industrial town of Bessemer. These African Americans called their new church Canaan Baptist Church.[31]

The founding of the St. Paul Christian Methodist Episcopal Church was similar to Canaan Baptist. Since its founding in 1818, African American slaves had worshiped with whites in a separate section of the Bethlehem Methodist Church. With the end of the Civil War, African Americans became dissatisfied with this separate section arrangement and formed several small circuits with a white minister serving as the circuit rider. In 1870 the Mt. Zion, New Hope, and Possum Valley circuits joined the Cedar Grove circuit to form to the St. Paul CME Church. Will McAdory gave them land in the Jonesboro area and helped them build a frame building. In 1887 St. Paul CME, like Canaan Baptist, moved to the new industrial city of Bessemer.[32]

Three churches began a few years after the Civil War on land donated by former slave masters. After the Civil War, African Americans in the Ruhama Baptist Church of present-day Birmingham, with the urging of white members, decided to remain as members of Ruhama. In 1868 thirty-seven of these African Americans with the consent of the white members withdrew and formed Mt. Zion Baptist. Obadiah Woods, formerly one of the largest slave owners in the area, gave the land for the church. African Americans in the community established a log cabin school behind the church, the first in the Zion City area offering African Americans a formal education.[33]

In 1867, according to a recently compiled church history, six former slaves who were farming on the Mims plantation in Powderly decided to have a church of their own where they and their children could worship as they desired. William Jemison Mims donated property on his plantation for the church to be built. He also gave land for a cemetery to be used by the members of the church. Not having an African American ordained minister in the area, a white minister came and assisted them in organizing the church. After much discussion they all agreed to name the church Mt. Pilgrim. The first building was a brush harbor which was built by the African American members.[34]

The First Baptist Church of Powderly had origins similar to the Mt. Pilgrim Baptist Church. During the Civil War several slaves on the

Mims plantation began to worship in an open field. After the war they begin to worship in a house. In the early 1870's they were given land by Williams Mims and erected a frame church building.[35]

At least one church in the county was an extension of a slave plantation church. During the Civil War, slaves in the Trussville area began worshiping in a log cabin provided by Sam Latham in 1857. After the Civil War, two African American brothers, William and Henry Talley, settled in Trussville and purchased land. In 1867 worship services began one-half mile southwest of Trussville on the land of William Talley. The Reverend Isom Talley became the first African American pastor. In 1868 Henry Talley donated land to the struggling church one mile north of Trussville. Members constructed a box frame building and adopted the name Mt. Joy Baptist Church.[36]

The Shady Grove Baptist Church of Oxmoor appears to have been the first African American church established in an industrial setting in the county. In 1862 John Milner and Francis Gilmer, two entrepreneurs from Southern Alabama, petitioned the Confederate government to build a railroad to Red Mountain and erect three furnaces and rolling mills. Returning to Oxmoor, Milner and Gilmer formed the Red Mountain Iron and Coal Company, which was destroyed by Union troops in 1865. In 1871 Daniel Pratt and Henry DeBardeleben purchased the facilities, and organized the Eureka Mining Company, with DeBardeleben as the first president. They rebuilt the furnaces and began to operate. African Americans were hired to work at the furnaces and mills. In the early 1870s the African American workers built a log cabin to use as a Baptist Church. This church became the Shady Grove Baptist Church of Oxmoor.[37]

Two churches in the eastern section of the county were the result of the initiative of an African American minister, the Reverend William Ware. Ware was born into slavery on the Ware plantation in East Lake, seven miles east of downtown Birmingham, on October 5, 1837. At the age of thirteen, he was baptized into the Union Baptist Church in 1856. Although limited in education, he was anxious to read the Bible and made strenuous efforts to attain a reading knowledge of the scriptures. Like the slave preachers throughout the South, Ware was a folksy preacher who delivered his sermons with imagination and power. He also lived a strong Christian and moral life. which endeared him to white leaders like the Reverend A. J. Waldrop, the white pastor of the Ruhama Baptist Church, who said of Ware that "We never had in Jefferson County a man of more stainless character." Because of his strong character and native ability, Ware was allowed to preach to both whites and African Americans. After emancipation, two white ministers ordained Ware to the ministry.[38]

After the war, Ware begin to form independent black churches for freedmen. In 1868 he built a small log cabin in Flat Ridge Valley and organized the Mt. Calvary Baptist Church. The church found a new location on Red Mountain in 1880 near the place of organization and erected a frame building, holding services there for several years. The church was also the location for a school until 1935 when a school for African Americans was erected in the Irondale community. The Mt. Pleasant Baptist Church of present-day Leeds sprang from the Mt. Calvary Baptist Church of Irondale and was also formed by William Ware. Ware and Taft Scott, an elderly member of the Mt. Calvary Baptist Church who lived in Leeds, saw the need for an African American church and began to hold services in the home of Taft Scott in 1870, which was a log cabin. Three years later the members built a frame building. Most of the churches in the Leeds area originated from the Mt. Pleasant Baptist Church.[39]

In addition to founding and pastoring the Mt. Calvary and Mt. Pleasant Baptist Churches, Ware pastored at least five other churches. Among these were the Canaan Baptist Church of Bessemer, the Mt. Joy Baptist Church of Trussville, and the Mt. Pilgrim Baptist Church of present-day Birmingham. In 1901 he was serving the Mt. Vernon Baptist Church and the Mt. Pilgrim Baptist Churches, both located in the city limits of Birmingham. During the years that he pastored the Mt. Pleasant Baptist Church, the church's compiled history reported that he walked from East Lake to Leeds in order to preach to the congregation. Ware was active in organizing fifteen churches during his long years in the ministry.[39] Because much of his ministry was done in his elderly years, Ware was known affectionately as "Father Ware."[40]

Ware was also one of the first denominational organizers among African Americans after the slavery period. In 1874 he helped organize the Mt. Pilgrim Baptist Association, the first African American Baptist Association in the county, and served as its first moderator. Because of Ware's leadership, the association had a membership of thirty-six churches in 1895. With his pastoral work, organizing, and denominational leadership, Ware did more to establish churches in Birmingham during this period than any other person. He also presaged the pioneer African American ministers who would move into Birmingham in the 1870's and 1880's to establish churches.[41]

Slavery, Religion, and African American Churches

Whether worshiping in camp meetings, plantation churches, or the churches of their masters, African Americans in Jones Valley developed their own version of Christianity which was a merger of African and evangelical features. This unique Christianity was the focus of life for the slaves. It was a source of hope, security, a means of meeting other slaves in the community, and most of all a way of viewing and understanding their own slave experience. Long desiring religious freedom and repelled by discrimination in white churches, African Americans after emancipation began to renounce their old religious connections and form their own churches. These churches chose their own African American ministers as pastors and with a great desire for education made these churches the location for at least two schools in the county. By the time that the city of Birmingham was founded in 1871, several churches already existed in the area and were important religious, educational, and social centers in the small rural African American communities of Jones Valley. With African American migration into the new city of Birmingham, migrants would establish many more churches.

II

Migration and the Formation of African American Churches in the New South City of Birmingham

The founding of Birmingham in 1871 and its emergence as an industrial center caused African Americans to migrate into the city seeking better economic opportunity. As African Americans moved into Birmingham, they found jobs but also a hard life in a hostile environment. Almost immediately they formed churches that mirrored those of the Alabama Black Belt and other parts of the rural South. The church had been the central institution in the community, providing support, comfort, and cooperation. The new migrants established churches everywhere they settled. They formed them in private homes, on vacant lots, and in storefronts. Most were Baptists, although several Methodist denominations established a significant number of churches. Some were the result of denominational missionaries and some white denominations established churches in the African American community. In addition, African American migrants also established churches in company villages, in the city area of Birmingham, and in industrial towns close to Birmingham.

The city of Birmingham was founded as the result of railroads and industrial development. The antebellum period of Jones Valley brought no industrial development to the area in spite of the report of the state geologist Michael Tuomey in 1850 that the area contained in close proximity the three elements necessary to produce iron: coal, iron ore, and limestone. The problem was that there were no railroads to transport these minerals to become manufactured into iron products, or to take finished products to markets. After the Civil War the Alabama Legislature of 1865-66 passed a law providing a state subsidy for railroads. Bonds and credit from the legislature made it possible for two different railroads to pass through Jones Valley with plans to intersect at Elyton: the Alabama and Chattanooga, and the North and South. Realizing where the railroads would cross and knowing the profits from land sales and industrial development, railroad and land speculators associated with the North and South Railroad organized the Elyton Land Company with $200,000 capital and bought 4,150 acres of farm land east of Elyton. John T. Milner, Chief Engineer of the North and South Railroad an early proponent of the area, cooperated to lay out the new town. These speculators completed the railroads and founded Birmingham in 1871.[1]

Before the end of 1873, however, the double blows of depression and disease shattered Birmingham's progress. A cholera epidemic in the summer, which killed 128 persons, was followed immediately by the economic panic of 1873. After five years of stagnation, Birmingham's economy began to improve in 1878 with the successful demonstration that coke made from local coal could be used to make iron cheaply. An economic boom began in Birmingham. The population increased from 3,086 in 1880 to 26,178 in 1890. These persons came to Birmingham because of a vibrant economy based upon mining, 25 blast furnaces, and 437 real estate offices.[2]

Among those migrating into Birmingham in large numbers were African Americans. Most came from the Black Belt of southern Alabama to escape the horrible life there where they lived and worked in a tenancy system which could be as exploitative as slavery. After obtaining freedom, African Americans in Alabama and the South had hoped that the federal government would provide them with their own land. With such hopes unrealized, African Americans were forced to return to the plantations and become tenant farmers. Most became sharecroppers. They preferred this arrangement to the gang system that reminded them of slavery.[3]

In the sharecropping system, the plantation owner equipped the sharecropper with mules, seed, fertilizer, tools, land, food, and a house in exchange for the labor of the sharecropper and his family. Often the sharecropper did not earn a profit but stayed in debt to the landlord, a circumstance that was repeated year after year.[4]

African American life was hard in all respects. Most lived in one or two-room cabins with leaky roofs, sustained barely by a monotonous diet that consisted primarily of salt pork, molasses, turnip greens, and coffee. Because of poor living conditions, African Americans were most susceptible to diseases such as tuberculosis, pellagra, pneumonia, and diphtheria. Despite the presence of a few private schools and some feeble efforts to provide public schools, educational opportunities for

African Americans were abysmally poor. Whites had little regard for African American life and especially during the times of economic depression blacks were easy targets for lynching. In addition, life was often boring, especially for the young who wanted more social activities.[5]

The main source of comfort, support, and cooperation for African Americans in the Black Belt was the church. It was the one institution that African Americans controlled. Because of its special place in the African American community, the church filled many needs. The church was first and foremost the worship center. Services consisted primarily of praying, singing, and preaching, with spirituals and meter hymns constituting the music. As time moved on, churches began to have choirs, but music remained a church-wide activity. Sermons were emotional and designed to inform, as well as move the worshiper through emotions. The strong emotions in the worship were a result of the unique worship which African Americans developed during slavery, and also a response to the harsh conditions under which they lived and worked. African American ministers frequently preached on Old Testament characters like Moses and Joshua. They also emphasized the return of Jesus when there would no longer be any cold, hunger, and pain, but food, beauty, and sunshine for all. There was a strong element of joy and happiness noted by observers of African American religion in the Black Belt.[6]

Besides its religious and worship functions, Black Belt churches provided a social function. With families and neighbors scattered over such a wide area, it was the institution that held together their sub-communities and families. By singing together, eating together, praying together, and engaging in other forms of fellowship at their churches a sense of community feeling was maintained. As a social institution the African American church afforded a large measure of relaxation and recreation from the physical stress of life by such activities as church suppers, picnics, and carnivals. Special church activities such as weddings, funerals, revivals, and baptizings served as social and religious functions. Revivals were an especially joyous time, looked forward to with great anticipation. Everything would come to a halt in the local community and there would be services two or three times a day. These revivals or camp meetings took place in late summer or early fall after the cultivation of crops, but before harvesting. The baptismal service came immediately after the revival accompanied by much shouting and rejoicing. Baptismal candidates generally wore white robes with the services taking place in a creek or river. It was perhaps the most picturesque of all the church functions.[7]

The church was often the educational center of the community. After the Civil War, African American churches provided a major supplement to the work of the Freedmen's Bureau and the northern benevolent societies like the American Missionary Association. Churches often housed the schools operated by these agencies. Sometimes, pastors doubled as teachers in these schools, especially before the establishment of public schools for African Americans. Some African American churches established their own schools. Baptist associations and Methodist conferences established several academies. In 1878 the Alabama Baptist State Convention founded Selma University, followed in 1889 by the African Methodist Episcopal Church of Alabama which established Daniel Payne College also in the city of Selma. In 1898 the AME Zion Church of Alabama established Lomax Hannon College in Greenville, Alabama.[8]

The key figure in the church was the pastor. Most were literate but had no formal education. African Americans expected their pastors to know the Bible and to be able to arouse the congregation. The preacher would often accomplish this with a chanting tone. The meaning of his words would be lost in the rhythm of the sounds the minister made and the loud amens of the congregation. Sermons, particularly in the churches of the common people, contained vivid imagery and parables. They frequently included references to Moses, the liberator of the Israelites, and the unquestioning faith of Abraham that God rewarded. The glories of heaven and the torment of hell were also common themes. Some sermons were very popular and often repeated during camp meetings and revivals. One of the most popular sermons was "Dry Bones," based on Ezekiel's encounter where the scattered bones of a human skull came together, symbolizing the rebirth of the sinner as a Christian. Another widely popular sermon was "The Eagle Stirs Her Nest," referring to how mother eagles stir their young from the nest to teach them how to fly, portraying God's concern and love for his people. "The Prodigal Son" was also a very popular sermon. Through the emotional power of worship, conveyed through the mesmerizing sermons of the preacher, African Americans received a sense of worth and the fortitude and faith to face a hostile world.[9]

When African Americans from the Alabama Black Belt and other rural communities in Georgia and Mississippi heard that jobs with wages were available in Birmingham, they began to flock to the area. What they found were jobs, but also a hard life in a hostile environment. African American migrants into Birmingham soon found themselves in a rigid and oppressive caste system that placed them at the bottom of the Birmingham community, a position reinforced by prejudice, inferior education, and job discrimination.

Most whites in Birmingham were southerners who brought their prejudices against African Americans with them. These white citizens also tended to judge African Americans in the city by the highly publicized activities of a few criminals. Most saw African Americans as irresponsible and unreliable and prone to commit crimes, especially crimes of passion. In 1889 the editor of the *Birmingham Age-Herald* declared: "The Negro is a good laborer when his labor can be controlled and directed, but is a very undesirable citizen." In 1909 a grand jury declared: "The white man's burden is the criminal negro. We are over whelmed with the amount of crime in this class of our citizenship." Because of this general attitude toward African Americans, whites insisted that the city government should do all within its power to control them, force them to work, and, most of all, protect whites from the criminal tendencies of African Americans. The Birmingham government responded and sought to control African Americans through several means: segregation, governmental regulation of saloons, vagrancy law enforcement, convict labor, and the county fee system.[10]

Some white groups opposed any education for African Americans, maintaining that it would give them a desire for equality with whites. In 1883 there were only two public schools for African Americans in the city and neither went further than the sixth grade. All of the African American residents of Birmingham who testified before the United States Senate Committee on Capital and Labor in 1883 pointed to inferior education as a significant factor in the lack of progress among the city's black population. Among the solutions they proposed were more industrial education, longer school terms, an African American superintendent, and federal aid to education.[11]

Housing for African Americans was the poorest in the city. Because of custom and the prevailing prejudice in the city, whites pushed African Americans into back alleys, along creek beds, close to furnaces, and near the central city area. Rental houses where most African American lived were often unpainted shacks with no sanitary sewers. Some families of three or more lived in one room tenement or apartment buildings. With such poor housing it is not surprising that the health of African Americans suffered in Birmingham. For example, the total number of deaths among African Americans from tuberculosis was two and one-half times greater than among whites.[12]

Job discrimination added to the oppression faced by African Americans migrants in the city. Skilled white workers feared the potential of African Americans in competition for jobs and preferred not to work with them. African Americans found themselves pushed to the bottom in the competition for jobs. They provided cheap and unskilled labor for the coal and iron industry. One study of workers in Birmingham during this period found that every skilled worker listed in the 1880 census, and all of those in the city directory samples before 1903, were whites.[13] Hope for black job achievement rose during the ten-year period of 1895 to 1905 when there were successful efforts to organize biracial unions. But biracial unionism collapsed during the early years of the twentieth century. The success of unionism created a strong challenge from business leaders beginning in the early 1900s. Second, economic competition between white and black workers led to more job discrimination at the turn of the century. White bricklayers, carpenters machinists, and telephone line installers engaged in strikes to protest the hiring of African Americans. With the unions losing ground among African American workers, interracial cooperation dissipated, and discrimination and racial hostility intensified. For these reasons, African American workers could expect to spend their lives in unskilled work that was physically exhausting and unrewarding. They were trapped in the dirtiest, most dangerous, and lowest paying jobs.[14] African Americans in Birmingham rarely found respect or self-esteem through jobs in Birmingham.

As they had done in the rural areas of Alabama, Georgia, and Mississippi, African Americans turned to the church. The churches established by the early migrants in Birmingham from the Black Belt were similar to those already established in Birmingham during Reconstruction by the ex-slaves who had remained in the area. They also mirrored rural churches in terms of denominations, worship, major events, and the charismatic leadership of the pastor. Most were Baptist, followed in numerical strength by the African Methodist Episcopal Church, the African Methodist Episcopal Zion Church, and the Christian Methodist Episcopal Church. These four denominations first established conventions and conferences in southern Alabama and later sent missionaries into Birmingham.

Most African Americans in the Black Belt were Baptists. By 1890 there were 61,030 black Baptists in the Black Belt, the largest number of any denomination. One reason was that during slavery there were more Baptist slave masters than any other denomination. Slaves joined the churches of their masters and many continued in those denominations after freedom. Among other causes for the growth of African American Baptists over other denominations were its emphasis on freedom and spontaneity in worship, a significant role for the laity, and a congregational polity that allowed African American Baptists to form churches and appoint ministers of their own choosing without formal educational qualifications. All these factors blended with the freedmen's desire to maintain their cultural roots and freedom from white control. Because most African American migrants into Birmingham were Baptists and Baptist churches were easy to organize, the overwhelming majority of churches formed by African Americans in Birmingham were Baptist. Although African American Baptists formed several associations by 1890, including the Mt. Pilgrim Association in 1874, most Baptist churches were the result of spontaneous organization by the laity or a local minister.[15]

The African Methodist Episcopal Church, known as the AME Church, had the second largest number of churches formed among African Americans in Birmingham. Founded in 1816 as the result of a racial dispute in the St. George's Methodist Church in Philadelphia when African Americans were forced from their seats, the church sent missionaries into the South after the Civil War who saw themselves as God's instruments to uplift the race. Their immediate concern was to establish churches. Missionaries formed the North Alabama Conference, which included Birmingham, in 1888. By 1890, the AME denomination had established churches in downtown Birmingham and five outlying towns and villages. Unlike the spontaneous pattern of church growth used by the Baptists, the success of the AME church in Birmingham was due to its organizational structure which sent traveling evangelists into areas to establish churches.[16]

The African Methodist Episcopal Zion Church, known as the AME Zion Church, followed a path into Birmingham similar to that of the AME Church but not with the same degree of growth or activity. Its major focus was in other states and other areas of Alabama. Formed in 1820 when the African American members of the Zion Methodist Church in New York voted themselves out of the Methodist Episcopal Church and formed their own denomination, the church moved into Alabama in 1867 and formed the Alabama Conference. Missionaries moved into the central portion of the state and in 1894 formed the North

Alabama Conference, which included Birmingham. The churches founded in the Birmingham area by 1890 were the Johnson Chapel Church in North Birmingham, the Petty's Chapel Church in Bessemer, and the Metropolitan Church in downtown Birmingham. By 1900 AME Zion missionaries formed two other churches, the Bethel Church in the Parker Springs community near Brighton and the Zion Church in the industrial community of Thomas.[17]

The Colored Methodist Episcopal Church, known today as the Christian Methodist Episcopal or CME Church, was a third African American Methodist denomination to establish churches in Birmingham. After the Civil War, some African Americans chose to remain in the white Methodist Episcopal Church, South rather than join the AME or AME Zion Churches. But in 1870, with African Americans forming separate conferences, whites and African Americans agreed that a separate church would enhance the growth of the church among African Americans. In that year, the African Americans in the Methodist Church, South, with mutual consent from the whites, separated and formed the Colored Methodist Episcopal Church in Jackson, Tennessee. CME missionaries formed the Alabama Conference in 1871 in Auburn, Alabama. In 1873 they placed churches in the northern portion of Alabama, including Birmingham, into the North Alabama Conference. Among the early churches established in the Birmingham area were the St. Paul Church in Bessemer in 1870, the Thirgood Church in Birmingham in 1879, and the Metropolitan Church in Ensley in 1900.[18]

A fourth group of African American Methodists who formed churches in Birmingham chose to remain in the Methodist Episcopal Church, North. Meeting in Philadelphia in 1864, the Annual Conference of the Methodist Church, North developed a plan for the evangelization of the newly freed blacks in the South which included the formation of separate annual conferences and the sending of missionaries and teachers into the South to aid the freedmen in adjusting to their new status as citizens. Moving into Alabama, Methodist missionaries assisted African American Methodists in forming churches and in 1876 organized the separate Central Alabama Conference in Randolph County. By 1890 missionaries had formed several churches in the Birmingham area including the Brownville Church in southwestern Birmingham in 1881, the St. Paul Church in downtown Birmingham in 1869, the Morning Star Church in Bessemer in 1882, and the Mt. Pleasant Church in the mining camp community of Sayreton in 1871.[19]

First generation migrants established few Pentecostal or Holiness churches in Birmingham. Only a small number of these churches had existed in the rural areas of Alabama, Mississippi, and Georgia where these migrants had lived. In the early twentieth century, as some African American Baptist and Methodist churches begin to drift away from the emotionalism that had characterized these churches, a small group of working class people began to turn to the more emotional Pentecostal and Holiness churches. This was a slow process in Birmingham. Many people kept away because of the belief that these churches were responsible for placing spells on people. Others saw little difference between their churches and Holiness and Pentecostal churches. For them, the worship and church life was similar. By 1900 only four such churches existed in the city.[20]

Other denominations that formed African American churches in Birmingham by 1900 included the Presbyterians, Congregationalists, Episcopalians, Roman Catholics, and the Cumberland Presbyterians. Their numbers, however, would remain small because of the lack of emotional outlet in worship and the lack of African American ministers because of the educational requirements for pastors. African Americans preferred those churches presided over by their own ministers and where they could express their own cultural and religious heritage.[21]

Many churches began and first met in private homes. In 1899 a layman, S.W. Wilson, invited his Baptist friends in the Kingston community to come and worship in his home. Out of these meetings came the First Baptist Church of Kingston. Similarly, the First Baptist Church of Pratt City began when African American families worshiped in homes. In 1880 these families built a log cabin and organized a church. The St. James United Methodist Church of Warrior first met in members' homes until 1891 when the members constructed a frame building.[22]

The early migrants who did not meet in homes built sheds on vacant lots, erected tents, met in storefronts, and constructed brush arbors until more permanent buildings could be erected. Churches of all the various denominations followed this early pattern. For example, the Brownville Methodist Church, composed of miners from the southwestern area of the county, first met in a tent until they could obtain enough money in 1886 to build a frame building. The New Salem Baptist Church of Bessemer began in 1884 when people in Muscoda camp built a brush harbor in that year. The St. James AME Church of Irondale started in 1868 in a log cabin, moved to a school building, and later built a frame church building. In 1879 a group of African Americans organized the Thirgood CME Church in downtown Birmingham in a frame storefront.[23]

Some churches began as prayer meetings. African Americans, with a desire for religious nurture and fellowship, would meet for prayer and Bible study where there were no churches in local communities. As these groups became larger, members purchased buildings and obtained a pastor. The New Hope Baptist Church of Birmingham began when a small group of African Americans who were workers at the Sloss-Sheffield Iron Company organized a prayer band in 1892 with persons going from place to place singing and praying together. Because of the rapid growth of the prayer band, the group changed the name to Community Bible Class. The members of the class obtained a building from the company located near the furnaces and organized a church.[24]

Whites organized a few churches in the African American community and often provided these churches with continuous assistance. The Ephesus Seventh Day Adventist Church of Birmingham emerged largely through the efforts of Elder M.C. Sturdivant, a white minister. Elder Sturdivant conducted house-to-house Bible study among African Americans. Having no building in which to worship, he gathered the believers in his home for Bible study. The group grew and by 1897 it became necessary to find a place of worship. Elder Sturdivant rented a house in downtown Birmingham and turned it into a chapel and school room. This was the first African American Seventh Day Adventist Church in Birmingham.[25]

Many churches, especially Baptist, began because of the initiative of local ministers in the community. Many of these men moved into Birmingham from rural Alabama and began to preach in homes until they could build or obtain other facilities. In 1887 the Reverend Samuel Perry moved to Birmingham from Uniontown in the Alabama Black Belt. Knowing that there was no Baptist church in the Graymont community, he invited the Baptists in the area to his home where he provided worship. Out of this gathering came the First Baptist Church of Graymont. In 1887 Rev. Paul Johnson came to Bessemer and began to hold worship services in his home. Out of these services came the Jerusalem Primitive Baptist Church. In 1878 there was no church in the Sayreton mining camp. The Rev. Joe Kappur moved into the area and organized the Mount Olive Baptist Church in his home. The Gaines Chapel AME Church began when the Rev. Richard Gray moved into the northern section of Birmingham and held services in the home of George Debro.[26]

In a few instances, African Americans from the same communities in the Alabama Black Belt came together in the Birmingham area to form churches. For example, many people came to Bessemer from Uniontown in the 1880s and 1890s and settled around Eighteenth Street. These people banded together to hold services and built a small frame structure in Eleventh Alley and Eighteenth Street, naming their church the New Bethlehem Baptist Church. Similarly, the Pleasant Grove Primitive Baptist Church began when several families moved from Belview in Dallas County to Jonesboro Heights, near Bessemer, all of the Primitive Baptist faith. They worshiped for a few years in the Mt. Zion Baptist Church and later purchased a lot and built a church on it, calling it the Pleasant Grove Primitive Baptist Church.[27]

Church formation among African Americans in Birmingham would also follow a geographical pattern with churches formed in company villages, the downtown area of Birmingham, and in industrial towns close to Birmingham. Company village churches sprang up in areas around furnaces and mines where the company provided the housing, usually a commissary, and sometimes a school and a doctor. Company village or camp churches, as African Americans called them, usually grew out of private prayer meetings, revivals, and Bible studies. After the residents started a church, the company would usually provide a building. Sometimes the company even assumed responsibility for building repairs and some support for the pastor. For example, African American Methodists in the Tennessee Coal and Iron Company quarters in Ensley organized the Bethel AME Church under a brush arbor in 1894. In 1898 the company granted them an old house where they worshiped until 1902. The First Baptist Church of East Bessemer had a similar beginning. African Americans moving into the Sloss Company housing in East Bessemer asked the company for permission to organize a church. The company built a building on the side of Red Mountain in 1886 and a church named Red Mountain Baptist Church began in that year. A third example is the New Salem Baptist Church of Muscoda, an iron ore mining camp on the northern slope of Red Mountain. In 1884 there was no organized Baptist church in the Muscoda Camp. People met in houses and also had services outdoors. In 1884 a group of Baptists built a brush arbor and organized a church. After a few months, TCI built a frame house for their use. It was used until 1901 when the company built another frame building.[28]

Company village dwellers often called the buildings that the company built for them to worship in "union churches" because frequently both Baptists and Methodists used the same building. They worshiped on alternate Sundays, but would have Sunday School together. Superintendents from the two churches would alternate in presiding on different Sundays. There was one union church built at the Muscoda Camp that had four congregations worshiping on an alternate basis. These were the New Salem Baptist Church, the Magnolia AME Church, the Starlight Baptist Church, and the Mason Chapel United Methodist Church.[29]

There were some planned attempts to organize churches in company villages by the various Methodist denominations, especially the AME Church. Bishops or presiding elders would locate an area where there was no church and assign a minister to move in and start a church. The strategy was to find persons in the camp who had been members of the particular Methodist denomination, get them interested in a church, and petition the company for a place to worship. Sometimes, the Methodist ministers would conduct a revival. For example, in 1894 the local AME Conference sent the Reverend Isaac Lewis, an AME minister, into the Woodward camp to organize a church. In that year he conducted a revival and organized the Woodward AME Church. A frame building was erected by the Woodward Iron Company for the church's use. In 1897 a site was chosen in the Brighton community where the members built a frame building and renamed the church St. Mark AME Church.[30]

The ministry of the Reverend G.W. Mitchell of the AME Church shows the strong organizational pattern and the capable church organizers that existed among African American Methodists in forming company village churches. In 1886 Mitchell moved to the Birmingham area from Tuscaloosa and joined the Bryant Chapel AME Church in Redding, a mining camp community located in the southwestern area of Jefferson County. In that same year Presiding Elder Winfred Mixon licensed Mitchell to preach and assigned him to the Woodward Ore Mine company village. In 1891 Mitchell reported at the Alabama Annual Conference that he had established a mission at the Woodward mines. The AME Church then assigned Mitchell to the Dolomite area in the western section of the county. After working three years among the miners of Dolomite, Mitchell had succeeded in establishing the Bethel AME Church with 300 members. In 1894 the church sent Mitchell to the Woodward mine in Bessemer where he spent four years and established the Woodward Chapel AME Church. In 1898 Senior Bishop Henry

McNeal Turner sent Mitchell to the company village community of Brookside where he founded the St. James Church and constructed a frame building. Between 1891 and 1898, Mitchell had established three company village churches and one mission.[31]

Baptists did not have the organizational structure that allowed them to assign ministers to particular areas on a regular basis. Their churches in company villages sprang almost exclusively from local initiative. After the Baptist group established a church, they would proceed to call a pastor of their own choosing. Because there were more Baptists than Methodists in the villages and they needed no denominational approval to form churches, Baptists soon outnumbered Methodist churches and were usually larger.

Company village churches were intensely emotional. The members judged pastors by their ability to evoke an emotional response. According to one pioneer camp pastor if the service ended without a strong emotional response the deacons would blame the pastor for his lack of spiritual power. Most camp dwellers in the Birmingham area had been sharecroppers in southern Alabama where worship was highly emotional in their rural churches. They expected the worship in the new camp settings to continue that pattern. Another reason was the horrible conditions and terrible life styles in which many camp dwellers were forced to live. Camp housing was worse for African Americans than for native whites or immigrants. In their sections of the camps, African Americans lived in overcrowded conditions with poor sanitation, and where there was often an unhealthy and inadequate water supply. Sometimes railroad tracks ran directly behind houses while creeks, running with water, flowed in front. Camp workers spent long days in dirty, hard, and often dangerous work. Layoffs were frequent in some camps and the pay scale for blacks was usually lower than for southern whites or immigrants. Because of overcrowded conditions and usually the presence of an immoral element, camps were difficult places to rear children. In these conditions, African Americans found hope and affirmation in worship but also an outlet for pent-up fears and worry that led to unbridled emotionalism.[32]

While African Americans were establishing churches in company villages, they were simultaneously starting them within the city limits of Birmingham. Most African American churches in Birmingham began primarily to the north and south of the downtown business district. These included churches of all denominations. The first church established on the Northside was the Sixteenth Street Baptist Church in

1873. A few African Americans who had recently migrated to Birmingham met in a building used as a tinner's shop on the fringe area of downtown Birmingham. They formed the church and called the Reverend James Readen as the first pastor. A few months later, a family by the name of Crawford, who operated a shoe shop, saw the need for a church and called a meeting of the other members of the AME Church in the area to see if they were also interested. They sent for the Reverend Zachary Taylor, a circuit rider, who came and organized the church. The small group named the Church St. John AME with the Reverend Thomas Coffee serving as the first pastor. Four years later, in 1877, a group of African American Methodists who lived on the Northside founded the Metropolitan AME Zion Church in a blacksmith shop.[33]

Other churches on the Northside soon followed as African Americans moved into the area. In 1887 a group of newly arrived migrants who wanted a church in their section of the Northside formed the Tabernacle Baptist Church. A group of Methodists in 1889 formed the Hopewell AME Church in a private home, moved to a brush arbor, and later constructed a frame building. In 1890 the moderators of the Mt. Pilgrim and Jefferson County Associations assisted a group of Baptists in forming the St. James Baptist Church.[34]

One of the oldest churches on the Southside was the Sixth Avenue Baptist Church, known originally as Second Colored Baptist Church. Its formation was largely due to the initiative of M.G. Kendrick who lived on the Southside but along with several other persons from that area attended the Sixteenth Street Baptist Church, known then as the First Colored Baptist Church. Kendrick and other members received letters of dismissal from Sixteenth Street Baptist in 1881 and formed the Sixth Avenue Baptist Church. The vision of Kendrick and the others was to form a church on the Southside that mirrored the Sixteenth Street Church. Another group of African American Baptists organized the Bethel Baptist Church near Sloss Village in a wooden frame building with the Reverend G.W. Parks serving as the first pastor. In 1887 the Allen Chapel AME Church began with members first worshiping in a brush harbor before moving to a frame building. In 1894 the Green Liberty Baptist Church began when a group of African Americans met in a two-room dwelling until members erected a frame church building in 1897 from scrap lumber.[35]

Occupational diversity was much greater among churches near the downtown area of Birmingham than in the company village churches where the residents were almost all miners and factory workers. By the

1890s a substantial professional class was developing that included teachers, doctors, lawyers, and business entrepreneurs. Although practically all churches reflected diversity in their memberships, some churches began to garner many teachers and business persons and became known as "class churches." In these churches, the members expected the pastors to have some education and to carry themselves with dignity and reserve but still preach with emotion and power. Maids, miners, janitors, and factory workers composed most of the membership of working class churches or "mass churches" as African Americans referred to them, where there was greater emotional fervor than at the "class churches." Education was not a prerequisite for the pastor, and the congregation expected pastors to preach with much emotion and power. The differences would develop more clearly among Birmingham churches in the first and second decades of the twentieth century.[36]

Churches also developed in towns adjacent to Birmingham. Bessemer was established by the industrialist Henry F. Debardeleben. In 1886 Debardeleben established the Bessemer Coal, Iron, and Land Company to plan the city that would include several residential areas for whites and African Americans.[37] As African Americans moved into Bessemer, they formed churches. In 1887 a group of African Americans migrated into the Jonesboro area of Bessemer and built a brush arbor for a revival. After the revival, they formed a church calling it the First Baptist Church of Old Jonesboro. One year later, a group of African American Baptists who lived to the south of downtown Bessemer formed the First Baptist Church, South Bessemer. Several African Americans living to the north of downtown Bessemer wanted to establish a church. From this group in 1889, the Jerusalem Baptist Church came into existence in that community. In 1893 Methodists who migrated into Bessemer wanted to form an AME Church. The Reverend George Mitchell came to the small group, and together they established the Allen Temple AME Church on the Northside of the new city. Others churches soon followed as African Americans moved into the Bessemer area. The Antioch Baptist Church began in 1904 in a storefront. In 1902 a group left the Jerusalem Baptist Church and formed the New Zion Baptist Church in a frame building belonging to white Methodists. A group of dissatisfied members left the Canaan Baptist Church in 1906 and formed the Fourteenth Street Baptist Church.[38]

Many churches established in industrial towns in Jefferson County were first formed in camps and later moved to industrial towns near Birmingham. The First Baptist Church of Ensley is an example of a church that began in a camp but moved to the new town of Ensley, which was formed in 1886 around newly built iron furnaces and coal mines. Initially most African Americans settled in Sherman Heights, an area located on a hill overlooking the Ensley furnaces. Later, African Americans in increasing numbers moved to the Tuxedo Junction area, about two miles to the east, where there was a popular dance hall, a few developing African American businesses, and new housing. Mount Zion Baptist Church, which African American furnace workers had formed in Sherman Heights in 1890 in a brush arbor, moved to the Tuxedo area. The members built a frame building changing the name to the First Baptist Church of Ensley. Several other groups organized in the area including the Macedonia Baptist Church in 1898 and the Metropolitan CME Church in 1900.[39]

The First Baptist Church of Brighton followed a pattern similar to the First Baptist Church of Ensley. In 1881 the Woodward family of Pennsylvania moved to the Birmingham area and formed the Woodward Iron Company. By 1886 there were two furnaces in operation and Woodward was a prosperous industrial community. Nearby, the town of Brighton sprang up along the street car line to the east of the Woodward furnace operation and was primarily a residential community for people working at Woodward and the coal mines at Mulga and Dolomite. In 1883 African American Baptists living in the Woodward Camp formed a church in a building designated by the company. After a few years the members moved the church across Jaybird Road to Brighton and conducted worship in a house, naming their church Shady Grove Baptist Church. In 1903 Shady Grove constructed a church building on 39th Street in Brighton that became known as First Baptist Church. As African Americans moved into Brighton from Woodward and other areas, other churches were formed. The St. Mark AME Church left the Woodward Quarters in 1897 and built a small frame building on the present site. In 1911 a group of members from the First Baptist Church formed the Shiloh Baptist Church. As the community expanded, residents of Brighton in 1908 formed the Oak Grove Baptist Church.[40]

To obtain a building where members could meet when they desired was the major reason for leaving camp sites and forming churches in suburban towns. Often the camp church building was used by several denominations and fraternal groups, which meant that it was unavailable when churches wanted to use it. Building their own church on land they owned gave churches greater freedom and access any time. A second major reason for leaving camp sites, both by churches and individuals, was to escape the immoral climate of camp life, which often attracted a criminal element. Third, building their own churches on land they owned was an act of independence. By moving from company villages, churches and individuals were seeking to better their condition and to be free from the company's dominance over their lives.[41]

Churches in the small industrial towns of Jefferson County exhibited the emotional worship experience found in most city churches and all company village churches. Pastors in company-village churches believed that people in industrial-town churches showed more vision and initiative than those living in camps in that the members owned their church building. Camp dwellers often lived for the immediate and depended on the company. In industrial-town churches, African Americans depended on their own resources and that accounted for more self-reliant and structured churches.[42]

Almost immediately after migrating into Birmingham, African Americans formed churches which resembled those they had established in the rural areas where they had lived in Alabama and other parts of the South. Churches had been the central institution in those communities, providing hope, support, and cooperation in a hostile environment. As they met similar conditions in Birmingham, African Americans moved expeditiously to establish similar churches. Denied economic and political power, the church became an omnibus institution. African Americans established churches everywhere they settled in the city and often in temporary and make-shift buildings. Churches began simultaneously in company villages, in the city of Birmingham, and in small industrial towns adjacent to Birmingham. The churches of the migrants developed a unique church life that provided basic needs for the first generation migrants who came to the city of Birmingham and would continue to do so as other African Americans migrated into the city.

III

Expansion and African American Church Life

Although African American migrants had established many churches by 1900, their numbers increased in the first two decades of the twentieth century. Several churches established by first generation migrants in make-shift buildings erected large and commodious edifices under the leadership of outstanding pastors. Church organizations expanded, and others came into being. Whether small or large, or established by first- or second-generation migrants, churches developed a distinctive spiritual life. Preaching was central in the life of these churches. Women composed the majority of the membership and served as the chief workers and fund-raisers. Through their spiritual life, churches filled many crucial needs. They assisted rural migrants in adjusting to the strange new life of the city, promoted moral discipline, and furnished a social life. Most of all, through the worship and spiritual life of their churches African Americans in Birmingham developed the fortitude, faith, and values to face life in the racist and hostile environment in which they were forced to live.

The growth of African American churches between 1900 and 1920 is reflected in the Birmingham City Directory. In 1900 the Directory listed only twenty-eight African American churches that existed within the city limits. By 1920 this figure had grown to 115 churches. Although one must consider the expansion of the city limits in 1910 which brought in areas like Ensley and Pratt City where there were churches already in existence, it nevertheless revealed the rapid growth of African American churches during this period.[1]

Baptists churches accounted for most of the growth as they had done in the last three decades of the nineteenth century. Of the 115 churches listed, sixty-seven were Baptist. Baptists continued to be the most popular because of the freedom to form churches, the emotionalism in worship, and the fact that most migrants into the city were Baptists. Another factor was the frequency of splits, usually caused by disagreements over pastoral leadership. For example, the Broad Street

Baptist Church that began in 1878 as the Spring Street Baptist Church had two churches formed out of its membership. In 1902 a dispute over excluding a member from the church for misconduct led a group to leave Broad Street and form the Trinity Baptist Church in Smithfield. In 1914 a dispute over pastoral leadership led to the formation of the South Elyton Baptist Church in 1914. Both Trinity and South Elyton grew rapidly to become large and flourishing congregations. Another example of growth through splits was the churches formed out of the Twenty-Third Street Baptist Church. Between its founding in 1899 and World War I, at least two churches grew out of it. In 1913 a group of members left with the pastor, the Reverend Hawkins, when deacons and a group of members challenged his pastoral authority. Reverend Hawkins and the members who left with him formed the Zion Star Baptist Church. Some years later, a dispute arose in the Twenty-Third Street Church over the pastorate of the Reverend C.S. Riddick. A group of members along with Rev. Riddick formed the Metropolitan Baptist Church.[2]

The increase in the number of Baptist churches led to more denominational organization among Baptists. Since 1873 the Mt. Pilgrim Association had included the churches of Birmingham and Jefferson County. As the churches in the Bessemer area increased, the need for an association in that area emerged. In 1900 the Baptists in the Bessemer area organized the Jefferson County Association. Similarly, churches in the Ensley and Fairfield communities felt a need for their own association. In 1910 Baptists in that area formed the Peace Baptist Association with six churches. At the first annual meeting in 1911, ten more churches joined the association. The charter of both newly formed associations stated that their purpose was to provide an agency of cooperation among churches, to promote doctrinal purity, and to sustain missions and Christian education.[3]

Although Baptist churches were autonomous, associations were important in the African American Baptist community in Birmingham. Associations had been an integral part of Baptist life in the Black Belt of Alabama where many African Americans had lived before coming to Birmingham. As these migrants moved into Birmingham and formed churches, they looked to associations to fill the same needs they had served in the rural South. In Birmingham, Baptist associations provided four basic needs. First, they helped establish churches. Once lay persons decided they wanted a church, they would call in the association in the area to assist them with the proper procedure for its formation. Second, associations provided order and discipline. Churches that taught false doctrine or engaged in improper activities were expelled from the association. Third, associations were also called to settle disputes. Judging by the number of splits in the area, it is clear that associations often failed in this regard, but in some cases they were successful in keeping churches together. Fourth, associations provided education. Both the Peace Baptist and Jefferson County associations joined the Mt. Pilgrim association in founding a school.[4]

The AME denomination established the second highest number of churches during this period. The AME Church composed twenty-two of the thirty-eight African American Methodist churches located in the city limits of Birmingham. Several factors accounted for this success. It was the first of the Methodist groups to move into the area with a significant number of missionaries, the organizational efficiency of the church, and capable leadership. The bishops assigned to the North Alabama Conference such as Henry McNeal Turner, Daniel Payne, and Wesley Gaines were strong religious leaders who brought with them a spirit of enthusiasm and missions that became contagious. Surrounding them were effective pastors and presiding elders with unusual dedication. Bishop Wesley Gaines, who presided over the North Alabama Conference in the late 1880s and 1900s, recorded in his history of the AME Church memories of the enthusiasm of the Alabama work, especially of the efforts put forth in the establishment and maintenance of Daniel Payne College. He wrote in 1889 that the Alabama Conference had strong men "with zeal and sanctified energy who were destined to make the AME Church a strong power in Alabama." Among those listed were Winfred H. Mixon who served several tenures as presiding elder in the Birmingham district and T. W. Coffee who pastored several churches in the area.[5]

The life and work of the Reverend Winfred Mixon shows how important AME leadership was in growing and sustaining churches in Birmingham. Unlike Baptists, who had many churches and grew through splits, the AME church was smaller and depended on capable leaders like Mixon who not only established churches but also maintained them for the denomination. Mixon was born into a slave family in Dallas County, near Selma, on April 25, 1859. After emancipation, his father sent him to work on a plantation in Virginia in his early years. Returning to Dallas County in 1876, Mixon was converted, baptized, and licensed to preach. In 1879 he was ordained and joined the "traveling connection," which meant that he became a full-time minister who would go wherever assigned. His early years were spent pastoring and founding churches. One of his major strategies was to conduct camp meetings and to harness the converts into AME Churches. His success as pastor and missionary caused the denomination to promote him to the position of presiding elder. Mixon's diary, which listed his activities as presiding elder of the Greensboro district from 1892 to 1895, showed his success and diligence. Besides establishing eleven new churches, Mixon attended 193 prayer meetings, forty-two funerals, twenty-one weddings, and 116 sick families. He baptized 115 adults and 128 children, delivered 1,152 sermons and lectures, traveled 24,000 miles, and administered the holy sacrament 14,910 times.[6]

Mixon brought that same energy and success to Birmingham where he served as presiding elder in 1887, 1897, and 1920. His diary entries of 1897 demonstrate his success in sustaining and enhancing the AME Churches in that area. His work as presiding elder included holding quarterly conferences, lecturing and preaching, appointing pastors and missionaries, and establishing churches. Two of his most noteworthy achievements were settling disputes, usually between pastors and members, and elevating the educational program of his churches. One of the disputes occurred in the St. John Baptist Church, the oldest AME Church in Birmingham, over a case of discipline. A committee of the church investigated an influential female member over a morals charge which led to her being excluded from the church. Many members blamed the pastor for acting in haste. After investigating the matter, Mixon found that the pastor had been misled and had the church restore the member. Mixon spent much of his time in 1897 keeping the church together. Another dispute occurred over pastoral leadership in the church at the mining camp of Brookside. The members voted that the pastor should be replaced. Mixon was not able to rescind the action of the church but salvaged the situation by providing a capable replacement.[7]

Mixon's educational leadership was most evident in his concern that the churches in his district have strong Sunday Schools. He established Sunday schools at his stations in Brighton and Pratt City. On September 2 he presided over the district's Sunday School convention which he had founded. His leadership resulted in two churches remaining in the AME denomination and the nine churches and four missions in his district being strengthened through a stronger emphasis on Christian education.[8]

Other Methodist groups in Birmingham had only a few churches. These other groups concentrated in other states and other parts of Alabama. The AME Zion Church was very active in the southern portion of Alabama and especially in North Carolina. Bishop George Clinton established the first AME Zion Conference in the South in North Carolina in 1864. That state became the headquarters for the denomination. The AME Zion Church placed both its publishing board and also its college, Livingstone College, in North Carolina. The Alabama Conference was founded in 1867 in Mobile, but the church did not establish the North Alabama Conference, which included Birmingham, until 1894. Similarly, the CME Church focused on Tennessee, establishing its college and publishing house in that state. It moved into Birmingham in the 1870s but with few missionaries. The AME Church got a headstart on all of the other Methodist groups.[9]

The large number of churches that African Americans founded in Birmingham and the financial support that churches received from them attests to the loyalty and importance of the church among African Americans in the city. With practically no support from whites, African Americans financed their churches and built places of worship. Some churches grew rapidly and built large sanctuaries at enormous cost and sacrifice. In 1884 the Sixteenth Street Baptist, under the pastorate of the Reverend William R. Pettiford, erected a new church costing $25,000. The Shiloh Baptist Church, pastored by the Reverend Thomas W. Walker, erected a sanctuary and basement at a cost of $45,000 in 1905. In 1909 the city condemned the Sixteenth Street Baptist Church because of structural problems in its foundation. Forced to relocate, the members under the pastorate of the Reverend Charles L. Fisher, constructed a new building costing $62,000. The St. John AME Church, the largest congregation in the city among Methodists, built a church building costing $25,000 in 1908.[10]

Some African American banks assisted churches in building new structures. For example, the Broad Street Baptist Church dedicated its new building in 1915. Among the invited guest at the dedication service was Mr. J.O. Diffay of the Alabama Penny Bank that had made the loan for the building. The People's Investment and Banking Company operated by W. L. Lauderdale also made church loans. In 1920 the St. John Baptist Church in Pratt City borrowed $5,000 from this banking company to erect a church building.[11]

Whether small or large, African American churches developed a distinctive church life. Sunday for its members was an all day affair. It also mirrored Sundays in the Alabama Black Belt where African Americans had spent all day at church, even eating on the grounds between worship services. For most churches that same pattern continued in Birmingham. In the typical church, Sunday's activities began at 9:30 in the morning with Sunday School. Following Sunday School was the regular worship service that usually began at 11 o'clock. At 3 p.m., the youth would hold their meeting. Evening service usually began at 7 p.m. On some Sundays there would be a special 5 p.m. service. Sunday at church was not only a time of worship but also a time of fellowship and socializing. Most members worked six days a week and regarded Sunday at church as a welcome break from a week-long routine of work.[12]

The most important Sunday service was at 11 o'clock in most churches. Observers noted the form and pattern that these worship services took in most churches. The service began with a praise service led by the deacons that usually lasted for at least thirty minutes. The purpose of the praise service was to prepare the worshipers for the main service. It consisted of meter songs and prayers. Favorite meter hymns were "I Love the Lord, He Heard My Cry," "When I Can Read My Title Clear," "A Charge to Keep I Have," and "Old Time Religion." The prayers were long and fervent. The person who prayed usually knelt before his or her pew. Some prayers have been recorded which were typical of those prayed in praise services during this period:

> This evening
> O Heavenly Father,
> I come to You in the humblest manner that I know how,
> I come
> Lord Jesus,
> With a humble heart and a bowed head.
> I call upon Your name,
> Lord Jesus,
> Because I know no other name to call.
> Lord Jesus,
> Bless the ones that are here under the sound of my weak voice.
> O Heavenly Father,
> We might be few, Lord, but You said where there are two or three gathered in My Name,
> You would be in the midst.[13]

Near the end of the praise service the pastor entered with his assistants. His entrance signaled that the devotion was about to close. At the end of the praise service the choir took the stand and provided a song service. By 1900 most church choirs sang spirituals, jubilee songs, and hymns. Although the hymns were standard or Euro-American hymns, African American choirs sang them in their own way. The African

American religious community took the Euro-American hymn tunes and gave them an exaggerated movement and rhythm. Among the favorite improvised or "gospelized hymns" were "What A Friend We Have in Jesus," "Never Grow Old," "I Must Tell Jesus," "At The Cross," "Amazing Grace," and "Blessed Assurance."[14]

Following the choir's singing was the time for announcements and offering. The pastor made the announcements and often gave words of instruction to the congregation. Deacons usually took the offering and occasionally would discuss with the congregation the needs of the church. Following one or two selections by the choir, the pastor delivered a sermon, which was usually from thirty minutes to one hour long and delivered with gusto. After the sermon came the pastor's appeal for sinners to express their faith in Christ and become members of the church. The service ended with the benediction.[15]

Although Sunday was the most important day for African American Churches, there were some week day and night activities. The frequency and nature of the activities differed from church to church. In most churches, there was a midweek worship service Wednesday nights. Other weekly activities were choir practices, deacons' meetings, usher board meetings, benevolent society meetings, deacons' wives meetings, and missionary society meetings. Some missionary society groups also met in homes during the week.[16]

The preaching of the pastor was the highlight of the worship and at the center of the church life that African Americans developed in Birmingham. Although there were exceptions, preaching in the early churches of Birmingham was done with wild excitement and emotion. Coming out of slavery where they had experienced a violent and emotional conversion experience, African Americans wanted a religion that would cause them to feel and experience the power of God. The notion of being possessed or filled with the spirit continued to be a vital part of their religious experience. African American worshipers expected preaching to be done with the spirit and cause them to be caught up in the spirit.[17]

Entirely impromptu, the preacher began in a conversational tone but steadily moved to a higher pitch, with the desired result that the congregation went into an emotional frenzy. One observer who attended a funeral at the Shiloh Baptist Church noted this pattern in the pastor's funeral sermon. She noted that the pastor, the Reverend T.W. Walker, began in a simple and dignified way by reviewing the best traits of the deceased as shown in her relations with family and friends. He then told of her work in the benevolent society and her many charities. As he continued, Walker's words came more slowly, his tones became more resonant, and he pitched his voice in a higher key. In this higher pitched voice, he began to describe in a graphic way the departure of the soul from the body to be with God in eternal rest. The mourners began to weep. As Walker's eulogy continued, his voice was raised even higher as he recounted the deceased's last words and reminded the audience that there will come a day of reckoning. The entire audience was now expressing grief in tears and moans and distressing cries.[18]

In most African American churches, the congregation aided the pastor by loud and encouraging responses. Such responses were a feature of camp meeting revivals that African Americans attended during slavery, but they were also a part of the call and response pattern that was an integral feature of the African religious experience after slavery. The audience responded with "amen," "all right," "that's right," "come on," "help him Lord," and "preach the word." The preacher often urged the congregation to continue the responses with interjections such as "Have I got a witness," and "You ought to say amen." The historian Walter F. Pitts has recorded portions of a sermon that described the call and response between the preacher and the audience:

> Jesus knew what he was gon' do
> "Yes!"
> The little boy, he know what he was gon' do-
> "Oh Yes!"
> But Jesus knew about the five thousand people-
> "Amen!"
> And they had traveled a long way with him-
> "Yeah!"
> And they don't know what it's all about-
> "Sho' you right!"
> I cain't let these people go back-
> "Yes!"
> Because they came a long way-
> "Yes!"
> I have to set out and feed these people-
> "Put you' soul in it!"[19]

The chanting style distinguished typical African American preaching from that of most white ministers. Although not used by all African American pastors, it was found in the Baptist and Methodist churches of working class congregations in the South, and in most Birmingham churches. Historians of African American preaching generally agree that its origins sprang from Africa where religious rituals were a combination of poetic recitation and music. On social occasions the Yoruba and Fulani tribes of West Africa performed their histories, prayers, genealogies, fables, and proverbs in a rhythmic fashion. Slaves in the United States in their secret religious services maintained this pattern in their preaching and praying, and after emancipation African American pastors continued this tradition.[20]

The chanting style added to the emotional intensity of the congregation. Preacher and people saw it as a way of bringing on the spirit of God. Most preachers who used this style began speaking in prose but end in a chanted, rhythmic pattern that galvanized the attention of the audience and evoked greater response from them. They repeated words and phrases so that loud "amens" and groans came from the congregation.[21]

Women were an indispensable part of church life in Birmingham. From the beginning of African American migration into the area, they had taken the initiative in starting churches. They began prayer meetings and Sunday Schools which later became churches. For example, the Mt. Zion Baptist Church of Bessemer began in 1905 because of a prayer meeting started by Mrs. Lizzie Campbell in her home. The Galilee Baptist Church in the mining camp community of Praco started when a group of women who were perturbed by the lack of religious opportunities for their children began a Sunday School class.[22]

The place of African American women in churches reflected their subordinate relationship to men. Men made the major decisions for the church and excluded women from the ministry and other offices within the church structure and organization. In Baptist and Methodist churches there were no female pastors during this period. Women did serve as traveling evangelists and deaconesses in some Methodist denominations but did not become pastors in Birmingham until the 1950s. In Baptist churches, pastors were adamant in their opposition to women serving as ministers in any form. But from within their subordinate position, women exerted a powerful influence on the organization and maintenance of the church. The overwhelming majority of women in Birmingham apparently saw their church work as an opportunity to engage in meaningful activities for themselves and their families. They made up the majority of the membership of every church in Birmingham. Without their support and labor there would have been no African American churches in the city.[23]

Women served as missionary workers, youth advisers, Sunday School teachers, choir members, ushers, and hosts. The missionary society was the exclusive and special domain for female work in the local churches. Most missionary groups had circles or units that met in various homes in different sections of the city. These circles were agencies for helping the poor and needy, Bible instruction, and fundraising. When a visiting minister or evangelist came to the church, they usually provided lodging and food.[24]

Once a month, all of the units of the missionary society would come together for a general meeting at the church. The general missionary meeting was a time of worship, fellowship, and instruction. It usually lasted all day. The general missionary society meeting of the Jackson Street Baptist Church in the Woodlawn section of Birmingham in 1895 followed this schedule:

Program

9:00 a.m.	-Praise Service
9:30 a.m.	-President's address
9:45 a.m.	-Hindrances to Christian usefulness
10:15 a.m.	-Best methods of governing children
10:45 a.m.	-Has each Christian a responsibility in bringing the world to Christ?
11:15 a.m.	-Reports of local societies
2:00 p.m.	-Praise Service
2:15 p.m.	-The true woman
2:45 p.m.	-Africa's need
3:30 p.m.	-The model missionary society
4:00 P.M.	-Business[25]

The women of the congregations in Birmingham played a key role in raising funds to keep the churches operating. They organized events such as bake sales, carnivals, suppers, dinners, teas, and balls to support the church. They were especially useful in raising money to pay for the construction of church buildings. Often in building fund drives, church auxiliaries such as the missionary society and other groups dominated by women were given a definite amount to raise for construction purposes or debt liquidation.[26]

The journalist Isabel Allen has left a written record of the church life of the Shiloh Baptist Church, founded by Thomas W. Walker in 1891 and built around his charismatic preaching and leadership. Like most African American churches in Birmingham, it was made up of working-class people. Most of the male members were miners, industrial workers, and household servants. Most of the women were homemakers or maids who worked for wealthy whites. Because of Walker's unusual preaching ability, African Americans flocked to the Shiloh Church. By 1895 it was the largest church in the city. Historian Charles Octavius Boothe referred to it in that year as the "marvel" church of Birmingham.[27]

Sunday always brought a full day of activities and worship at Shiloh. Adapting their Sunday activities to the needs of the members, Shiloh's first worship service began at 6 am. This gave those members who had to work all day on Sunday an opportunity to attend worship. The early morning service was followed by Sunday School at 9:30 am. Instead of an 11 o'clock worship service, Shiloh held its main worship service for its members at 3 pm, an hour that was most convenient for his female members who had to work as maids or cooks on Sunday mornings but were free to come to Shiloh at 3 pm. The evening service, usually attended by 1,500 persons, began at 7:30 pm and occasionally lasted until midnight, depending on the enthusiasm of the preacher and his congregation.[28]

Shiloh Baptist Church's activities continued every day and night of the week. The choir practiced, the ushers deliberated, and the missionary convened. On Monday evenings, the Baptist Young People's Union met. On Thursday night there was prayer meeting. On any afternoon the minister might hold a baptism, a marriage, or a funeral. Other church societies meeting included the Christian Relief Society, the Children's Mission Band, the Afro-Benefit Association, and the Tenth League, whose members agreed to give one-tenth of their earnings toward paying off the church's debt. Besides its religious and benevolent activities, the church sponsored social activities such as dinners, banquets, and teas. On these occasions, members wore their best clothes and enjoyed much laughter and fun.[29]

Thomas Walker dominated Shiloh with an uncommonly autocratic rule. Pastors were generally acknowledged as the leader of the church, but they were expected to consult with deacons, stewards, and members before making major decisions. Splits occurred in some churches because of charges that the pastor was too dictatorial. Because Walker had founded Shiloh, preached with unusual ability, and developed it into the largest church in the city, he could assume an absolute authority rare in Birmingham churches. By 1905 Walker directed a staff that consisted of an associate pastor, a choirmaster and a clerk trained in office and business procedure. Walker also had a board of eight deacons who followed his direction. He headed every department and every church leader answered to him.[30]

Throughout its life, the African American church filled many needs for those who migrated into the city. Perhaps most immediate was socialization and adjustment to urban life. The migrants who moved into the city were unfamiliar with big city life. Coming from rural Alabama and other southern states, they were accustomed to small communities where there were intimate personal relationships. In Birmingham they experienced anonymity and an impersonal environment. The churches provided a sense of community in this new and strange environment that gave the former rural dweller a sense of belonging. Although located in a big city, the churches provided a style like the one they had left in the rural areas. Well-known hymns were sung; prayers were offered for familiar needs; and ministers preached with familiar emotion. African Americans maintained their cultural roots, and through the language and emotionalism of the worship they found a sense of well being in a new and hostile environment. First-generation migrants created the churches to fill this need. As later migrants moved into the city of Birmingham, they found churches already established which ministered to their spiritual, social, and psychological needs.[31]

In the sense of assisting new arrivals in adjusting to a strange environment, African American churches were similar to the Greek Orthodox Church and the Roman Catholic Church. Greek immigrants, like African Americans, came to Birmingham seeking better economic opportunity. Arriving in Birmingham in the 1880s, most Greek immigrants, operated either restaurants, grocery stores, or fruit stands. They sought to preserve their heritage. In 1907 they organized a Greek Orthodox church that quickly became the center of the Greek community, and through its worship and activities became the primary agency of cultural identity. The Holy Greek Orthodox Church, the seventh Greek Orthodox church organized in the United States, had a membership of approximately one hundred members who paid dues of twelve dollars a year. Many Greeks moved into the neighborhood near the church. The Greek immigrants also established a Greek school to help the children maintain their language and heritage.[32]

The Italian Roman Catholic Church played a similar role. Most Italian immigrants came to Birmingham from Sicily and southern Italy where the Catholic religion was an integral part of village life. On coming to Birmingham, many Italians drifted from the church primarily because the worship services were in English, which many did not understand. Birmingham Italians were fortunate that in 1904 the Catholic Church sent a young priest, Father John Canepa, to build three churches in the city. The three churches became the hub of life for Birmingham's Italian immigrants and their children. The use of the their language and the celebration of the traditional feast days gave Italians the cultural roots that helped them maintain a sense of community and well-being in a new environment.[33]

Through its many activities and spiritual life, the African American church in Birmingham supplied other important needs: a social life, self-esteem and hope, and a refuge against white hostility. For many African Americans, the church was the social center. Churches sought to provide wholesome activities in a community which neglected African American social and recreational needs. The activities were similar to the ones the church had provided in the rural areas. Picnics, teas, fundraising dinners, banquets, and socials were offered by most African American churches in Birmingham. Churches also functioned as music schools, concert halls, recreation clubs, and sites for political debates and town meetings. For the children the church provided Sunday School, youth meetings, and picnics. Special programs for Christmas and Easter furnished young people a chance to express their talents. Most of all, the church was the place where young and old heard the latest news, and even sometimes, courted and met their mates.[34]

No service rendered by the African American church was more important than building self-esteem. Given only the dirtiest and most unskilled jobs of the iron and steel industry and viewed by whites as inferior, African Americans found little in the wider society of Birmingham to give them a sense of worth. The church was one place they could feel good about themselves. Whenever whites stripped blacks of their humanity, the church offered dignity. Called "boy" or "uncle" on the job, they were "brother" or "mister" at church. They were deacons, trustees, stewards, ushers, choir members, and heads of organizations. Similarly, an African American woman might work as a maid her entire life, but she could maintain self-respect by teaching a Sunday School class or coordinating a youth program. African Americans were somebody in their churches and received respect.[35]

The preaching of the pastor was an integral part of the self-esteem and hope that the African American church provided for the African Americans who migrated into Birmingham. The exodus experience remained as strong as it had been in slavery. Though African Americans were no longer in slavery, they lived in a caste system that segregated and oppressed them. Sermons such as "Moses at the Red Sea," "Dry

Bones in the Valley," and "The Eagle Stirreth Her Nest" were a few favorite sermons in which preachers continued the identification with the Israelites. African American preachers assured their audiences that the God who had led them out of slavery was still working on their behalf.[36]

The constancy of Old Testament preaching did not keep African American preachers from dwelling on Christ and the heaven that awaited the faithful. This emphasis was not sheer escapism but reinforced the notion of deliverance. African American preachers combined this-worldly and other-worldly salvation into a positive whole that supported each other. The heaven that preachers described was neither white nor black but could be achieved only because of the quality of one's spiritual life. If such was the case, spirituality and not color was most important. Segregation therefore had no standing with God. All persons were equal in the sight of God and had worth. African Americans gravitated toward this kind of preaching because it revitalized their spirits and gave hope and worth despite their circumstances.[37]

The church was the place where African Americans could go to escape the hostility of the white world. Placed in a position of powerlessness because of disfranchisement, denied justice from the courts, looked down upon as inferior, subject to mob violence and lynchings, African Americans could move within the confines of their churches and find warmth and security. In their churches, they felt free from the white world. They were free to express their deepest thoughts. Although whites might scoff at their style of worship, it was one of the few places where African Americans felt whites would not enter. In Birmingham, the church served as their refuge and shelter in a hostile environment.[38]

The African American church constantly urged moral discipline on the early black migrants into Birmingham. Away from the watchful eye of family and members of their rural communities, many migrants, a large portion of whom were young men, engaged in gambling, drinking, and prostitution. Much crime was attributed to African Americans. Living in crowded quarters, at the lowest economic level, unaccustomed to the temptations of city life and always under the close surveillance of police officers, African Americans composed about 60 percent of the Birmingham's criminals. Some churches began as a means of combating unlawful and riotous behavior. The Evergreen Baptist Church in the coal mining camp of Lewisburg, was started to address the lawlessness of the camp. Two ministers came into the area, and with the support of the religious people in the company village built a brush arbor and started religious services that resulted in the Evergreen Baptist Church. Similarly, the Mt. Zion Baptist Church of Ishkooda was founded in 1896 in an iron-ore mining village so that the children in the village would get moral and Biblical training to challenge the lawless influences there.[39]

African American churches sought to enforce moral discipline through the act of expulsion. Imitating their experience in the Alabama Black Belt, Birmingham's churches expelled members found guilty of immoral behavior such as drunkenness, adultery, fighting, fornication, and stealing. Females guilty of becoming pregnant out of wedlock and church officers who created discord in the congregation also faced expulsion. Persons expelled were required to come before the church and ask for forgiveness so they could be reinstated as members, a process similar in all the denominations. The threat of expulsion had the effect of deterring what churches considered immoral behavior, especially among church members who did not want to be embarrassed and who feared the prospect of being cast out of God's church.[40]

Drunkenness came under special fire from African American clergy. They witnessed many African Americans victimized by liquor. Its use led many persons, especially men, to neglect their families and to perform poorly on the job. Testifying before the U.S. Senate Committee of Capital and Labor in 1883, the Reverend Isaiah Welch of the St. John AME Church declared that prohibition of alcohol would go far to correct the ills among African Americans in Birmingham. Most African American clergy supported the temperance movement and used their pulpits to agitate for it. In 1885 the Alabama Conference of the AME church supported Senior Bishop Henry McNeal Turner's description of temperance as the greatest question then being discussed in the civilized world. At the same time, Senior Bishop James Hood of the AME Zion Church, insisted that intemperance was a sure sign that one was not yet a Christian and had fallen from grace. Such preaching represented an an earnest attempt by African American clergymen to solve what they perceived as a social problem that was destroying people.[41]

African American ministers encouraged strict morality in marriage and family life. In slavery, slave masters often separated families through the sale of one of the spouses. Slave marriages generally had no legal standing. Although many African Americans sought to find and reunite with their mates after emancipation, others formed relationships without marriage. The many young males migrating into Birmingham often lived with women out of wedlock. Such arrangements were frowned upon by churches and often resulted in expulsions. Many

African American pastors maintained that the race could never succeed without strong Christian families.[42]

William R. Pettiford, pastor of the Sixteenth Street Baptist Church, believed Christian family life was essential for the uplift of African Americans. In 1895 he wrote *Divinity in Wedlock*, in which he sought to strengthen the consciousness of African Americans in Birmingham about the sacredness of marriage, to advise them on principles for choosing a mate, and to give advice on how to have successful marriages. Marriage, Pettiford insisted in his book, was ordained by God. God instituted it for the general happiness of mankind and to bring children into the world. To dissolve it without regard for the divine law of God was to commit adultery. To bring children into the world outside marriage was to commit fornication. In selecting a mate, Pettiford counseled, a person should avoid a drunkard, a loafer, or someone too old or too young. One ought, he insisted, never marry simply for beauty or in haste. A Christian should never marry a nonbeliever, and he urged persons to marry those of their own religious faith. Giving special advice to young men, he said that they should have three things before entering marriage: money, education, and a home. On the subject of what makes a successful marriage, Pettiford discussed love, respect, honesty, faithfulness, good manners, kindness, and sound economic principles.[43]

Sermons by two of the most well-trained pastors in Birmingham during this period show the strong concern for moral discipline. The Reverends Charles L. Fisher and James H. Eason pastored in Birmingham in the 1890's and early 1900's. Their books of sermons reflected their concern that African Americans develop the doctrinal soundness, moral discipline, and character necessary to advance themselves and the race, in spite of the segregated system in which they lived. Their sermons shared little in common with the "social gospel" adherents of the day. Individual sin and personal salvation were basic concerns of the sermons of Birmingham's African American ministers.

Fisher, pastor of the Sixteenth Street Baptist Church from 1898 to 1910 and also from 1921 to 1930, highlighted in his book of sermons, *Social Evils*, six sins that were destroying not only African Americans in Birmingham but also the American family and free institutions. For him any action that opposed a Biblical command or did not contribute toward spiritual edification was wrong.

Basing his first sermon on the familiar parable of the prodigal son, Fisher examined the evil of wastefulness. He insisted that this sin needed discussing because of the tendency of many African Americans to spend their money unwisely. He maintained that so many "throw away in a day what it takes a year to accumulate." The solution, Fisher maintained, was to teach thrift in the home, school, and church.[44]

Fisher used the story of Samson and Delilah to denounce lust and sex outside of marriage. He showed how Samson, a strong man and child of divine promise, was reduced to a pitiful "dwarf" of a man because he yielded to sexual passion. The moral of the story, Fisher pointed out, was not to be deceived by beauty or driven by lust.[45]

Fisher also considered dancing a cardinal sin because it aroused passions. It did not enhance the "mission of the church and the work of Christ." The ball room, Fisher insisted, was "the devil's hot house."[46]

Fisher agreed with Bishops Turner and Hood that alcohol led to the breakdown of character, the home, and the government. Fisher suggested that the church needed to teach the biblical doctrine of temperance, which he defined as "total abstinence from anything that was physically injurious and moral degrading." According to Fisher, when Jesus said "watch and pray that ye enter not temptation," he had alcohol in mind. Training our children early through Sunday School to abstain and to support temperance societies was the most effective way of destroying this menace to our world, Fisher maintained.[47]

Fisher viewed with alarm the growing popularity of the theater in his series of sermons. He referred to the theater as "Satan's Reception Room," where the devil promised good, clean entertainment but instead tempted us with vulgar and degrading entertainment. Immoral displays of feminine figures characterized many dramas. Because such plays were all that the public would support, Fisher maintained that the theater could not correct itself. The only solution was for people to refrain from attending these plays.[48]

Fisher also examined the evil of poverty, which he attributed to laziness, reduction of wages, and the encouragement of vagrancy by the upper classes. Poverty encouraged crime and the weakening of government. As a remedy, Fisher proposed the cultivation of strong work habits and industry by the home and school starting at an early age. He closed this sermon by reminding his readers that "riches, wisdom, and length of days are the heritage of those who work patiently, and wait, and murmur not."[49]

James Eason, pastor of the Jackson Street Baptist Church, in his book of sermons and addresses, *Sanctification or Fanaticism*, emphasized the need for doctrinal soundness and purity. For him, it was important that African Americans exercised correct thinking, especially in terms of their religion. Concerned with the teaching that a person could live a perfect life, many of his sermons dealt with refuting this doctrine. According to Eason the Bible taught that sanctification was a life-long process in which the person was growing spiritually but never achieved a finished position of perfection on earth. It was important that people be moral but not perfect, Eason insisted. Eason, a controversial figure, also gave forceful comments on other issues. The only true churches, he insisted, were those that followed the congregational pattern of the New Testament. In a brief address on fraternal lodges, Eason compared the imperfection of lodges to the perfection of the church. Lodges, Eason maintained, were against the best interest of the church because they took a person's first loyalty from the church. Only the church can lead one to eternal salvation, Eason insisted.[50]

Although primarily dealing with doctrinal issues, Eason did address the moral and spiritual elevation of the African American race. Eason pointed out that African Americans were living in a time of crisis which resulted from the growing hostility of whites that was most evident in the spread of segregation, disfranchisement, the discrimination of labor unions, and the unequal expenditures for African American education. To remedy the situation, Eason insisted that African Americans needed men with vision and courage who could organize blacks to build institutions to elevate themselves. He also urged African American men to work hard, achieve a broad education and develop moral principle. "Remember," he insisted, "in his last sermon, "men of principle rule the world."[51]

In providing a spiritual community and structured social life, the African American church in Birmingham was the institution through which African Americans could express their deepest feelings and at the same time achieve status, find security, and create a meaningful existence. The preaching of pastors was central to this community. Through the preaching of the pastor and the many activities of the church's life, rural migrants learned to cope with life in the city and were taught the values and moral discipline to survive in a hostile environment. Women found an opportunity to be involved in useful work. The African American church in Birmingham not only provided social, moral, and spiritual functions but also was able to reach beyond its spiritual life to build economic, educational, and other institutions to fill the secular needs of African Americans who migrated into the city during this period.

IV

Leadership, Institution-Building, and the African American Church in Birmingham

As African Americans migrated into Birmingham, the church served not only their moral and spiritual needs but also was in the forefront of establishing institutions to meet their physical and secular needs in a segregated city. As the central institution in the community, it supported and enhanced the other institutions established by African Americans in the city. Because of their unique role in the churches, pastors became the key leaders in the wider community. Using their churches as a base, they established institutions to fill the economic, educational, and welfare needs of African Americans in the city. Although these pastors did not make a frontal attack on segregation, they joined others in protesting what they saw as the excesses of the Jim Crow system.

Segregation in Birmingham grew increasingly harsh over time. From the beginning of their arrival in Birmingham, African Americans were segregated both by custom and law. The increase in the number of African Americans in the city to 40 percent by 1890 caused whites to insist that even tighter controls be placed on them. This segregation was especially strong in housing and on street cars. By custom and the design of real estate companies, the city maintained rigid housing segregation. The private utility company that operated street cars for the city segregated African American in the back of the cars. Beginning in 1903 the superintendent of parks began to deny African Americans access to the city's parks. By 1910 African Americans could not enter the city's parks except as servants for whites, unless given permission by the city commission.[1]

The city and state of Alabama also disfranchised African Americans during this period. In the 1870's, approximately 30 percent of the registered voters in Birmingham's elections were African American, and in the 1880's it ranged from 45 to 48 percent. But in 1888 Democrats established an all-white city primary that eliminated African

American voters from the election that mattered most. The new Alabama constitution of 1901 disfranchised African Americans with property and literacy requirements and a poll tax. The number of African American voters declined from 100,000 to 3,700. As African American political power diminished, the city ignored their interests.[2]

In the segregated community that African Americans built in Birmingham, the church supported the other institutions that were vital to the community, especially women's clubs and fraternal organizations. Often ministers in the city were the principal speakers for these occasions. For example, in 1906 the Knights of Pythias of Birmingham, which had about 5,000 members in Alabama and was one of the strongest fraternal orders in Birmingham, held their annual Thanksgiving service at the Shiloh Baptist Church with the Reverend Thomas W. Walker preaching the sermon. Several ministers in Birmingham, including the AME minister George W. Mitchell, were leaders among the Pythians. For many years, the sisters of the Mysterious Ten, a women's social club, held meetings at the AME Church in Birmingham. The United Brothers of Friendship, a men's fraternal order, also called the UBF, was organized at the St. John AME Church in 1887. The Old Ship AME Zion Church of Montgomery was the site of the organizing meeting of the State Federation of Colored Women's Clubs of Alabama. The Alabama Women's Clubs held several of their early meetings in Birmingham churches. The Sixteenth Street Baptist Church was the setting for the second session in 1900.[3]

African American churches supported the small but important black business community in Birmingham. Many leading business people were ministers, including William R. Pettiford and W. L. Lauderdale, both bank presidents, and Thomas W. Walker, who operated several businesses, including an insurance company. Other ministers were also involved in all kinds of businesses from grocery stores to loan companies. African American businesses regularly advertised through churches and religious meetings. The *Churchman*, the newspaper of the Sixteenth Street Baptist Church in the early 1900s, listed several advertisements from Diffay's Barber Shop, North Side Pharmacy, Cloud's Studio, Kumfoot Shoemaker, Dunbar Cafe, and Birmingham Undertaking Company.[4]

A similar relationship existed between the church and the African American press in Birmingham. Many ministers served as editors of African American papers, including H. S. Doyle of the *Negro American*, William McGill of *Hot Shots*, William R. Pettiford of the *Negro*

Enterprise, and Charles L. Fisher of the *Sparks*. Several became agents and investors in papers; for example, the Reverend T.L. Jordan, pastor of the Sixteenth Street Baptist Church, bought shares in the *Negro American* and was an agent for the paper. Most papers carried news of church events and some churches paid for advertisements. The many prominent pastors involved in the African American press no doubt encouraged their members to purchase African American papers.[5]

A close relationship existed between the African American church and the schools. Of the twenty public schools that the Birmingham Board of Education started and funded between 1883 and 1921, three began in churches and most of them at one time met in church buildings. For example, the Thomas Elementary School had its beginning in 1887 in the basement of the St. John AME Church. When the building housing the Avondale school burned in 1915, it met in the St. James AME church. The Kingston school began in 1902 in the Pilgrim Rest Baptist Church. William R. Pettiford and other pastors petitioned the city to form the first public high school for African Americans in the city, Industrial High School. Once Industrial High School and other schools began, churches and schools worked together. African American schools often held graduation services and other school programs in local churches. Often ministers were speakers for chapel services, baccalaureates, and commencements. *The Truth*, a paper that constantly advertised happenings at Tuggle Institute, advertised the speakers at its school. Most of the speakers at special events were pastors. Rev. W.C. Owen, pastor of Sardis Baptist Church, served as the school's chaplain and was a frequent chapel speaker.[6]

African American pastors were the leaders of the wider community during this period. Several factors accounted for their leadership and influence. Beginning in slavery, the African American preacher emerged as a key figure in the slave quarters, giving hope and security through their preaching, singing, and praying. After slavery, preachers created the main independent African American institution, the church. Although some had no formal education, pastors were among the most educated in the African American community. They were leaders because they had a following through their churches, whereas no other persons had such a natural constituency. Pastors were in close contact with many people. They also had an economic independence that most African Americans did not have. They naturally led the African American community.[7]

The most significant institutional builder and leader in the African American community during this period was William R. Pettiford. He was involved in almost every area of African American life in the city. Like many leaders and ministers of his era, Pettiford shared Booker T. Washington's emphasis on self-help, economic solidarity, and thrift as the keys to uplifting the African American race. Pettiford and Washington supported and admired each other and appear to have been warm friends. Pettiford was a supporter of Washington's National Negro Business League, serving on the executive committee in 1900 and giving major speeches at most of the annual meetings. Washington strongly influenced Pettiford's appointment as an Assistant Commissioner from Alabama for the Cotton State and International Exposition that met in Atlanta in 1895. In 1900 Washington delivered a speech in Birmingham in which he extolled the work of the Alabama Penny Savings Bank of which Pettiford was president. One year later Washington recommended Pettiford to President Theodore Roosevelt to be the United States Revenue Collector from Alabama. In his book, *Future of the Negro*, Washington pointed to Pettiford as an example of the success of his philosophy that through economic success whites would accord African Americans the proper respect. When the southern press was criticizing Washington for having dinner with President Theodore Roosevelt, Pettiford wrote Washington in 1901 stating that he regarded him as the Joseph of the race. Pettiford assured Washington that, like the ancient Israelite Joseph was sold into Egyptian slavery by his brothers but was elevated to a significant position of power by the Pharaoh, he too would come out victorious.[8]

Mirroring the experience of other African American leaders of his era, Pettiford rose from low beginnings to prominence. Born of free parents in North Carolina in 1847, he moved to Alabama in 1869 to seek better financial opportunity. With little money but a determination to improve his education, he entered the State Normal School at Marion, Alabama, now Alabama State University. After seven years of study mixed with work during the summer, Pettiford completed his education and became a pastor and school principal in Uniontown, Alabama. In 1877 he resigned these positions to become a teacher at Selma University and entered the theological department of the school. In 1880 he was ordained to the ministry and soon afterward became pastor of the First Baptist Church of Union Springs, Alabama, where he also was principal of the city school for African Americans. At the Union Springs church, Pettiford liquidated a large debt, remodeled the building, and greatly increased the church's membership. Such success brought him to the attention of the First Colored Baptist Church of Birmingham. In 1883 he accepted the pastorate of the First Colored Baptist Church, later named the Sixteenth Street Baptist Church. He was urged to do so by many state leaders, including Booker T. Washington, who insisted that he could provide the necessary leadership for Birmingham's growing African American population.[9]

Pettiford's first years in Birmingham were spent in revitalizing and enhancing the Sixteenth Street Baptist Church. When he became pastor the Membership was only about 150 and the church was holding services in a downtown store room. It had a debt of $500. He directed his first efforts toward canceling the debt and erecting a building suitable for present needs and future growth. By 1884 the church paid off its indebtedness and started a building fund. Members also erected a new building in 1885, the largest and most commodious in the city. The membership grew during this period to more than 400. It became known as the "people's church" because the community held so many of its meetings there. The church also served as a center for missions and evangelism. Pettiford formed the first missionary society in the city at Sixteenth Street Church. In 1887 the church began assisting four mission churches in other areas of the county and city.[10]

Because of his success in developing the Sixteenth Street Baptist Church, Pettiford quickly became one of the most outstanding and respected religious leaders in the city and state. His fellow pastors elected him president of the Ministerial Association of Birmingham. In 1887 the Baptist in the city and county chose him as moderator of the Mt. Pilgrim Baptist District Association, the largest organization of churches in the city and county. As moderator he established new churches in communities where none existed. Among the churches were the Harmony Street Baptist Church of Avondale and the First Baptist Church of Wylam. In 1889 he became president of the Alabama Baptist State Convention. Resigning that position in 1892, he assumed the position of financial secretary.[11]

Pettiford's leadership expanded beyond religion to include benevolence, education, and business. The major avenue for his leadership in these areas was the Representative Council, which he formed in the 1880s. The council was composed of delegates from Sunday Schools, social clubs, conventions, societies and lodges, and business organizations whose purpose was to reach African Americans "by furnishing them with information of self-help" and "to study the condition of African Americans in Birmingham with a view of finding remedies and the best method of applying them." It succeeded in organizing chapters throughout the city. The organization of the Representative Council consisted of three departments: missionary, educational, and business. The business department's major concern was establishing and enhancing African American businesses in the community. The educational department sought to start needed educational institutions, literary societies, and homes for disadvantaged persons. The missionary department focused primarily on starting churches where none existed. Through the Representative Council and working with the women's clubs, Pettiford was successful in forming such benevolent organizations as the Children's Hospital and the Old Folks Home. The club women and others assisted in the two projects, and Pettiford provided the leadership and inspiration.[12]

Pettiford's educational leadership was most evident in the establishment of the first African American high school in Birmingham. In 1899 he and Mrs. B.H. Hudson led a group of African American citizens in requesting such a school in Birmingham. With the assistance and support of Samuel Ullman, chairman of the Birmingham Board of Education, and J. Herbert Phillips, superintendent of schools, the institution was established in 1900. The board appointed Arthur Harold Parker, a protege of Pettiford, the first principal and only teacher of the new school which became known as the Industrial High School. The high school officially began in September 1900 in one room on the second floor of the Cameron Building with eighteen students. Among the persons present at the formal opening was William R. Pettiford. Parker reported that because of the great enthusiasm and happiness of those present over the beginning of the school, they sang and made speeches most of the morning. Pettiford continued to support the school, especially in its early years. The high school held its first graduation at the Sixteenth Street Baptist Church in 1904.[13]

Pettiford's most ambitious project was the establishment of the Alabama Penny Savings Bank. Pettiford later explained that he was riding on a streetcar one Friday night in 1890 when he observed an African American woman drinking whiskey who had just received her weekly pay. That experience, he maintained, led him to think about some kind of business where African Americans could save their money rather than wasting it on alcohol or other foolish endeavors. Pettiford's inspiration also came in part from William Washington Browne, president of the Savings Bank of the Grand Fountain United Order of

True Reformers of Richmond, Virginia, who expressed an interest in opening a branch of his bank in Birmingham. Pettiford and the local African American business elite took the initiative to establish their own bank after deciding they could do a better job than a person from outside the community.[14] Three months of agitation, speeches, and advertising were necessary before there was enough sentiment in support of the project. Some African Americans distrusted black-operated banks because of the failure of the Freedmen's Bureau Bank. William Pettiford led a cadre of leaders who were determined to push the project to success. They included Peter F. Clarke, vice-president; B.H. Hudson, Sr., school teacher, grocer, and cashier of the bank; N.B. Smith, a real estate broker, manager of the Metropolitan Mutual Benefit Association, and superior master of the Afro-American Benevolent Society; Arthur H. Parker, who in 1901 became the principal of the Industrial High School; J.O. Diffay, who owned several barber shops and later held the position of president of the Peoples Mutual Aid Association; and Thomas W. Walker, pastor and founder of several businesses. These men had already become involved in successful business ventures. Among the board of directors were Reverend J.I. Jackson, a local pastor; Professor F.S. Hayzel, a school principal; and Reverend J.Q.A. Wilhite, president of the Birmingham Mutual Burial Association and pastor of the Sixth Avenue Baptist Church.[15]

Pettiford accepted the position of president of the bank with some reservation. He had undertaken the formation of the bank as a missionary project that he saw as an extension of his pastoral duties. When asked at an early meeting of the directors to assume the presidency, he declined. The directors threw down an ultimatum: "You'll be president or there will be no bank. Your name is necessary for confidence." Pettiford consented to serve for one year while continuing his pastoral duties. At the end of the one year, the confidence argument and the ultimatum again confronted him. After serving for four years on a one year basis, Pettiford resigned his pastorate. "Though I'll have you understand," he told the board of directors, "I'm still a preacher." He became the full-fledged president of the Alabama Penny Savings Bank, an office he held for twenty-three years. Throughout those twenty-three years, Pettiford continued to preach in churches and denominational meetings and for a brief period assumed the pastorate of the Tabernacle Baptist Church.[16]

The Alabama Penny Savings Company achieved immediate success. The bank opened its doors on October 15, 1890. It received on deposit that day, $555, which along with the $2,000 already paid in from the sale of stock, constituted its working capital. The bank was not incorporated at first because under the Alabama laws of the nineties a capital of $25,000 was needed. It was incorporated as the Alabama Penny Savings Bank in 1895 with its required capital of $25,000 and the privilege of increasing it to $100,000. During the bank's first decade, Pettiford engineered many real estate transactions that proved to be highly productive for the bank. For example, in 1896 bank officials bought a building for $6,500 and sold it one year later for $20,000. Pettiford and the directors then bought a house for $18,000 which they sold several years later for $35,000. During its lifetime the Penny Bank may have had 10,000 depositors in its main bank in Birmingham and its branches.[17]

Part of Pettiford's success as leader of the Penny Bank was the result of his cultivation of members of the white power structure. Accepting Booker T. Washington's emphasis on self-help and racial solidarity, Pettiford also agreed with Washington's emphasis on developing partnerships with powerful whites. Pettiford entered working relationships with other banks. Needing someone to train his workers in bookkeeping and banking procedures because no institution provided such training for African Americans in the city, Pettiford was successful in obtaining assistance from white financial institutions in Birmingham. Help from the Steiner Brothers appears to have been one major factor for the Penny Bank's survival of the economic crisis of 1893, when some white owned banks failed and many depositors withdrew their savings.[18]

Pettiford's move to the position of president of the Penny Bank strengthened his belief that thrift, frugality, and economic self-help were essential for African American uplift. While serving as both pastor of Sixteenth Street Baptist Church and president of the bank from 1890 to 1893, Pettiford increasingly called the church together to discuss practical concerns of thrift and economic solidarity. Pettiford became convinced that it was necessary for African Americans to establish a financial base on which to uplift themselves. In 1895 he published a book entitled *God's Revenue System* in which he gave a Biblical basis for this belief. When he became full-time president of the bank in 1893, Pettiford sought to spread his message of economic liberation. His addresses at various National Negro Business League meetings and conferences on the Negro held annually at Hampton Institute in Virginia revealed his philosophy of economic liberation. In 1903 Pettiford gave an address entitled, "The Importance of Business to the Negro," which he emphasized this idea: "No substantial progress can come to any race unless the race is developed in a very large degree along business lines . . . the substantial progress of an individual, a race, or a nation is measured by its ability to rise from the position of earning wages to that of profitably directing its own business." He also decided that it was not enough for African Americans to own their own businesses but that they had to commit to a practice of patronizing black-owned businesses. His views reflected his recognition of the benefits of a self-imposed segregated economy, an idea that other leaders of the time were also groping with: "The colored wage-earner must be prevailed upon to spend his earnings so that a portion of the same may be retained by his people. Any class or race of people who fail to get this idea clearly in their minds and act upon it are past redemption."[19]

Pettiford's philosophy of economic liberation included a strong advocacy for homeownership. At several meetings he revealed both his commitment to help African Americans own their own homes through the bank's lending policies and the extensive benefits to the community when members of the African American community engaged in property ownership. In an address before the Sixth Annual Convention of the Negro Business League, Pettiford insisted that one of the great features of the Alabama Penny Savings Bank was to teach the art of saving money and of purchasing homes. He said that out of the bank's 8,000 depositors more than 1,000 had purchased their homes. At the Thirteenth Annual Convention he said that the very presence of an African American bank in a community gives Negroes a better chance to own their own home. He further maintained that the presence of African American banks had saved thousands of homes owned by Negroes from foreclosures.[20]

The Penny Bank under Pettiford's direction proceeded aggressively to promote home ownership through carefully engineered real estate transactions. The board of directors agreed to spend half of the money invested in the company to purchase real estate in large quantities that they then subdivided and sold in small packages to encourage home ownership. Such a strategy motivated many African Americans in the city to purchase their own homes. Mortgage records, particularly in the new suburb of Smithfield, show that the Alabama Penny Savings Bank had loaned most of the residents the funds to purchase property in that subdivision.[21]

True to the perception of his bank movement in missionary terms, Pettiford sought to spread his gospel of economic liberation to other sections of the state. He established branches of the Alabama Penny Savings Bank in Selma, Anniston, and Montgomery. When the Alabama Legislature passed a law prohibiting the further extension of branches in Alabama, Pettiford was not completely checked. The fame of the Penny Bank had spread to other parts of the United States. Pettiford received many offers to come to other cities to assist in starting African American banks in those locations. He accepted some of these invitations, remaining in the place he visited until the bank was underway. For example, in 1908 Pettiford assisted African Americans in Atlanta in starting the first bank in that city. It was also during this period that Pettiford helped organize the National Negro Banker's Association, an organization committed "to foster and encourage the establishment of banks among our people and to look after the interests and welfare of those already organized."[22]

In 1913 the Penny Bank built its own building on 18th Street in Birmingham's thriving African American business district. The five-story building also housed other African American businesses on its upper floors. Of its sixty-four rooms, black businesses occupied all of them except one. The rent paid to the Penny Bank amounted to $8,000. The architect, Wallace A. Rayfield, who designed many churches in Birmingham, had his office there. The *Birmingham Reporter*, *Birmingham Messenger*, and the *Voice of the People*, all African American newspapers, were housed there. The building was a projection of Pettiford's commitment to the philosophy of self-help and economic solidarity: African Americans cooperating to assist African Americans.[23]

By the time of Pettiford's death in 1914, the Alabama Penny Savings Bank was the largest and strongest African American owned bank in the United States with a capitalization of $100,000 and an annual business exceeding $500,000. In 1915 the bank merged with another black-owned bank and became the Alabama Penny-Prudential Savings Bank with J.O. Diffay as acting president.[24]

Despite the Penny Bank's success and its merger, the institution failed in 1915, less than one year after Pettiford's death. Several reasons have been given to explain the demise of the Alabama Penny Bank. One explanation suggested that when B.H. Hudson's son, the bank's teller, fell short in his accounts, a run on the bank began which the officials could not halt. A second explanation maintained that the bank tied up too much of its money in long-term church loans and did not have the necessary cash flow to meet the $35,000 necessary to pay the Christmas fund depositors. Other reasons given were the merger with the

Prudential Bank that further weakened its cash flow and the excessively rapid expansion of branches. Another rationale offered by a former official of the bank suggested that when the Penny Bank ran into trouble the Steiner Brothers, who were financial agents not only for this bank but also the First National Bank that also was having financial difficulty, chose to meet the needs of the First National Bank. Thus, the Penny Bank could not solve its difficulties. Any or all these factors could explain the bank's demise. The major reason, however, was probably the death of William Pettiford. From the beginning Pettiford had been the inspirational leader and had exercised sound judgment. He also had strong respect in the African American community and had nurtured a unique relationship with the white power structure. His successors probably were not able to maintain his strong connections. It was necessary therefore to liquidate the bank's assets and to sell the $150,000 bank building to the Knights of Pythias for $70,000.

Next to Pettiford, the most outstanding leader in building institutions in the African American community of Birmingham was the Reverend Thomas W. Walker. Pettiford greatly influenced Walker and both worked together in several community projects. Like Pettiford, Walker was also a part of the "Tuskegee Machine," a term generally referring to those who supported Booker T. Washington as the leader of the African American community and subscribed to his philosophy of economic solidarity and self-help. Washington served on the board of directors of the Grate Coal Company in Birmingham that Walker operated. Walker gave a speech at the National Negro Business League in 1900 in which he discussed the coal company. In 1902 Washington spoke at the National Baptist Convention meeting at the Shiloh Baptist Church, an occasion at which a stampede occurred that resulted in the death of several persons.[25]

Walker was born into slavery in Coosa County, Alabama, in 1852. He remembered being sold with his family while still a lad, a memory that lingered with him throughout his life. After emancipation, he moved to the Montgomery area where he was converted, joined the Elam Baptist Church, and assumed the position of Sunday School superintendent. In 1881 Walker moved to Birmingham, joined the Sixteenth Street Baptist Church, and entered the ministry. Three years later Pettiford licensed and ordained Walker. Soon afterward, Walker accepted the pastorate of the Sixth Avenue Baptist Church which grew to become one of the largest churches in the city. After the first building was destroyed by fire, Walker led the effort to erect an even larger sanctuary in 1890.[26]

Walker's powerful preaching was the key to his immediate success. The working class in Birmingham relished his emotional speech. Walker had imbibed the folksy preaching style of his father, who had been a slave preacher, and the pastors of Elam Church. Limited in education but gifted with imagination and power, Walker attracted the rural migrants who continued to move into Birmingham from the Black-Belt of Alabama and other Southern states. An observer noted that his exposition of the Bible, combined with his recital of how God had delivered him out of slavery and had kept him through trials and temptations, caused congregations to go into emotional frenzies. Walker's preaching style and charisma, however, did not appeal to all members of Sixth Avenue. Many wanted a less emotional worship experience, and others felt that Walker was too arrogant and conceited. Walker left the Sixth Avenue Baptist Church in 1890 and for a year pastored the First Baptist Church of Brighton, located in the western section of the county.[27]

In 1891 Walker returned to Birmingham and with six members formed the Shiloh Baptist Church. The membership numbered two thousand by 1895. Often during the worship services hundreds of people could not get inside to hear Walker preach because the sanctuary was already full. Urgently needing more space, Walker led the Shiloh Church into building a second church costing nearly $40,000. By 1900 Walker had baptized more than 3,000 new members into the Shiloh Baptist Church.[28]

As pastor, Walker concerned himself with more than just the spiritual life of his congregation. He devoted a substantial part of his preaching to educating his African American parishioners on spending their money wisely. He constantly stressed that money spent on sensible clothing, a decent home, education for their children, church maintenance, and a reasonable portion for savings in an African American owned savings institution would raise their standing and self-respect among both other African Americans and whites. To meet the practical economic needs of his large membership and those of African Americans generally in Birmingham, Walker opened several businesses. These included a shoe store, a livery stable, a cemetery, a newspaper, a funeral home, a coal company, and a relief society with sick and death benefits. Walker also chaired the board of directors of the Alabama

Penny Savings Bank. Although not formally educated, he was one of the founders of Birmingham Baptist College.[29]

Perhaps Walker's most important creation outside of his church was an insurance company. Originally called the Afro-American Benevolent Association, it began in his church as a benefit society with sick, accident, and death benefits. By 1894 it was a standard insurance company, renamed the Union Central Relief Association of Birmingham. Walker sought to put it on a business-like basis by establishing benefit rates that were closely tied to premiums, setting the maximum death payment at $100. He hired as many as 125 agents at the company's peak and in 1894 petitioned the state legislature for a charter. Finally, in February 1901 after several failures, Union Central became the first African American insurance association to be officially chartered in Alabama. In 1897 Walker moved into Georgia and established the Union Mutual Relief Association of Atlanta, with Walker as its president. It became the first African American insurance association chartered in Georgia, receiving authorization to write policies for a maximum benefit of $500.[30]

Walker's motivation for establishing the Union Central Relief Association derived partly from the discrimination of white insurance companies. White insurance companies generally refused to write personally priced insurance policies for African Americans, rating them higher risks because of poverty, greater exposure to disease, and shorter life spans. Those companies that did insure African Americans, beginning with the Prudential Insurance Company in 1881, charged high and discriminatory premiums, which they could not pay. Walker noted in Birmingham that Southern Mutual Aid Association, the only company of its kind doing business among African Americans, refused to employ black agents even to solicit from African American clients. The behavior of the white agents of Southern Mutual also outraged Walker. He observed that upon entering African American homes these white agents frequently failed to give proper respect, especially to black women, addressing them by their given names or referring to them as "auntie".[31]

No issue concerned the African American church and its leadership more than education. Coming out of slavery, African Americans craved the opportunity to receive formal training. They flocked to the schools of such agencies as the Freedmen's Bureau and the American Missionary Association, desiring to learn to read and write. African Americans wanted an education because they saw it as a means of liberation and of extending their freedom. Their concern with reading the voting ballots and safeguarding themselves against the fraud and manipulation of written contracts from planters provided significant reasons for their desire to become literate. Others saw education as a means of equality with whites. And still others wanted to read the Bible for themselves. After the demise of Reconstruction circumscribed political rights, education became an even more compelling priority of many African American church leaders.[32]

Like other clergyman in the South, African American pastors in Birmingham sought to provide education with a Christian dimension. For these ministers, Christian education was imperative for the moral progress of the race. Bishop Wesley Gaines, who presided over the AME Church in the state for several years, made it clear in his opening address to the Negro Young People's Christian and Education Congress of Alabama in 1902 that only the combination of Christianity and education would uplift the race. Speaking as president of the congress, Gaines said that "Our young people must be educated, but it is our business to see that their education is permeated with the spirit of the great Teacher who in the Sermon on the Mount laid down the great elemental propositions and principles upon which all education worthwhile is to be based and built-up." The Reverend J.S. Jackson, pastor of Birmingham's AME Zion Church, speaking at the first annual banquet of Tuggle School in 1908, praised the school for providing an intellectual, moral, and religious education. Most clergy valued education because they felt that it helped develop one's God-given abilities. Only a Christian-based education could help people learn how to use their abilities to understand and respond to the demands of God.[33]

Most clergymen in Birmingham and the South championed both industrial and liberal arts education. There appeared to be no debate about the merits of one type of education over the other. Ministers in the city agreed with prominent school founders Isaac Lane and J.C. Price that those African Americans not capable of completing the demands of a liberal arts education needed industrial training as an alternative. They insisted, however, that those with the ability should pursue a liberal arts education. William Pettiford, who had received a liberal arts and a theological education, maintained that students in Birmingham needed industrial training along with the liberal arts because of the industrial economy of the city. Some schools in the city sought to provide both. Industrial High School, the first public high school for African Americans in the city offered both liberal arts and industrial courses. As late as 1915, the school required all students to take five hours of industrial arts courses. The boys took courses in carpentry and tailoring, the girls cooking and sewing. Similarly, the St. Mark Academy, the first private high school for African Americans in Birmingham, had primarily a liberal arts curriculum but also offered several industrial arts courses. Despite its liberal arts orientation, St. Mark's also had a cordial working relationships with Tuskegee Institute. In 1914 Booker T. Washington wrote C.W. Brooks, principal of St. Mark's, thanking him for the good students he had sent to Tuskegee and urging him to send others to take the course in agriculture.[34]

Some individual African American churches operated schools and kindergartens, including the Shiloh Baptist Church and the St. John AME Church. But many of these schools operated only sporadically or for short periods. Miller Memorial School and St. Mark's Academy were the two schools operated by individual churches which were the largest and of the longest duration. Both received substantial support from white denominational agencies. The Miller Memorial School was primarily an elementary school located in an annex to the Miller Memorial Presbyterian Church. In 1914 the school had a total of seven teachers, including the pastor, and 176 pupils. The financial report of 1912-13 showed the school with an income of $1,325, of which $1,000 came from the Presbyterian Board of Mission for Freedmen and $325 from tuition.[35]

The Protestant Episcopal Diocese of Alabama founded St. Mark's Academy in 1892. It offered a secondary education for African Americans in Birmingham, the first school to do so. Two white women from New York and Michigan served as the first teachers, but in 1899 the Reverend Charles Brooks, an African American clergyman from Baltimore, became the pastor of St. Mark's Episcopal Church and the principal of the school. In May 1900 the school issued its first high school diploma. By 1914 St. Mark's enrolled 171 elementary pupils and 21 secondary pupils, with seven teachers and workers. The land was valued at $5,000 and the two story brick structure at $15,000. The school charged tuition and fees, but most of its support came from the Episcopal Board of Missions and the American Church Institute for Negroes.[36]

In the first decade of the twentieth century African American denominations in Birmingham pooled their resources to form schools. The Methodist Episcopal Church, Baptist, and Colored Methodist Episcopal Church established schools in Birmingham that they called colleges, but these schools offered little more than elementary and high school courses. These "colleges" which mirrored those founded earlier in the Black-Belt and served the peculiar needs of African Americans.[37]

The Freedmen's Aid Society of the Methodist Episcopal Church established Central Alabama Institute and College in Huntsville, Alabama, in 1878. In 1904 the institution moved to Mason City in the Birmingham area and constructed six large buildings, including two dormitories. Although the Freedmen's Aid Society owned and financed Central Alabama College, a board of trustees from the all-black Central Alabama Conference governed the institution. The faculty generally consisted of from six to ten members, with graduating classes numbering three to twenty-three members. Its first class graduated in 1907. Available records show that about 153 persons received the high school diploma, and these graduates usually succeeded in passing the Alabama State Board Examination for teachers. In 1915 the Bureau of Education reported that the school had an enrollment of 190 students and 11 teachers and workers. The institution offered primarily liberal arts courses with a few classes in industrial arts. In 1922 Central Alabama Institute and College sustained a tragic loss when fire destroyed its main building and other facilities. When the Freedmen's Aid Society decided not to rebuild, the school ceased to exist.[38]

Miles Memorial College was the result of efforts by the CME Church in Alabama to provide Christian education for the state's youth. Out of this effort emerged a high school in Thomasville, Alabama in 1898. Four years later, the CME Church of the Alabama Conference established a high school at Booker City, now Docena, in the Birmingham area. But in 1907 the Tennessee Coal and Iron Company, also called TCI, which held mineral rights to the property, wanted to open a mine there and use convict labor. TCI and the school's trustees negotiated a deal to exchange the Booker City property for the present location of thirty acres. The trustees considered this property, located only four miles from the heart of Birmingham and situated near the North Bessemer car line, more desirable for a school. According to the agreement there would be an even exchange for the real estate, and the school would receive $25,000 to construct a building in exchange for the building and land at Booker City.[39]

With the merger of the Thomasville High School and the move to the new site, Miles College came into being in 1907 and was chartered in 1908. Most of its first students enrolled in elementary grades, with small numbers in the secondary and college programs. The institution graduated its first class in 1910, with four persons receiving the high

Leadership, Institution-Building

school diploma. By 1914 enrollment reached 246 pupils and 14 teachers and workers, but the school carried a heavy financial debt.[40]

The need for a trained ministry led to the formation of another school in Birmingham by African American Baptists called Birmingham Baptist College. Ministerial education had been an initial concern of African American churchmen after emancipation. Since the minister was to be the leader of his people, he could be most effective with a formal education. The fear that an untrained clergy would misinterpret the Bible and misinform the people also undergirded the demand for an educated ministry. Daniel Payne, a patriarch of the AME Church who served as bishop in Alabama, agreed with the negative assessment of the typical African American pastor that Booker T. Washington advanced in August 1890. Washington had complained that most black ministers, being uneducated, failed to expose the masses to the truths of Christianity. Payne and other church leaders admonished ministers to seek theological training at a variety of levels, suggesting the creation of Bible schools for ministers of average abilities. Ministerial leaders also believed in the power of their own example, expecting that others would follow their example in this area.[41]

The rapid proliferation of Baptist churches in the Birmingham area resulted in untrained persons filling pulpits and assuming leadership positions. Baptist leaders began to make efforts to provide ministerial education. The initial effort begin in 1904 when Reverends C.O. Boothe and W.R. Pettiford held classes in the basement of the Sixteenth Street Baptist Church. Sometime later, the Reverends John W. Goodgame, Sr. and J.J. Green started similar efforts at the Sixth Avenue Baptist Church. Soon afterward, several district associations in the Birmingham area were engaged in educational efforts. In 1912 three associations in the area ceased operating their schools in favor of a single institution which they named Birmingham Baptist College. They formed the Colored Baptist Educational Association, which became the owner of the institution. The trustees purchased ten acres of land and built an administration building in 1913, largely due to the inspiration and leadership of John W. Goodgame. In 1914 the school was in such an embryonic stage that the Bureau of Negro Education felt it did not warrant a discussion in its report at that time.[42]

Women's religious groups in the city played a significant role in the support of educational institutions. Mrs. William Pettiford organized the first Baptist women's convention in the city, assembling thirty-seven women from the various Baptist churches in the city who had a desire to do missionary work both at home and on the foreign field. The women met at the Broad Street Baptist Church in 1883 and formed the Mt. Pilgrim Baptist Women's convention. They affirmed their commitment to missions and their belief in the Bible as the sole guide in all matter of faith and practice in Baptist churches. This group also became a major supporter of Birmingham Baptist College.[43]

Methodist women's groups followed a similar pattern to the Baptists. Although they supported home and foreign missions, their chief function was to support the newly established colleges of their denomination. CME women groups supported Miles College in Birmingham, AME Zion women groups raised funds for Lomax Hannon College in Greenville, Alabama. The North Alabama Conference of the AME Church formed its women's auxiliary in 1878. This group of women began immediately to support Daniel Payne College.[44]

The African American church also provided important aid to Birmingham's poor and needy. Moving into Birmingham to improve their economic condition, African Americans found themselves in the poorest paying jobs. Unemployment and chronic layoffs were a problem for many. With few resources, African Americans had little to put aside for periods of illness, unemployment, and expenses at death. Inadequate public charity failed to meet the needs of the masses of African Americans and whites. Many found it difficult to obtain any form of insurance or relief. Poverty and a low standard of living made many African Americans unacceptable as members of some fraternal organizations that operated insurance departments. Most African Americans in Birmingham could not afford the high premiums of the white insurance companies.[45]

The church stepped into the gap to provide relief and to assist the growing pauper class. The poor often called upon churches for donations to feed their families or for assistance during times of sickness and death. Benefit societies and Christian unions provided a major part of the church's benevolence. These societies had been a part of church life in the Black-Belt of Alabama. Inspired by a spirit of Christian charity and common need, African Americans supported these societies with the pennies which they could scrape together in order to aid each other in times of sickness. But the major emphasis was to insure themselves a decent burial. These societies often gave themselves vivid names that showed their Biblical and charitable bent. Among these names were "Love and Charity," "Builders of the Walls of Jerusalem," "Sons and Daughters of Esther," and "Brothers and Sisters of Love."[46]

Leadership, Institution-Building

Benevolent societies and Christian unions sprang up in churches throughout the Birmingham area. For example, the *Negro American* reported on March 17, 1894, that the Coalburg AME Church had recently established a benevolent society. Earlier the Reverend W.R. Pettiford had established the Christian Aid Society at the Sixteenth Street Baptist Church. Its object was "to aid the sick members and bury its dead, and to do such work as may be agreed upon from time to time by vote of the society." In 1920 members of the Oak Grove Baptist Church in Brighton formed Christian Union #16 the primary purpose of providing death benefits to its members. Many other churches formed similar groups, including the New Zion Baptist Church of Bessemer, Macedonia Baptist Church of Ensley, and the St. Luke Baptist Church in the Cairo area of Birmingham.[47]

Pastors and ministerial groups also organized protests aimed not at overthrowing the South's system of segregation but at pointing out what they viewed as gross injustice. Even when ministers were not the major leaders, protesters usually held their meetings at churches. For example, in 1895 African Americans met at the Shiloh Baptist Church to protest the shooting of a black thirteen-year-old girl by a Birmingham police officer. The girl had been picking up coal from a railroad car. Protesting both this shooting and the frequent shootings of African Americans by white police officers in the city, the mass meeting presided over by laymen in the community issued the following resolution and appeal:

> To the Humane and Christian-hearted White People of Birmingham Jefferson County: We, the law abiding Negro citizens living in your midst, in mass-meeting assembled in Shiloh Baptist Church, December 19th, feeling seriously effected by a defect in public sentiment which admits of so frequent murders of our people by the officers of the law, as well as others, the same being allowed to escape without dire punishment, realize that it is our bounden duty to make this earnest and urgent appeal to you.
>
> Feeling that the security of human life is uncertain and the peace and dignity of our commonwealth has been outraged; that the common good of all the people, white and black, may appear, and the ties that bind us as a people of a single state be cemented, let there be a careful prosecution of all such deplorable crimes.

> Be it remembered that the strength and character of a people are manifested as much in protecting the weak and helpless as in conquering the mighty. When will justice be crowned?[48]

On several occasions, black ministers joined other prominent African Americans in Alabama in protest. In 1901 William Pettiford, Booker T. Washington, and others sent a resolution of protest to the Alabama Constitutional Convention against the disfranchisement of African Americans. These leaders wrote in a conciliatory, even subservient tone and explained their pleas as the only way by which blacks could make their views known to the all-white members of the Convention. Each petitioner represented himself as a good citizen and taxpayer. African Americans, they insisted, had rendered much service to the white people. The petition maintained that African Americans were disfranchised in Alabama twenty years ago and they saw no need of additional measures that would serve no useful purpose beside that of humiliating the race. The petition also urged the convention not to take away educational opportunities from African Americans in Alabama.[49]

Individual ministers and ministerial groups protested against lynchings and the treatment of African Americans on railroads. In 1894 a group of Alabama leaders called a Colored Convention to discuss the present and future state of African Americans in the state. In addition to Pettiford, Birmingham ministers present were Winfred Mixon, presiding elder of the AME Church and chairperson of the resolution committee; H.S. Doyle, pastor of the St. James CME Church; and T.L. Jordan, pastor of the Sixteenth Street Baptist Church. The meeting issued a protest resolution against lynching with the Reverend Robert T. Pollard of Selma giving an address on the issue. A committee also sent a resolution to the Alabama Railway Commission protesting discrimination on the railroads.[50]

Similarly, African American ministerial groups in the city protested the abuses of street car operators. Streetcars in Birmingham had always been segregated. African Americans were required to sit in the back of the car and to give up their seats if whites were standing. Streetcar employees, usually of white working class origins, often expressed deep-seated racial antipathies in discourteous and even violent treatment of African American riders. In 1918 the problem centered on white conductors' abusive treatment of African American women. An incident in March of that year, in which a streetcar conductor struck a black woman and had her arrested for disorderly conduct angered African Americans. Similar instances of verbal abuse of African American women by streetcar workers brought protests by a local minister's organization, the Interdenominational Ministerial Alliance, and a local civic group, the Colored Citizens' League of Bessemer.[51]

The African American church served an important function in Birmingham by establishing institutions that served the secular needs of the people. Pastors led both the churches and the wider African American community. They were close to the people, commanded their respect, and enjoyed the freedom to engage in community leadership. The two most important leaders, William Pettiford and Thomas Walker, built economic, benevolent, and educational institutions. Although not making a frontal assault on segregation, churches hosted protest meetings, and pastors joined others in the community in denouncing what they saw as the excesses of the system of segregation. With the coming of World War I, many African Americans would leave Birmingham and migrate to the North. Changing circumstances would require new religious responses, even as churches continued their traditional functions.

V

The African American Church Between the World Wars: Continuity and Preservation

In the period from 1920 to 1940, African American churches of the mainline denominations continued to fill many of the same needs they had met before World War I in an atmosphere of dashed hopes, white intimidation, and economic insecurity. Many African Americans migrated from Birmingham to the North, but a large number moved into the Birmingham area from rural Alabama and other areas of the South seeking better economic opportunity. These migrants formed many churches, primarily small Baptist churches, which met the crucial needs they had supplied for first-generation migrants. African American churches also continued to be social centers. Although people of all classes worshiped together in many churches, a few churches were composed almost exclusively of the small group of African American professionals in the city. Pastors of the traditional Baptist and Methodist churches continued to be leaders in the community. Pastors were greatly concerned and involved in enhancing businesses and in preserving the educational institutions formed before World War I. Most pastors continued to adhere to the philosophy of self-help, but there emerged a stronger sense of injustice among them and louder cries for fairness. The Reverend J.W. Goodgame, Sr. was a towering figure among African American clergymen in the city, and one of the most effective ministerial and community leaders during this period.

Because of their loyalty during World War I, which included serving in the armed forces, sponsoring liberty bond drives, and forming speaker's bureaus to dispense government information about the war, African Americans in Birmingham expected to be granted greater civil rights. Many felt their wartime sacrifices entitled them to the same rights as white Americans. When such rights did not come after the war, African Americans in the city began to agitate and protest.[1]

Protest took several forms. For example, in 1919 a group calling itself the Negro Betterment League of Alabama presented to Governor

Kilby, Lieutenant Governor Miller, Speaker of the House Merrit, and to both houses of the legislature a petition of grievances and proposals for changes concerning African Americans in Alabama. During the same year, the Interdenominational Ministerial Alliance and the Birmingham Colored Citizen's League objected to the showing of the film, *The Birth of a Nation*, which they saw as causing serious damage to the image of African Americans. No organization was more important during this period than the National Association for the Advancement of Colored People (NAACP). A group of citizens formed a branch of the NAACP in Birmingham in 1919 and sought to attain equal rights for African Americans through education, protest, and litigation. Among their many involvements in the 1930s was the Willie Peterson case, in which an African American man with a crippling physical deformity was shot by a white man in his jail cell and ultimately sentenced to death for killing two white society women and wounding a sister of one of the victims.[2]

Despite protest from the NAACP and other organizations in the city, there was no significant change in race relations. The depression and general harsh economic times of the 1930s worked against betterment of African American conditions. Fear and intimidation caused by violence and white resistance accelerated during the 1920s and 1930s and served to thwart any real change in race relations. Many African Americans being beaten and killed by the police with questionable justification. While the police used open and legal means to press violence against African Americans in Birmingham, the Ku Klux Klan employed clandestine and extra-legal methods such as beatings and violent threats to "keep blacks in their place." During the 1920s the Birmingham Klan became one of the largest in the nation, with the Robert E. Lee Klan group boasting a membership of 18,000 by 1924. To show its power and influence in the city, the Klan staged large rallies. In 1923 the Nathan Bedford Forrest Klan group attracted 50,000 people to a rally that included an initiation ceremony, a barbecue, a fireworks display, and the giving away of a car. Although the Klan aimed its violence at several groups, African Americans in Birmingham felt the Klan represented a special threat to them because of the activities of the post-Reconstruction Klan. They believed that random acts of violence by the Klan were a warning to them to stay in their place. The coal strike of 1920 also contributed to the atmosphere of fear and intimidation. African Americans composed 70 percent of the miners. The local press and company officials portrayed the strike in racial terms. After Governor Thomas Kilby sent in Alabama troops to end the strike in favor of the company, many African Americans migrated to the

North. Those who remained were forced to work in an atmosphere of intimidation.[3]

The municipal government also undertook measures to inhibit African American progress. Rigid segregation by law became an established fact with little protest. In 1923 the city enacted a streetcar segregation ordinance. Three years later the city passed a law mandating segregated housing. Disfranchisement also continued. In 1928 only 352 African Americans out of a population of 85,280 were eligible to vote in Birmingham. Only 456 African Americans voted in the whole of Jefferson County in 1935.[4]

Despite the segregation and generally harsh conditions in Birmingham, African Americans from the Black Belt of Alabama and other southern states continued to migrate into Birmingham. Although conditions were far from ideal in the city, they were simply much better than life for many tenant farmers in southern Alabama. Many moved to states in the North, but some chose to come to Birmingham. The principal reason was to improve their economic opportunities. For example, Will Prather came to Birmingham from the Black Belt. He maintained that the lure of a steady job earning monetary wages motivated him. George Brown reported that he came to Birmingham from Dallas County in the 1920s to survive. He felt that if he had remained in Dallas County he might have starved to death because of the bleak conditions for blacks. Working his way to Birmingham, he first got a job at the Tutwiler Hotel, then in 1926 or 1927 he began to work on a part-time basis at Sloss Furnaces. Finally, in 1931 he received a permanent job at Sloss Furnaces. This urban migration by persons such as Prather and Brown meant that African Americans continued to make up approximately 40 percent of Birmingham's population.[5]

With continued African American migration into the city, the number of churches increased. Among the denominations, the Baptists far outdistanced any other. A Works Progress Association (WPA) survey of African American churches in Birmingham and Jefferson County in 1939 showed clearly the primacy of the Baptist church among African Americans. According to the study, there were a total of 314 African American Baptist churches out of a total of 429 African American churches in the city and county. African Americans established approximately sixty-two small Baptist Churches in the Birmingham area between 1920 and 1939. Other denominations, including the Methodists, established few churches. The WPA survey listed less than twenty Methodist churches of all denominations founded during this period.[6]

One reason for the rapid growth of Baptist churches was that recent migrants to the city formed numerous churches of that denomination. These persons preferred smaller churches to the larger and more established churches. The established churches already had their leadership, and the new migrants saw little chance of moving into these positions. Many of these new migrants were poorer than many persons in the established churches, had less education, and did not dress as well as most of the other members. These concerns led them to form smaller churches where they felt more comfortable, churches that reminded them of the churches in the rural areas where they had worshiped. For example, a group of recent migrants established the Twenty-Third Street Baptist Church of Ensley in the home of Mrs. Nora Moore. Mrs. Moore and others in the Ensley community gave as their reason the need for a church for the "poorer classes" where they could worship and where there would not be as many calls for money as in the larger and more established churches. Another group of recent migrants started the New Kingdom Baptist Church in North Birmingham in 1935, saying that they felt discriminated against in the larger churches.[7]

Splits, which had accounted for Baptist growth before World War I, led to the formation of many new and small Baptist churches in the period between the wars. Almost without exception, the splits occurred over the issue of pastoral leadership. With few places to exercise leadership in Birmingham's segregated community, members anxious for power and recognition often questioned the pastor's authority. This questioning often led to bitter internecine conflict and ultimately to splits. One such split occurred in 1924 at the Lively Hope Baptist Church when a group of members broke away to organize the Peace Baptist Church of Pratt City. In 1926 members left the New Canaan Baptist Church to form the Pleasant Hill Baptist Church of Ensley. In 1938 a group of twenty dissatisfied members left Sixth Street Peace Baptist Church and formed the Antioch Baptist Church of Smithfield. Members from the Zion Baptist Church of Titusville broke from the Goldwire Baptist Church in 1936 over the issue of whether to call another pastor when the current pastor of Goldwire became ill. In 1933 a group of dissatisfied members left the Harmony Street Baptist Church and formed the First Baptist Church of Irondale. In 1931 the Reverend J. A. Martin, pastor of the Jackson Street Baptist Church of Woodlawn, led seventy members from the church to form the First Baptist Church of Woodlawn after a group of deacons questioned his authority.[8]

Some observers in Birmingham cautioned the community that there were too many churches. A study by Benjamin Mays and James

Nicholson in 1933 reported that they had found 216 churches of all denominations within the city limits of Birmingham. The study suggested that some of these churches needed to merge to make for stronger ministries. The Reverend E. O. Woolfok, pastor of St. Paul's Methodist Church, reached a similar conclusion. In his Emancipation Proclamation address on January 1, 1930, he insisted that African Americans in Birmingham had too many churches and denominations and were trying to build an over abundance of buildings. Such extensive building programs, he insisted, were taking excessive amounts of money from the African American people of the city. Despite the observations of Mays and Nicholson and the protests of Woolfok, there was no letup in the formation of African American churches in Birmingham. Smaller churches simply met needs that the larger churches did not meet, especially for the new migrants, who found a more satisfying emotional outlet and greater recognition in these small churches.[9]

Church life in the "Bear Marsh" area, about twelve blocks southeast of the center of the city, was typical and shows the preponderance of small churches. Although there were three large churches nearby — the Sixth Avenue Baptist Church, the Shiloh Baptist Church, and the Payne Chapel AME Church — residents preferred smaller churches. At least eleven small churches, some in alleys where many of the people lived, were located close together in this fifteen block area. In these churches the worship was similar to that in the Black Belt churches where these migrants had once attended. In the Black Belt, typical worship services consisted of meter hymns, long prayers, spontaneity, shouting, and emotional preaching by the pastors. In the small churches they established in Birmingham, members worshiped in the same style, responding to the singing of the choir and the preaching of the pastor with loud "amens" and shouting. "Whooping" and chanted preaching, in which the preacher pitched his voice in a musical fashion to evoke emotions, remained popular in these churches.[10]

Besides providing an emotional outlet, these smaller churches were also important in giving the new migrants and working class a sense of self-esteem and worth, as churches had done for first- and second-generation migrants before the war. Although some major industries had built more adequate housing and health services for miners and industrial workers in the area, African American life was often dreary and precarious. African Americans continued to have the dirtiest jobs, jobs that accorded them little or no status. Especially in the churches they had formed, recent migrants to the city could receive recognition and be somebody. In their study, Mays and Nicholson insisted that in these churches the working class felt a part of something they could own and control. Although most did not own their own homes, they took pride in being a part of a church that they owned. Their church was the product of their own hands and brain. Mays and Nicholson concluded that in African American churches in urban areas, including Birmingham, 80 percent of church members were domestic workers and common and semiskilled workers. In Birmingham during this period, these persons earned from $21 per week as porters in stores to $36 as workers in the coal mines and some furnaces. With these meager funds, they supported their churches and often built impressive buildings.[11]

These small churches also provided the masses with training and gave them an opportunity to develop their talents. A truck driver of average ability became chairperson of the deacon's board. A hotel man of some ability became superintendent of the Sunday school. A woman that the larger community would barely notice, socially or otherwise, became a leading figure in the missionary society. A young woman of little or no education became a leading singer in the choir. Frequently, these persons did not feel at ease in the more sophisticated clubs or even fraternal groups, but they found their niche in the church.[12]

These smaller Baptist churches did not represent the creation of new denominations or religious forms. The new churches became a part of the denomination and subscribed to its polity, doctrine, and practice. Many of these churches joined the established Baptist associations, and their pastors became members of the Baptist Minister's Conference. By 1940 the Mt. Pilgrim Baptist Association had grown to 124 churches. The smaller Baptist churches established after 1920 were responsible for this rapid growth. Among the churches joining the Mt. Pilgrim Association during this period were the First Baptist Church of Woodlawn, the Lily Grove Baptist Church of North Birmingham, the First Baptist Church of Rising, the Mt. Zion Baptist Church of East Thomas, the New Zion Baptist Church of Pratt City, and the Mt. Hebron Baptist Church of North Birmingham.[13]

Although many recent poor migrants preferred to start their own churches, others assimilated into established churches. In time, some of these persons assumed positions of leadership. Churches such as the Sixth Avenue Baptist Church on the Southside and the St. James Baptist Church on the Northside showed a balance of professional and working-class persons worshiping together in the same church. The African American professional class in Birmingham was small, consisting of teachers, businessmen, some skilled artisans, a few doctors and dentists, and ministers of the larger churches. All classes of African Americans lived in the same communities, and people tended to join the churches in those communities that included many factory workers, miners, and domestics. Teachers who taught in the various communities tended to live in those communities and to attend the local churches.[14]

One reason that many middle and working-class people worshiped in the same churches was the generally democratic spirit in Birmingham churches. In their 1933 study of 609 African American churches in sixteen cities, including Birmingham, Mays and Nicholson concluded that generally the church was the one place where African Americans of different social status could mingle in a Nicholson found that 67 percent of black professionals went to church weekly and 56 percent had specific church duties, such as teaching in the Sunday school or singing in the choir. In their visits to Birmingham and other areas they studied, Mays and Nicholson found in these churches a congenial atmosphere in which a timid or tense person was set at ease immediately. This congeniality, they noted, came from a hearty handshake from a member of the church or by a cordial greeting from an usher who seemed to sense that this person was a stranger or by some word from the pastor in his sermon or at the end of the service. The atmosphere, they insisted, was one of "at home-ness."[15]

Both small and large churches of the mainline denominations met other needs they had supplied before the Great War. They continued to be meeting places in the African American community. Besides hosting regular meetings that included several worship services on Sunday, plus prayer meeting on Wednesday night and church auxiliary meetings for choirs, ushers, and the missionary society, churches were the places of special meetings by such groups as the Masons, Pythians, Elks, and women's clubs. Some churches allowed civic organizations, such as the NAACP, to hold meetings in their churches. Denominational organizations, such as Baptist associations and Methodist district and general conferences met regularly at certain churches. Among the various Methodist groups, the favorite meeting places for denominational meetings were St. John AME Church, Metropolitan AME Zion Church, and Thirgood CME Church.

Because of their size and central location, the Sixth Avenue Baptist Church on the Southside and the Sixteenth Street Baptist Church on the Northside were the sites of many special community meetings when there was a need to accommodate large numbers of people. For example, in 1923 the Sixth Avenue Church hosted a meeting for Marcus Garvey, the black nationalist leader. Whether the meeting was approved by the ministers of the city is not known. Garvey did attract a large audience.

The Pythians held their Thanksgiving program at the Sixth Avenue Church in the same year. Famous African Americans who spoke at Sixth Avenue during this period included Mary M. Bethune, W.E.B. Dubois, William Pickens, and Countee Cullen.[16]

The Sixteenth Street Baptist Church was the scene of several citywide revivals during the 1920s conducted by nationally known evangelist G. Wilson Becton that brought unusually large crowds to the church. Newspapers reported that worshipers filled the sanctuary and basement of the church an hour before the meetings started. Many clubs held important meetings at the church, including the Periclean Club, which annually brought some of the most outstanding African Americans in the country to the city during Negro History Week. Both the Semper Fidelis Club and Club Imperial used the Sixteenth Street Church to host their annual programs. The Alabama State Teachers Association held many of its annual meetings at Sixteenth Street. The Chambliss Recital, sponsored by Mrs. Minnie E. Chambliss with some outstanding pianists participating each year, was one of the highlights of the year for the church and the community. The Birmingham Baptist Minister's Conference and the Interdenominational Alliance of Ministers usually met at the Sixteenth Street Baptist Church. Each year on the first of January, the community presented a program at Sixteenth Street celebrating the signing of the Emancipation Proclamation. Editor Oscar Adams of the *Birmingham Reporter* insisted that Sixth Avenue Baptist and Sixteenth Street Baptist were the leading churches in the city because of their value as meeting places in the community, size, and the numbers of significant community leaders in their memberships.[17]

For many African Americans in Birmingham, the church continued to be the main social center. Most of its activities took on a social dimension. Churches sponsored fashion shows, singings, plays, debates, banquets, picnics, and dinners. Most church auxiliaries provided their own forms of social activities. For example, missionary societies often met in private homes. Often these meetings ended with refreshments and fellowship. During the 1920s, the *Birmingham Reporter* summarized the missionary society meetings of the First Congregational Church. The group met regularly in the home of a member. The major business was the presentation of a paper by a member or guest. Afterward, there would be fellowship and refreshments. One of the missionary society's major yearly activities was a banquet for the pastor's anniversary.[18]

Churches and denominations provided activities for the youth. These activities in the church consisted of picnics, fairs, and plays. The main youth organization for the Baptists was the Baptist Young People's

Union (BYPU), which met every Sunday at 3 o'clock p.m. Its purpose was to train the youth for work in the church. Its programs consisted of youth leading the devotions, classes, plays, and fellowship. By the mid-1920s the Mt. Pilgrim Baptist Association had instituted a BYPU Convention headed by P.D. Davis of the Sixteenth Street Baptist Church. Its purpose was to convene the BYPU workers and youth from its ninety churches for training, fellowship, and spiritual renewal. Among the AME churches, the youth met every Sunday in an organization called the Allen Christian Endeavor Society. Its actions were quite similar to those of the BYPU.[19]

A church youth program that grew in popularity during the 1920s and 1930s was the Junior Church. It consisted of youth deacons, youth ushers, and a youth choir. Each fourth or fifth Sunday in a particular month the "Junior Church" was responsible for performing the roles in the church that adults usually did. The "Junior Church," BYPU, and Allen Endeavor Society provided African American youth with training for leadership positions in the church and in the secular world. It also gave them significant social and religious outlets in a city that did not provide them with adequate parks and other recreational facilities. For the leaders of the church, the church's youth activities provided an alternative to such demonic activities as card playing and dancing.[20]

There were, however, a few churches in Birmingham that catered almost exclusively to the professional class. They were not new in the African American community and were the result of denominational affiliation, educational attainment, and occupational mobility. They first emerged during the years immediately following emancipation. Many African American churches came into existence with the aid of northern-based white missionary groups, such as the American Missionary Association and the Freedmen's Aid Bureau of the Methodist Episcopal Church. These missionaries saw the indigenous religion of the slaves as barbarous and heathenistic. Through the founding of churches and schools, they sought to reform slave religion and place it within mainline Protestantism. Many African American professionals had attended colleges supported by white denominations and had absorbed their style worship, which was more formal than that of most black churches. A large percentage of the elite or professional blacks — doctors, lawyers, physicians, teachers, nurse — were Congregationalists, Presbyterians, and Episcopalians, having attended churches supported by these denominations.[21]

W.E.B. DuBois found this denominational pattern of professional churches in his study of the thirty-three elite families in the Alabama

Black Belt town of Marion in 1899. His study showed that these families were members of the Congregational Church rather than the "shouting" Methodist and Baptist churches in the city. Among the males of the thirty-three families, there were seven farmers, six ministers, five barbers, five carpenters, four bakers, two clerks, two teachers, one mail agent, one drayman, one government employee, one missionary, one plumber, one porter, one sailor, one nurse, and one gardener. Among the females there were seven teachers, two nurses, two cooks, one merchant, one dressmaker, and one washerwoman. The reason for their membership in the Congregational church was that the American Missionary Association operated Lincoln Academy in Marion, where many of these persons had attended school and where they had accepted their formal style of worship.[22]

In a similar study of African American professionals in Charleston, South Carolina, from 1880 to 1920, Williard B. Gatewood found that many of these persons gravitated toward the Episcopal, Presbyterian, and Congregational churches, with the Episcopal Church having the highest percentage. These persons were members of old-line families; many of whom had been free in slavery. Other African Americans who became successful doctors, lawyers, and educators broadened their numbers. Education and affluence set them apart from other blacks, and they saw themselves as the "better class." In some cases, they were set apart by the light complexion of their skin, and for the most part other African Americans saw them as occupying a lofty status. Although some in this class that Gatewood describes were also members of Baptist and Methodist churches, with a substantial percentage being the descendants of founding families in those churches, they eschewed emotionalism in worship. For them the "moaning and shouting" preacher was a major obstacle to racial progress.[23]

A striking example of an upper-class or professional church described by Gatewood was St. Mark's Episcopal Church in Charleston, South Carolina. Founded in 1865 by fair-complexioned people of color who had been freed before the Civil War, St. Mark's comprised the social elite of the city. It had the reputation of not welcoming dark-complexioned African Americans or those who were a part of the working class, as Ed Barber was to discover. "When I was trampin' 'round Charleston, dere was a church dere called St. Mark, dat all de society folks of my color went to. No black nigger welcome dere, they told me. Thinkin' as how I was bright 'nough to git in, I up and goes dere one Sunday. Ah, how they did carry on, bow and scrape and ape de white folks . . . I was uncomfortable all de time though, 'cause they was too 'hifalootin' in de ways, in de singin', and all sorts of carryin' ons." Wealth, color, and antebellum social status produced a gulf that existed between the members of St. Mark's and the rest of the African American community.[24]

There was no church in Birmingham comparable to the St. Mark's Episcopal Church. African Americans migrated into Birmingham seeking employment opportunities. Most black men were mine or factory workers. Black women were primarily domestics and laundresses. Most had received little formal education. There were, however, among these African American migrants persons who were teachers, business people, barbers, and a few doctors and lawyers. By the 1920s several blacks had attained semi-supervisory jobs in the mines, factories, and at the railroad companies. Others had become officers in the black fraternal and Masonic groups that gave them status in the community. It was these kinds of persons, distinguished by occupation and education, who made up the African American middle class in the city. The model for Birmingham was closer to the DuBois study of Marion, Alabama, than what Gatewood found to exist in the urban areas of northern and southern cities that had an antebellum heritage. Many of the people who migrated into Birmingham tended to cluster into some of the same churches.[25]

Among Birmingham churches with professional or upper-class memberships, there was one Presbyterian, one Episcopal, and one Congregational church in the 1920s. The Presbyterian and the Episcopal church followed a similar pattern. White missionary groups formed both churches and gave continuous support. The Protestant Episcopal Diocese of Alabama, with strong support from James A. Van Hoose, an energetic deacon in the Episcopal Church and mayor of Birmingham from 1894 to 1896, established St. Mark's Episcopal Church in 1891. The next year the Episcopal diocese sent two white teachers, Miss Konan of Brooklyn, New York, and Miss Patcher of Battle Creek, Michigan, to start St. Mark's Academy. The Central Alabama Presbytery organized Miller Memorial Presbyterian Church in 1892. Shortly after its founding, the church operated a school in the basement. As African American Presbyterians or Episcopalians moved into the city, they joined these churches. Others became members because they received their education at the schools these churches operated. The two churches did not attract the working class because of their formal style of worship.[26]

The First Congregational Church of Birmingham was similar in origin and membership composition to St. Mark's Episcopal and Miller

Memorial Presbyterian but was larger than the other two churches and included members who were quite influential in the African American community. First Congregational was founded in 1882 by B.H. Hudson, his wife Hattie, and a few other persons who wanted to establish a Congregational church for African Americans in Birmingham. Hudson was a graduate of Talladega College, a Congregational school supported by the American Missionary Association where he had become a member of the Congregational Church. Coming to Birmingham, Hudson served as one of the first principals of the Thomas School. He gathered a small group, and in 1882 they began to worship together in a small store-front at Seventeenth Street and Second Avenue North. Soon, the group appealed to the American Missionary Association of the Congregational Church for money to build a small frame church at Third Avenue and Twenty-Sixth Street North. The church was admitted to the Congregational Association of Alabama in 1883. The Congregational yearbook for the year ending December 31, 1883, gave the following statistics for the newly formed church: nine males, eight females, and fifteen in Sunday school.[27]

During its early years, the American Missionary Association assisted the church by sending a missionary named Miss Evans to help build the membership. Miss Evans helped to organize the Women's Missionary Society to bring youth and adults into the church. This organization proved invaluable in attracting new members. The First Congregational Church's relationship with Talladega College was also of major significance to the church's growth. Through the years, youth from the church attended Talladega College. On returning to Birmingham, they continued to be members of First Congregational. As African American congregationalists moved to Birmingham, they also joined First Congregational. For example, the Butler family lived in Marion, Alabama, and was associated with the Lincoln Normal School and the First Congregational Church of Marion, both established by the American Missionary Association in 1870. When the family moved to Birmingham in 1911, they became members of First Congregational.[28]

First Congregational was also fortunate in having two pastors with long tenures during the church's formative years: Reverends Fountain G. Ragland and Eugene C. Lawrence. Reverend Ragland was pastor from 1901 to 1917. During his pastorate, the church relocated and became self-supporting. Reverend Lawrence was pastor from 1922 to 1932. He had a strong community ministry and was a scholarly preacher and teacher. Both men were well educated and gave the church stable leadership during important periods in its history.[29]

Because of its educated ministry, and because it drew so many persons from Congregational schools, professional blacks almost completely made up the membership of First Congregational. Its formal style of worship was characteristic of the Congregational Church but did not appeal to the working class in Birmingham. In the 1920s and 1930s First Congregational became known as the "education church" because of the large numbers of teachers, principals, and educators in its membership. Among these were A.H. Parker, first principal of Industrial High School; Arthur Shores, principal of Dunbar High School in Bessemer; Carol Hayes, director of African American schools in Birmingham; and E. Paul Jones, supervisor of African American schools for Jefferson County. Besides many educators, there were also doctors, dentists, labor leaders, and nurses in the membership of First Congregational. Most of its two hundred members were professionals. First Congregational had the largest percentage of upper class persons in its membership of any black church in the city.[30]

Although churches of the African American professional class followed a denominational pattern, there were a few such churches in Birmingham among the Methodists and Baptists. Of the African American Methodist churches in Birmingham, none equaled First Congregational in the percentage of members who were professionals. There were Methodist churches in which significant numbers of professionals were members in the 1920s. These churches included Metropolitan AME Zion, St. Paul's Methodist Episcopal, Thirgood CME, and St. John AME. They were among the first churches of their denominations established in the area and were known as "mother" churches. They were also the primary places for their denominational meetings. Located in the downtown area, they attracted business people, teachers, and other professionals who were members of the various African American Methodist denominations. Many of these professionals were offspring of pioneer and founding families. After receiving their education at various black colleges in the state and nation, many returned home and resumed their membership in the churches. Lay leadership in these churches was in the hands of professionals and the pastors were among the most well educated in their denominations. Worship in these churches was to some degree emotional, but it was more restrained than in the working class churches.[31]

The Sixteenth Street Church was exceptional among Baptist churches, which tended to be the most democratic in terms of attracting members from all backgrounds and classes. The ministry of William R.

Pettiford largely determined the nature and character of the Sixteenth Street Church. Although the church was the oldest within the city limits, established in 1873, it was Pettiford who led in erecting the first significant church building and who enlarged the membership. Coming to Birmingham in 1883, he assumed the pastorate of Sixteenth Street when its congregation was worshiping in a store on Third Avenue with a membership of 150 and $500 in debt. Within a short time, he had paid the church out of debt and built a new sanctuary. Being a well-educated minister with an aggressive ministry, Pettiford attracted to Sixteenth Street Church upwardly mobile blacks and many of the few professionals in the city who were Baptists. Because of its size and location, the church became the center for public meetings in the African American community. By the time Pettiford resigned in 1893, the Sixteenth Street Church had become the leading African American church in the city, attracting people of all classes but especially those Baptists who were considered professionals. As African American teachers, business people, nurses, dentists, and doctors moved into the city, many joined the Sixteenth Street Baptist Church. In 1893 the church claimed 450 members, including a large group of professional African Americans and leaders in the community. Among these were A.H. Parker, first principal of industrial High School and U.G. Mason, a community leader and one of the first physicians to practice in the city. There were also fraternal leaders, teachers, women club officials, and Masonic leaders.[32]

The pastors who succeeded Pettiford were educated and eminent men. One of the most notable was the Reverend Charles L. Fisher, who served two tenures as pastor from 1898 to 1911 and from 1921 to 1930. Fisher had attained the most formal education of any African American pastor in the city and was one of its most eloquent preachers, having graduated from Leland College and Baptist Union Theological Seminary (now Chicago Divinity School). During Fisher's tenure, Sixteenth Street began to build its present structure and its membership grew to over 1,000. While working-class people worshiped there, the church continued to attract the Baptist elite of the city. Fisher was also active in religious and civic affairs during both of his tenures. During his first tenure, he served as moderator of the Mt. Pilgrim District Association, the largest in the state. During his second term, he was a lecturer on Baptist history at the National Baptist Sunday School and B.Y.P.U. Congress, an editor of the Advanced Sunday school Quarterly of the National Baptist Publishing Board, president of the Interdenominational Ministerial Alliance of Birmingham, and twice appointed by Governor

Bibb Graves to represent the State's black ministers before the International and Inter-denominational Ministerial Alliance in Washington, D.C. African American Baptists throughout the nation regarded Fisher as a ripe scholar, safe leader, and a "Prince of Preachers." A man of Fisher's education and talents attracted the elite of the community.[33]

Professionals and community leaders made up the lay leadership of the Sixteenth Street Church during the 1920s and 1930s. T.C. Windham, one of the wealthiest African American contractors in the South, served as chairperson of the Trustee Board. Other leaders included R.A. Blount, head of the Masons, P.D. Davis, Masonic leader and businessperson, and J.O. Diffay, the leading barber in the city. Among women were Mrs. A.M. Brown and Mrs. L. M. Gaillard, both having served as president of the Women's Federated Clubs of Alabama. Women of the prestigious women's clubs, including the Periclean, Imperial, and Semplis Fidelis were made up of Sixteenth Street women. There was also a host of teachers. Through the years the sons and daughters of Sixteenth Street Church received their education from black colleges, with many returning to the city to assume leadership roles at the Sixteenth Street Church. Sixteenth Street Baptist Church had the largest number of professionals of any African American congregation in the city. It continued to be, in spite of internecine conflict, the leading African American church in Birmingham.[34]

In the period between the World Wars, pastors continued to be leaders in the Birmingham community, although there were no leaders like W.R. Pettiford and T.W. Walker who operated businesses, banks, and other secular endeavors while also serving as spiritual leaders of the community. The chief reason for this change was the emergence of laymen who provided leadership in these secular areas. These men proved to be competent and had been in the community long enough to amass a following. Furthermore, most pastors preferred to spend their time with church and spiritual concerns. Among outstanding laymen was A.H. Parker who was the educational leader in the African American community, serving as principal of Industrial High School and supervisor of black education. Businessmen Charles M. Harris, T.C. Windham, and Arthur G. Gaston emerged as leaders. In the African American Masonic world, significant leaders included R.A. Blount, P.D. Davis, and J.O. Diffay. The most outstanding leader in the African American press was Oscar Adams. These lay persons, most of whom were strong churchmen, led the way in forming businesses, public educational institutions, and civic organizations that pastors had led before World War I. For example, Arthur G. Gaston formed the Booker T. Washington Burial Society. T. C. Windham formed Windham Brothers Contracting Company and Jones Valley Finance Company. Oscar Adams organized the *Birmingham Reporter* and the Birmingham Civic Association. James McPherson, a medical doctor, was the leading figure in the formation and maintenance of the NAACP in the city.[35]

Pastors remained the leaders of the churches, and despite sharing leadership with lay persons, remained powerful community leaders. Through their preaching, they gave hope and self-esteem to persons that the larger Birmingham community considered inferior. As leaders of the church, touching the lives of the people from birth to death, pastors continued to assume a position of eminence and importance among their parishioners and in the community. Lay leaders coveted the support of pastors and their churches, support that they knew was indispensable to their success.

The pre-World War I emphasis on self-help, racial solidarity, race pride, and building character continued in the sermons and addresses of African American pastors. In 1926 C.L. Fisher preached a sermon at the Sixteenth Street Baptist Church in which he compared black progress with that of the Israelites crossing the Jordan River. Fisher maintained that for African American to cross the Jordan to freedom they must overcome three barriers: the belief that other races are better, the lack of thrift, and the lack of dedication to God. In a 1926 article in the *Birmingham Reporter*, P. W. Wells, an AME Zion pastor, counseled the African American community on the importance of self-reliance. "If you wish to live," he insisted, "stand on your own resources. Walk on your own legs." He went on to say that environment and conditions need not defeat African Americans. If African Americans developed their own resources, they would greatly improve themselves and their community. Part of that self-reliance, Wells insisted, was the support of African American business. "White businesses," he maintained, "takes out of our community and puts nothing back." In 1927 F. W. Alstork, pastor of the Metropolitan AME Zion Church, urged African Americans "to develop independence, in character, industry, finance, intelligence, and Christianity." He insisted that African Americans needed to abhor radicalism, including the *Chicago Defender's* call for African Americans to leave the South. He urged Birmingham's blacks to stay here and commit themselves to honesty, dependability, and industry.[36]

Although self-help continued to be the dominant theme, a stronger voice for fairness and the right to vote was clearly noticeable in the African American ministerial community. African American pastors stopped short of calling for the immediate end to segregation but otherwise took a more militant stance in their protest than the pre-World War I ministerial leadership. In a Fourth of July sermon, Bishop Benjamin J. Shaw of the AME Zion Church, who lived in Birmingham, said that he could not celebrate Independence Day because the Negro was not free. He was, according to Bishop Shaw, still in chains. One reason was that African Americans could not vote. Shaw called on America to do what was right by giving the franchise to all. In a similar speech in 1923, Rev. H. N. Newsome of the St. John AME Church projected a similar theme. Newsome said he was against race mixing, but that African Americans should be given fair play in the courts and at the ballot box, and he urged a law against lynching. He called for equal justice for all. In a sermon at the Metropolitan AME Zion Church, Rev. W.W. Matthews lashed out at a statement by Governor O'Neal of Alabama in which O'Neal said that black women should not vote because they had no character. In 1928 Rev. Frank W. Alstork of Metropolitan AME Zion Church gave the Emancipation Address. He maintained that African Americans had been loyal to the nation by shedding their blood in every war. "If blood is the price of liberty," he insisted, "African Americans should have liberty."[37]

On some occasions, clergyman expressed their growing concern through petitions. For example, in 1923 the African American community held a meeting to protest the zoning ordinance that mandated segregated housing in Birmingham. Those at the meeting decided to send a petition to the city council. Among the signers were several key pastors, including Reverends R.H. Hall, president of the Baptist Minister's Conference, F.G. Ragland, pastor of First Congregational Church, C.L. Fisher, pastor of Sixteenth Street Baptist Church, H.N. Newsome, pastor of St. John AME Church, and J.A. Bray, general secretary of education for the CME Church.[38]

Pastors gave top priority to two concerns: the promotion of community-based African American businesses and the maintenance of colleges and schools. They supported black businesses in several ways. Some pastors promoted African American enterprises through their personal example. For example, the Reverend Robert Richardson, pastor of the Harmony Street Baptist Church, in an article in the *Birmingham Reporter* in 1923, stressed that he was insured with an African American company and that he was on the board of directors of the Jefferson County Burial Society. Rev. William Boyd of the Trinity Baptist Church in a similar article said that both his sick and burial insurance were with an African American company. Besides setting personal examples, these pastors supported African American business from their pulpits and on special speaking occasions. In his Emancipation Address to the citizens of Birmingham in 1923, H.N. Newsome said that "Negroes in Birmingham spend a million dollars a year." More money, he insisted, "should be spent with Negro businesses." Newsome maintained that this would further help to emancipate African Americans. Ministers sponsored resolutions to support African American business. In 1930, at a meeting of the Jefferson County Burial Society, two outstanding ministers, C.L. Fisher, pastor of Sixteenth Street Baptist Church, and William Atmore, moderator of the Mt. Pilgrim Baptist Association, sponsored a resolution that African American ministers should support African American businesses. Pastors also took an active part in organizations that sought to boost businesses. One such group was the Jones Valley Booster Club, which African American business leaders had formed for mutual support. The organization held meetings all over the area in churches, with pastors often being the principal speakers.[39]

The founding and development of the Booker T. Washington Burial Company, later called the Booker T. Washington Insurance Company, shows the strong relationship between the church and African American business. Returning to Birmingham after serving in the armed forces in World War I, Arthur Gaston had a strong desire to go into business. With no money, he worked first in a laundry and later went to work for the Tennessee Coal and Iron Company at its Westfield plant. Gaston noticed that many co-workers were unable to live from week to week on what they earned and were eager to borrow money and pay interest. Gaston began to lend money and opened a peanut and popcorn stand. All these endeavors did a thriving business.[40]

Enthusiastic about his early successes, Gaston began to think of other ways to make money and help the community. He noticed that in Westfield people were always giving money to those who did not have money to bury relatives. The idea came to him that people might be willing to pay a small regular sum to a burial society to obtain decent burials. He called a meeting at a church in Westfield. Rev. J.L. Miller, pastor of the St. Paul AME Church, and Rev. S.H. Ravizee, pastor of the Hopewell Baptist Church attended the meeting. Both ministers and the others present thought well of the idea but were not willing to invest any money or commit their churches to do so. Gaston decided to launch the business on his own. He began to write up people in his burial society, promising the purchasers a hundred dollar funeral for twenty-five cents a week for the head of the family and ten cents a week for any additional family members. Before he had taken in one hundred dollars in premiums, one of his members died. Gaston contacted Rev. S.H. Ravizee, who counseled him to keep his word by burying the person even if he had to borrow the money. At the funeral, after he had delivered the eulogy and taken up the customary offering for the family, Ravizee informed the congregation that this would be the last funeral offering in the church since there was a burial society in the community that would keep its word. He asked Gaston to stand and urged the people present to join Gaston's burial society immediately. That day many people at the funeral and in the community joined. This event launched the Booker T. Washington Burial Society.[41]

Realizing the importance of pastors and the churches for galvanizing support in the African American community, Gaston involved both in promoting his business. In the organizational meeting of his burial society, he placed three pastors on the advisory committee, Ravizee, Miller, and G. F. Moore. As the business grew to include a funeral home, agents went to churches and denominational meetings to publicize the company. Sometimes the company gave discounts on policies to people at various church meetings. Gaston noticed that quartet singings drew large crowds and decided to sponsor some of these groups as a way of gaining publicity. He also put them on radio, hiring William Blevins, one of the areas top gospel singers, who hosted the program. The radio program was a huge success. In addition to it, the company promoted musical extravaganzas at the Municipal Auditorium and at Legion Field. Famed national groups such as the Wings Over Jordan Choir and the Golden Gate Quartet performed at these concerts. Thousands of people flocked to hear them. These promotions made the Booker T. Washington Burial Company familiar to people throughout Alabama and directed a large amount of business to the company.[42]

African American pastors and their denominational groups in Birmingham during the 1920s and 1930s met with success and failure in their strenuous efforts to maintain their schools. One school burned and another was forced to close. In 1922 Central Alabama College, which had moved to Birmingham in 1904 and was operated by the Freedman's Aid Bureau of the Methodist Episcopal Church, sustained a tragic loss when a fire destroyed its administration building. The Freedman's Aid Bureau chose not to rebuild and the school thereby ceased to exist. Birmingham Baptist College was forced to close because of limited support, internecine conflict that led to the emergence of a rival school, Easonian Baptist Seminary, and the devastation of the depression. The college was unable to pay its teachers and a mortgage indebtedness of $23,000. The trustees leased the school's buildings to the

County Board of Education for the operation of a county high school, Powderly High School. Former faculty members held classes in churches in an attempt to keep the school spirit alive. In 1936 the Baptists of Birmingham liquidated the mortgage and the institution reopened in 1939 with J.H. Wrenn as president and T.D. Bussey as his assistant.[43]

One college moved from Selma to Birmingham. Daniel Payne College, supported by the AME Church of Alabama, was on the verge of closing. Debate emerged among pastors concerning the best ways of salvaging the institution. Some pastors wanted it to remain in Selma. Others suggested moving it to a more urban location. One group wanted it moved to Montgomery, while another group favored Birmingham. Because of the influence of Presiding Bishop William Allen Fountain, the institution relocated to Birmingham in 1927. The AME Church bought forty acres in Woodlawn for $25,700. The trustees planned three buildings: an administration building, and two dormitories to house 200 male and female students. The school was to be known as Greater Payne College. It would consist of a junior college and a school of religion. By 1930, when the institution celebrated its fortieth anniversary, it was in full operation in Birmingham. Bishop Fountain showed that in its forty years of operations 75 percent of its graduates had become teachers, 8 percent ministers, and 5 percent doctors.[44]

Miles College, operated by the CME Church of Alabama, was the most successful of the African American colleges in Birmingham during this era. During the 1920's and 1930's, the CME Church of Alabama financed two important buildings: the Brown Administration Building and a practice building for teacher training. Miles consistently had a student body of several hundred persons. In 1931 Miles dropped its high school program and went to a standard college program, conferring only baccalaureate degrees. Despite its progress, by 1939 the institution was $60,000 in debt because of the depression.[45]

One of the most outstanding African American pastors in Birmingham during this period was the Reverend John W. Goodgame, Sr. Among pastors he had one of the longest tenures, serving one church, the Sixth Avenue Baptist Church, for approximately thirty years. He was highly respected as a man of character and integrity, and excelled as a community and race leader. His philosophy and activities in Birmingham reflected what pastoral leadership was all about between the wars. Like many significant pastors of his day, Goodgame's early life was a struggle. Born into a poor family, he sacrificed to obtain an education, graduating from Talladega College with a degree in theology.

After serving brief pastorates in his home church in Talladega and in Anniston, Alabama, he came to Birmingham in 1908 to assume the pastorate of the Sixth Avenue Baptist Church.[46]

Although Goodgame's philosophy and leadership would in many ways mirror that of William Pettiford, there was a basic difference between the two. Goodgame's identity was that of a pastor. Unlike Pettiford and other ministerial leaders of the post-Reconstruction South who felt compelled to become full-time political, business, and educational leaders, Goodgame remained exclusively a pastor. Instead of operating businesses or other secular concerns, he supported lay persons who provided leadership in those areas. For example, B.L. Windham, who served for many years as a deacon and clerk at Sixth Avenue Church, was president and founder of the Booker T. Washington Life Insurance Company, a company founded earlier than the burial society of Arthur G. Gaston, and one of the most successful African American businesses in the city. One way that Goodgame supported Windham was by urging members of Sixth Avenue Church to take out policies with Windham's company. He also served on the company's board of directors. In the 1920s, Goodgame became the national grand treasurer of the Mosaic Templers of America, a Masonic order. In 1929 he had an opportunity to become grandmaster, but refused the position on the grounds it would take too much time from his duties as a pastor.[47]

Goodgame excelled as a builder, organizer, and administrator. During the second year of his pastorate at Sixth Avenue Baptist Church, the sanctuary burned to the ground. He led the congregation in building a new edifice costing $65,000. In 1920 Goodgame succeeding in liquidating the mortgage, raising $11,457.38 in one drive to achieve his goal. He led the church in 1927 in building a Sunday school annex that cost $30,000. Under Goodgame's tenure, Sixth Avenue Baptist became one of the leading churches in the city. Commenting on Goodgame's Twenty-third anniversary as pastor at Sixth Avenue, the editor of the *Birmingham Reporter* noted some of Goodgame's accomplishments. The church claimed a membership of 4,500 and a building that could seat 2,000. Among its outstanding features were a brass band, a boy scout unit, and a Sunday school that had an enrollment of 800 to 1,000. During his twenty-three years at the church, Goodgame had presided at 365 weddings and 1,287 funerals.[48]

While primarily a pastor, Goodgame took seriously the role of the African American pastor as a community and race leader, and the role of the church in serving the needs of the community. He stated at the special service that marked the retirement of the mortgage on the church in 1920 that "our church is an organization of community uplift, spiritual inspiration, and Christian guidance." He maintained that the retirement of the debt would only increase the church's duty to the community. As community leader, Goodgame was active in promoting the uplift and well-being of African Americans in the city. For example, in 1920 he led in organizing the fight against tuberculosis in the African American community. In 1928 Goodgame headed the Negro division of the Community Chest Drive. For many years, he was president of the Emancipation Association of Birmingham, the organization that each year sponsored the program celebrating the signing of the Emancipation Proclamation. He also headed the ministerial alliance in the city.[49]

As community citizen and leader and in the tradition of William R. Pettiford, Goodgame was in contact with white leaders and often represented the desires of the African American community to the power structure. Goodgame maintained a strong relationship with Reverend James E. Dillard, pastor of the Southside Baptist Church, the leading white Baptist church in the city at the time. Dillard assisted Goodgame and the Sixth Avenue Baptist Church in structuring the Sunday school and the general church program at Sixth Avenue. Goodgame also built a strong friendship with the Reverend Henry Edmonds, head of the Alabama Interracial Council and one of the most liberal white pastors in the city. Both men were present at the service celebrating the mortgage liquidation of the Sixth Avenue Church.[50]

Goodgame believed that self-help, moral character, and racial solidarity were the best ways of uplifting the race. Although he called for fair play, his basic philosophy supported African Americans to use their resources to advance themselves. His philosophy of uplift called for African Americans to build institutions to fill their needs. In an address entitled, "Negro Baptists, Their Rise, Progress, and Their Contribution to the Advancement of the Race," Goodgame maintained that the greatest contribution of Baptists was in supporting education and in buying and building homes and businesses. One of the persons he praised as a Baptist hero was William R. Pettiford, who founded the Alabama Penny Bank in Birmingham. Goodgame also lauded Booker T. Washington for his work at Tuskegee Institute. He insisted that others should duplicate what these two men had done.[51]

Goodgame constantly and persistently stressed the development of moral character in his sermons and addresses. In the Emancipation Address to the African American citizens of Birmingham in 1920, Goodgame stressed that if progress were to continue African Americans must build strong character and help reform the criminal element. For Goodgame, developing character and discipline would help African Americans overcome the obstacles of race prejudice and would promote achievement. In a memorial address for A.C. Freeman, an African American that one of the major industries elevated to a supervisory job, Goodgame insisted that race prejudice was not the only reason for the African American plight. Part of the problem, he maintained, was lack of work, discipline, and will. Goodgame insisted that man was the architect of his own fate and that if African Americans developed character, determination, and will, they could make marvelous achievements as A.C. Freeman had done. Members who were alive during Goodgame's pastorate recalled that during his years at Sixth Avenue Baptist, the church expelled persons for offenses such as gambling, drunkenness, and immoral sexual behavior.[52]

Goodgame best summarized his emphasis on achieving through the development of character and determination in a brief address entitled, "The Growth of Adverse Opinions towards the Negro." In this address he acknowledged that prejudice against African Americans was growing. He pointed to job discrimination, lack of funds for schools, lynching, police brutality, and the growth of the Ku Klux Klan as evidence of this renewed hostility. He counseled African Americans not to despair but to develop strong values and habits. Goodgame discussed education, religion, frugality, family support, morality, and racial solidarity in his address. He insisted that men especially needed to practice these virtues. African American men, he asserted, "must be men."[53]

Education was also a top priority for Goodgame, both as pastor and denominational leader. Influenced by the Sunday school movement, he led Sixth Avenue in having one of the largest Sunday schools in the city, with a membership between 800 and 1,000. As pastor, he encouraged parents to send their children to college. During his tenure at Sixth Avenue, many young people went to college because of his influence and assistance. Goodgame's interest in educational institutions was a part of his denominational concern that Baptists have an educational presence in the city. A denominational leader among Baptists, serving as treasurer of the Alabama Baptist State Convention and chairperson of the enrollment committee of the National Baptist Convention, Goodgame had a desire to see the establishment of a Baptist school in Birmingham to train the large number of illiterate pastors and ministers. In the early 1900's, he conducted classes in the church basement along with the Reverend L.L. Green, pastor of Broad Street Baptist Church. In

1913, when the Baptist associations of the Birmingham area came together to form a college, Goodgame chaired the board of trustees. It was largely due to his efforts that Baptists purchased nine acres of land and erected an administration building. He continued to serve as chairperson of the board of trustees of Birmingham Baptist College until the financial crisis that temporarily closed the college.[54]

Although there were some deviations from the past, a great deal of continuity characterized the mainline African American churches in Birmingham between the two great wars. With the influx of a large group of poor migrants into the city after World War I, many small Baptist churches emerged, supplying crucial needs for recent arrivals. Churches continued to be social centers and places of meeting. A small number of professional blacks made up the majority of the membership of a few churches in the city. These churches had a formal style of worship, but most churches of the mainline Baptists and Methodist denominations continued to worship in their traditional way. Although some pastors showed an inclination to be more outspoken on racial matters, especially in their call for the ballot and fair play, most continued to stress self-help as the basic philosophy of uplift. As leaders in the community, pastors spent much of their time seeking to preserve the gains of the past, especially in education and business. The Reverend John W. Goodgame, with his strong pastoral skills and concern for self-help, discipline, character, and education emerged as a key pastor and community leader. With the devastation of the depression and the increase of migrants into the city, new forms of religious expression also emerged in the Birmingham community during this period.

VI

The African American Church Between the World Wars: Communism and New Religious Responses

Although the church continued to perform the roles and functions that it had provided in Birmingham before World War I, African Americans created some new religious responses to the economic depression and continued racial hostility after the war. The depression and continued migration of African Americans to Birmingham contributed to the emergence of a radical organization, the American Communist Party. This organization sought to use the churches for recruitment but met rebuff and opposition from pastors and lay leaders in Birmingham. Two religious responses came into being that were more successful and became an integral part of the religious landscape in the city: gospel music and churches of the Pentecostal, Holiness, and Spiritualist traditions. These religious forms served the particular needs of African Americans as they sought to survive harsh economic times and the racist atmosphere that existed in Birmingham.

Few events devastated Birmingham more than the economic depression of the late 1920s and the 1930s. Economic conditions forced several banks to close. Industry canceled orders so that by 1933 the city's mills and factories were operating at only one third of capacity. In 1932 the district's member of Congress, George Huddleston, testifying before the United States Relief Committee, stated that only 8,000 of Birmingham's 108,000 wage earners were receiving their normal income, with at least 25,000 having no work at all. The city's tax revenues declined, which meant that there was little money to meet the city's financial needs. President Franklin Roosevelt labeled Birmingham "the worst hit town in the country."[1]

No one was hit harder in the city than the African American population. Already occupying the dirtiest and lowest-paying jobs, they were often the first targeted for layoffs. Black unemployment reached as much as 75 percent during this period. Many African American women were unemployed because of a reduced demand for domestic work. Shackled with the burden of raising children and limited by poor public and private relief, their lives were particularly hard.[2]

African Americans turned to all sorts of survival techniques. Drawing on their rural experience, many planted vegetable gardens in sizes ranging from small plots to forty acre farms. African Americans planted gardens on company property, in coal and ore mines, in back alleys, and in industrial towns all over the area. Many raised pigs and cows in the city. Others did odd jobs for food, gathered grocery store throwaways, sold peanuts on the streets, and hauled and sold coal obtained from mines or railroads. In a desperate effort to obtain fuel, some African Americans tore down vacant houses. To prevent the demolition of homes, some real estate companies employed men to stay in empty houses to prevent them from being stripped for firewood.[3]

In the midst of the depression a radically new organization, the American Communist Party, came into Birmingham. Stressing the economic exploitation of the workers by capitalists and the need for a new economic order, the organization attracted several hundred African Americans to its ranks. The party did not attract whites in Birmingham because of its stand on racial equality. It therefore focused most of its attention on the African American community. Communists used several methods to attract members. Recruiters came in and formed Communist units among industrial workers. They held meetings and marches in the community to demand more adequate relief, staged boycotts against the Community Chest and Red Cross, formed neighborhood committees to fight evictions and foreclosures, and endorsed an African American candidate for governor. By far the Party's most effective effort in attracting African Americans was its defense of the Scottsboro boys, nine African Americans accused of raping two white women on a freight train traveling through Jackson County in Alabama. The depression had hit the poor black working class so hard that despite being warned against the evils of the party, many of them viewed hunger and joblessness as a greater threat.[4]

One of the most effective African American Communists in Birmingham was Hosea Hudson. Born in rural Georgia in a poor and racially hostile environment, Hudson became a sharecropper. By selling peanuts he was able to pay off his sharecropping obligations and move to Atlanta. In Atlanta Hudson worked in a railroad shop, but when he saw no chance for advancement there he came to Birmingham, where he got a job at the Stockham Pipe and Fittings plant as a molder. He soon became dissatisfied with the poor working conditions, lack of advancement opportunities, nonpayment for overtime, and verbal abuse by the whites who supervised African American workers. Hudson first became aware of communism during the Scottsboro trials. Communist recruiters approached him on his job. For him the Communist Party, through worker solidarity and self-determinism, offered a way of improving the harsh conditions under which he lived. In 1931 he joined the party with eight other Stockham workers. Before the company fired him a few months later, Hudson had set up six other communist groups.[5]

An examination of Hudson's life and experiences in Birmingham also shows the relationship between the churches and the poor working classes and how African American Communists fared in their relationship with the church. In his early years in Georgia, Hudson had become a member of the Baptist Church, a relationship that he continued as a sharecropper. Moving to Birmingham from Atlanta, he joined the New Bethel Baptist Church in the Avondale section of Birmingham, where he rose to the position of junior deacon. Soon he was attracted to the quartet singing in the Birmingham area and joined a group called the L and N Singers. His group, along with other quartets, went from church to church participating in singing conventions. The singing conventions were a major form of recreation for the churchgoing working class in the city. After joining the party in 1931, Hudson continued to be a member of the New Bethel Church. The church was a place where people congregated regularly and where he could talk to friends and neighbors about communism. In 1932 Hudson made the mistake of inviting a Communist to speak at the church, an incident that brought harsh rebukes from the pastor and members who felt that the church was not the place for such political involvement. Hudson left the church, but in 1938 he returned at the urging of the Communist Party. The Party hoped to build alliances with other groups in the community and knew that the church was the place where the masses congregated. After returning to the church, Hudson formed a singing group known as the Smithfield Vocal Singers but did not openly try to proselytize for the Party in his church again.[6]

New Bethel Church's rebuff of Hudson typifies the attitude of pastors and church leaders toward the work of the Communist Party in Birmingham. With one or two possible exceptions, pastors joined the NAACP and the African American middle class in opposing the party. They saw it as idealistic and impractical. For them the Party's lack of recognition of the color line made its chances of success nil in the South.

Some pastors joined Oscar Adams, editor of the *Birmingham Reporter*, in maintaining that communism among African Americans in Birmingham was merely the emotional response of an ignorant and uninformed people, which could only lead to violence and bloodshed. A few pastors also agreed with the 1931 report of the Commission on Interracial Cooperation that the Party was manipulating blacks for its own ends. These pastors, including the Reverend M. Sears and the Reverend John Goodgame, insisted that blacks and whites were too interlinked for the races to pull apart from one another. Sears and Goodgame joined white liberals such as the Reverend Henry Edmonds, pastor of the Independent Presbyterian Church and state chair of the Committee on Interracial Cooperation, in calling for cooperation between the races and fair law enforcement. Some pastors in the city opposed communism because of its doctrine of atheism; other pastors simply did not understand communism's philosophy and opposed it because of newspaper reports and the negative information they received.[7]

Occasionally, the Communist Party in Birmingham criticized African American pastors by deprecating their character and impugning their motives. The *Southern Worker*, the official organ of the Party in Birmingham, from time to time accused prominent ministers of stealing funds from their congregations, citing for example, the Reverend J.H. Eason of Jackson Street Baptist Church and Bishop Socrates O'Neal of a Pentecostal denomination. Most of the criticism leveled against pastors had more to do with what the Communists regarded as their political shortcomings. For Communists, the pastors were preaching a "pie in the sky" message that failed to deal with the pressing problems of unemployment, starvation, and discrimination. They insisted that pastors who advocated the notion of African American labor allying with white capital were keeping workers in subjection and poverty. Those pastors, the Communists maintained, were supporting an economic and political system that should be destroyed.[8]

In Birmingham there was at least one instance of near violence between African American Communists and a pastor. The Reverend M. Sears, pastor of the Bethel Baptist Church in North Birmingham, was among the leading anti-communists in Birmingham and a co-author of the Committee on Interracial Cooperation's damning 1931 report, "Radical Activities in Alabama." Tension between Sears and the Communists emerged in 1933 with the arrest and beating of Randolph Carter, a Red Cross relief worker. Carter had become embroiled in a heated debate with his white project director, who drew a pistol and shot at him. Carter then went into seclusion. Sears convinced him to come out of hiding and turned him over to the police, who beat him. Local Communists in the community held Sears responsible for the beating. The Communists led a march to Bethel Church to confront Sears. When they entered the church, Sears brandished a shotgun he had hidden behind the pulpit, causing a near riot in the church. Because of the incident, the members forced Sears to resign from the Bethel Church. The incident served to further alienate pastors from the Communist Party in Birmingham.[9]

New forms of music emerged in the African American religious community as a response to the insecurity of the depression and the formal music that had become a regular part of many church worship services. Many larger African American churches, in an attempt to move into mainline Protestantism, had stopped singing spirituals and jubilee songs. Among Methodists, hymns from the regular Methodist hymnals and anthems had become the norm in worship services. Many Methodist churches had disbanded the praise services where the congregation sang meter hymns. Among Baptist churches formed by the first-generation migrants in Birmingham, music and worship had lost much of its emotional fervor. Both the Sixteenth Street Baptist Church and the Sixth Avenue Baptist Church installed pipe organs; each also had a church orchestra. Some smaller Baptist churches followed similar musical patterns.[10]

Gospel music signaled a departure from the more formal music that was emerging in the larger churches of Birmingham. Gospel songs were spontaneous and full of strong emotions. They were songs of faith that rallied the hopes and aspirations of people in the face of the devastating social conditions of the depression. Arising out of urban settings where blacks suffered from dashed hopes and poverty, these songs, with their intricate rhythms, strong beats, and alternated scales, gave attention to blessings, sorrows, woes, and the joys of the "after life." Gospel songs tended to be more individualistic and otherworldly than the spirituals of the slaves. Jesus rather than the Hebrew children dominated the gospel songs. The focus was on heaven, and in gospel songs, unlike the spirituals, the idea of heaven remained firmly fixed in the future. The world was a place of suffering, and one had to take comfort from the blessings and the assurances of the almighty. Mainline Baptist and Methodist leaders discouraged the use of gospel songs in their churches, seeing them as too worldly and emotional. Gospel songs were first performed in Pentecostal settings and gradually made their way into the smaller Baptist and Methodist churches of the working class.[11]

Although Thomas Dorsey was the first person to use the term *gospel* songs, to form a gospel choir, and to add blues and jazz features to this music, gospel-like music began in Birmingham before the emergence of the gospel music of Dorsey. There were other influences that preceded the blues and jazz additions of Dorsey in Birmingham. Chief among these was Charles Tindley, an African American Methodist minister. Born in Maryland in 1859, Tindley gained prominence as a camp meeting preacher and singer there. By 1900 he had settled in Philadelphia, where he founded the church that now bears his name, Tindley Temple United Methodist Church. Tindley's church became famous for its concerts and gospel hymns, most of which he had written. In these songs Tindley used African American imagery to attempt to address and interpret the oppression African Americans faced as they settled in the cities, as spirituals had done in the slavery era. Unlike the spirituals, the Tindley gospel hymns made few references to Old Testament characters and events and were meant primarily for congregational singing. They admonished those who suffer the storms of life to stand fast in Christ. In 1916 Tindley published a collection of his songs entitled *New Songs of Paradise*, the first published collection of gospel hymns. The collection included such songs as "The Storm Is Passing Over," "Stand By Me," "We'll Understand It Better By and By," and "Some Day." By the 1920s these gospel hymns had made their way into Birmingham churches.[12]

In 1921 the Sunday School Publishing Board of the National Baptist Convention published the *Gospel Pearls*. It was a landmark in promoting the gospel sound in Birmingham and in the United States. A small collection of 165 songs, the *Gospel Pearls* contained songs for Sunday schools, revivals, churches, conventions, and other religious gatherings. The songbook was divided into three sections. The third section contained African American gospel hymns and arrangements of spirituals. Charles Tindley dominated this section contributing six of his songs while Dorsey contributed only one. Since most Baptist churches were members of the convention, the gospel sound of Tindley and others had a ready market in Birmingham.[13]

A third major influence on Birmingham were gospel composers and hymn writers. Among these persons were ministers such as J.M. Gates and A.W. Nix, along with laymen Kenneth Morris and J.H. Brewster, and laywomen Sallie Martin and Roberta Martin. These people were also gospel soloists, who in the late 1920s and 1930s, began to give concerts around the nation, including in Birmingham. Along with Thomas Dorsey these persons began to transform Tindley's congregational gospel hymns into songs for church choirs, soloists, and quartets. The popularity of this new kind of singing which ranged from congregational hymns to songs for specialized soloists and groups, had an important consequence for worship in the African American churches. While through hymns and meter music worshipers were united through the collective activity of singing, the new gospel style required the congregation to assume the role of audience. Worshipers became bystanders who witnessed the preaching and personal testimonies of singers. Most of all, they began to witness a new religious experience in which singers sang the gospel in a very emotional fashion. The congregation's reply came through "amens," noddings, humming, clapping, swaying, or occasionally by singing along with the performers.[14]

The main avenue for gospel singing in Birmingham's churches was the emergence of "number two" choirs. From their founding most churches in the city had formed a choir. In the 1920s singers in churches began to request an additional choir. Sixth Avenue Baptist Church started a number two choir in 1922, as did the New Pilgrim Baptist Church in 1929, and the Zion Star Baptist Church in 1938. The primary reasons were age differences, with young adults preferring to sing with their own age group, and the attraction of the new gospel singing that was making its way rapidly into the churches. Although both choirs sang gospel hymns, the new number two choirs specialized in the songs from the *Gospel Pearls* and later began to sing the solo-oriented songs of Dorsey and the other composers. By World War II Gospel music in most Baptist churches was well on its way to becoming the most popular of all the music in those churches. Baptist churches accepted the new music faster than the Methodist churches, which was another reason they grew more rapidly.[15]

While choirs became popular in Birmingham, quartet singing made the greatest contribution to gospel music in the area. In the 1930s the Birmingham area was the center for quartet singing in the United States. Only Norfolk and the Virginia Tidewater area could compare in the popularity of quartet singing and its influence on the rest of the nation. Between the early 1920s and late 1950s over 100 quartets sprang up in the area. Practically every local community, including the industrial communities such as Dolomite, Westfield, Docena, Edgewater, and

Fairfield, had its own quartet. There was intense competition among the groups. Birmingham area churches and high school auditoriums became staging grounds for quartet competitions and programs. This competition was epitomized by the monthly battles staged at Council School in Ensley between the Famous Blue Jay Singers and the Birmingham Jubilee Singers. The competitions were not just for the most popular groups but extended to all the quartets who wished to compete. Large crowds filled churches and school auditoriums to witness these competitions.[16]

Several factors accounted for the emergence of quartet singing in the Birmingham area. One was stimulation from African American education. At Tuskegee Institute, Booker T. Washington and Robert Moton cultivated a heritage of African American religious folk music based on the examples of Hampton Institute and Fisk University, whose musical groups had traditionally performed a cappella. The music departments of Fisk and Tuskegee had an effect on musical training in the broader African American community through their graduates who taught in southern rural communities and secondary schools. Richard C. Foster, who organized the first known quartet in Bessemer, received instruction in quartet singing while attending high school in Lowndes County. His teacher was Vernon Barnett, a graduate of Tuskegee who had learned quartet singing there. Professor Malachi Wilkerson, principal of Parker High School and the early director of the annual Negro Folk Song Festival in Birmingham and his wife Julia Wilkerson, of the Parker High music department, both of whom had been trained at Tuskegee, encouraged a cappella singing in the area.[17]

A second factor in the emergence of quartet singing was the migration from the rural to the urban areas. In the rural areas of Alabama, Georgia, and Mississippi, quartets were an important form of singing. Moving to the industrial camp areas of Birmingham and Jefferson County in the 1920s and depression years, migrants brought this style of singing with them. Denied access to other forms of popular entertainment, they embraced quartet singing as a popular pastime. It provided a time of fellowship, socializing, and a means of expressing one's faith.[18]

A third factor that encouraged the emergence of quartet singing in Birmingham was innovation. The large number of people moving to the city brought with them a variety of regional experiences in a cappella singing. Birmingham was fortunate in having a number of persons who added new techniques to the harmonious rhythm of quartet singing in the area. Silas Steele of Brighton perfected an emotional sermonizing lead singing style that became inseparable from gospel quartet performance. A few years later Lewis Porterfield Lewis popularized the "pumping" bass technique in which the bass singer essentially mimics a tuba rather than singing the words in harmony with other forces. These two features, along with an emphasis on harmony, combined to give Birmingham its unique quartet sound, a sound in which four or more singers sang a cappella in close and complex harmony with a strong lead and a creative and powerful bass part.[19]

Quartet singing in the Birmingham area was also closely allied with the African American churches. Churches were a main setting for quartet appearances. Although quartets rarely appeared at regular church services, they were featured guests at homecomings, anniversary programs, and at other musical events in the churches. Several singing groups were at one time members of the same church. The Ravizee Singers were once all members of New Zion Baptist Church in Bessemer and were brothers and sisters of its pastor, the Reverend Shelton H. Ravizee. The Golden Leaf Quartette came out of Mount Moriah Baptist Church in Pratt City. Another group came out of Starlight Baptist Church in the Muscoda Mining Camp located a few miles from Bessemer. The format of the quartet's weekly rehearsals borrowed elements of the church service: the groups opened rehearsals with a devotion and special song and closed with a final prayer.[20]

Because of the church background of the singers, the theology and world view of the quartets was that of the African American church. Quartet singers emphasized the power of God and his ability to reward the faithful. They believed in the assurance of blessings through suffering. As God had rewarded the slaves because of their faithfulness, he would be with them in their new industrial setting. In their singing quartets used a call and response method that was similar to the dialogue between the preacher and congregation in the church. This style of performance encouraged crowd participation. It was common for audiences to respond with expressions such as such as "Go ahead," "Sing it," and "That's all right." Finally, many songs were the same as those performed by church choirs. Among these were the jubilee spirituals, such as "Low Down Chariot," the hymns of invitation such as "Lord I Come to Thee," and Protestant metric hymns, such as "Jesus Is All the world to Me."[21]

Although quartet singing served several important purposes, none was more important than expressing the longing for a better life. Almost all of the first-generation singers were mine and mill workers who had migrated from rural Alabama. They had moved to Birmingham to better their economic condition. Through their songs they showed a new identification with and hope for life in the city. A song that expressed this identification most clearly was "Birmingham Boys," which was the song that the Famous Jubilee Singers opened their performances with, and which other groups in the area also used. Although the song referred to domesticity and family life, it clearly expressed the expectation of a better life.

>Birmingham boys are we,
>Jolly as can be.
>Rolly, jolly, Birmingham boys are we.
>You can tell without a doubt,
>When the Birmingham boys are out,
>Rolly, jolly, Birmingham boys are we.
>I was tired of living in the country,
>So I moved my wife to town,
>And there I bought a cottage,
>And then I settled down.
>Where the boys in the valley they go
>>bow-wow-wow,
>
>And the pigs in the pen go
>>wee-wee-wee
>
>And the cat joins in with a meow,
>And the rooster on the fence goes
>>cock-cock-a-doodle-do-do
>
>All them biscuits in that oven,
>How I wish I had some of them.
>Ha, ha, my goodness I declare.
>Birmingham, Birmingham, Birmingham
>>boys are we.
>
>If you could hear those Birmingham boys,
>How happy you would be
>>(oh, you would be).[22]

The desire for a better life gave quartet singing a dimension of protest. The industrialists of Jefferson County perpetuated the South's traditional racial hierarchy by relying on African American migrants for low-paid, untrained, or unskilled labor. These industrialists also sought to suppress union activities. Although unions had led several strikes in

Birmingham, the passage of the National Industrial Recovery Act in 1933 caused such unions as the United Mine Workers of America and the United Steel Workers of American to achieve steady and significant growth in the area. Although there were tough battles between management and labor, African Americans achieved better wages, benefits, and working conditions through the unions. Through the singing of quartet groups, they expressed their support for labor unions. Union backers used the song, "Union Boys are We," a variant of "Birmingham Boys" to show this pro-union position as workers joined in struggle against the company and its agents for a better life.

> Union boys are we, happy as can be,
> Rolly, rolly, jolly, jolly,
> Union boys are we.
> Progressives in de valley go
> bow-wow-wow
> Scabs in de pen go wee-wee-wee,
> An' snitchers in de barn go hee-haw-hee
> Popsicles on de fence go
> cock-cockle-do-do-do,
> All dem biscuits in dat oven,
> How I wish'd I had some of 'em,
> Ah, ha, g-goodness I declare;
> All dem 'lasses in dat plate,
> Sop, sop, sop befo' it be too late,
> Ah, ha, g-goodness I declare,
> Union boys, union boys, are we,
> If you could live a union life,
> How happy you would be.[23]

Although most quartets favored the union movement, there were some groups that identified more closely with it than others. One example was the CIO Singers. This group was composed of employees from United States Pipe Shop in Bessemer, Tennessee Coal and Iron Company, and the Louisiana and Nashville Railroad. They performed on radio station WJLD along with Tiger Thomas, a local labor organizer and president of the United Steel Workers of America Local 1466. They sang during the breaks after Thomas had discussed union affairs. Along with other groups, the CIO singers also sang at labor union functions, such as banquets, meetings, and conventions.[24]

Some union songs had a clearly biblical and theological character. These songs sanctified the union movement and described it as a "holy cause." Those fighting against management were children of God who would succeed if they held on. Some of the songs pictured union leaders as heroes in the same light as Biblical characters like Moses. Two songs written by the Reverend Rosco McDonald, lead singer of the CIO Singers, show this explicit spiritual emphasis. In his song "The Spirit of Phil Murray," the labor leader is a type of Moses who came to earth to set the working people free but is now gone to heaven to get his reward. Another song, "Satisfied," places the origin of unionism in the Bible:

> Well you read in the Bible
> You read it well
> Listen to the story
> That I'm bound to tell
>
> Christ's last Passover
> He had his communion
> He told his disciples
> Stay in union
>
> Together you stand
> Divided you fall
> Stay in union
> I'll save you all
> Ever since that wonderful day my soul's
> been satisfied.[25]

Birmingham's unique quartet singing style gave it a nationwide appeal. Beginning in the late 1920s these groups began to export their uniqueness around the nation. The first Birmingham group to receive national recognition was the Birmingham Jubilee Singers. In 1926 the group recorded an album for the Columbia Record Company. One year later they toured the East with Ethel Waters. In the same year the Birmingham Jubilee Singers joined the vaudeville circuit. Among its most famous songs were "Birmingham Boys," "Southbound Train," and "He Took My Sins Away." The success of the Birmingham Jubilee Singer's success opened the door for other groups in Birmingham. Before 1940 at least ten Birmingham quartets had made commercial phonograph records, including the Dunham Jubilee Singers, the Ravizee Singers, and the Blue Jay Singers.[26]

The Birmingham style moved to other parts of the United States not so much via the phonograph as by the singers themselves. The famous Blue Jay Singers, led by Silas Steele, was among the first groups in the state to go on far-flung barnstorming tours, tours which eventually took them over most of the United States. In the mid-1930s the Kings of Harmony introduced the New York metropolitan area to the gospel quartet style. Some individual Birmingham singers and quartet groups moved to other cities and became highly successful. During the 1930s the Famous Blue Jay Singers set up operations in Dallas before moving to Chicago around 1940. The Kings of Harmony moved to Houston in the late 1930s. Both the Kings of Harmony and the Heavenly Gospel Singers used Cleveland, Ohio, as their home base in the 1940s. The Heavenly Gospel Singers ultimately settled in Los Angeles. Two outstanding Bessemer trainers, Norman McQueen and Gilbert Porterfield, carried the Birmingham quartet ethos to Chicago and New Orleans respectively, when they relocated in those cities around 1930. Silas Steele moved to Memphis in the 1940s to sing with the Spirit of Memphis. There he became very popular and successful. The profound influence and spread of gospel quartet singing from Birmingham to Chicago, Cleveland, New Orleans, Nashville, Memphis, and other cities was an important chapter in the story of African American gospel music.[27]

The rapid growth of Pentecostal, Holiness, and Spiritualist churches also represented a new religious response to the economic insecurity and the racism of the times. At the end of World War I only six such churches existed in the city limits of Birmingham. By the beginning of World War II, this number had increased to thirty-six. Many of these churches were meeting in houses and storefronts, and started because of recent migrants into the city or ministers who were sent by their denominations. These persons would usually conduct a revival in a home, gather a few converts, and establish a church. After they established the church, ministers continued holding revivals as the primary means of evangelism and fundraising for these churches.[28]

The growth of Pentecostal, Holiness, and Spiritualist churches was not only the result of migration and revivalism but also a reaction against the formalism of worship in many mainline churches. As new migrants moved to the city, some formed smaller Baptist churches to meet their particular needs. Others joined the small Pentecostal,

Holiness, and Spiritualist churches that were more congenial to their emotional and psychological needs. These churches were most amenable to African Americans during the depression years when life was insecure. Rather than searching for political and secular solutions, many substituted the spiritual power and certainty that these churches offered. In these churches people sought to escape the troubles of this world by dwelling on the rewards awaiting in the next.[29]

In addition to the emotional fervor, spiritual certainty, and otherworldly perspective that appealed to many African Americans in Birmingham, there were three other elements that drew African Americans to these small Pentecostal, Holiness, and Spiritualists churches. One of these was a recovering of the spiritual emphasis of the past. These churches claimed that they constituted a revitalization of the African and slave elements that made up the original religion of African Americans that the mainline churches had rejected with their sedate hymns and formal liturgy. In their music, these churches reached back to the traditions of the slave past and out to the rhythms of the secular African American musical world around them. They brought into the church not only the sounds of ragtime, blues, and jazz but also the instruments. Drums, tambourines, guitars, saxophones, trumpets, trombones, and whatever else seemed appropriate to accompany the singing. The people clapped their hands, danced, and shouted to the beat of the music. It was in these churches that gospel music was first performed before it became accepted in many mainline churches. The masses felt at home in these churches. In explaining the appeal of the Church of God in Christ, which he founded, Charles Mason maintained that his church had "the original rhythm of colored people."[30]

A second appeal was a sense of recognition and dignity. While mainline churches in the African American community had always provided these needs, in the 1930s positions in these churches were in the hands of middle-class persons. Recent migrants and poorer blacks felt alienated and saw no hope of attaining key positions. In the small storefront Pentecostal, Holiness, and Spiritualists churches a person could more easily rise to a position of leadership. In a society where he was considered inferior, an individual of humble standing could become in a Spiritualist church a bishop, minister, elder, deacon, or prophet on his ability to communicate with the spirit world. Some Spiritualists churches created quasi-royal positions such as King, Queen, Prince, and Princess. Thus, a person with a marginal status in society could become

Baptism Service in Black Belt from C.O. Boothe, Cyclopedia of Negro Baptists in Alabama *(Birmingham, 1895)*

Baptism Services were joyous occasions in the Black Belt of Alabama where most blacks lived before migrating to Birmingham.

St. Paul CME Church, Docena

Starlight Baptist Church, Bessemer

Many of the earliest black churches in Birmingham were brush arbors. The first permanent buildings were plank buildings looking much like the two churches shown above.

Shiloh Baptist Church, 1895 from C.O. Boothe, Cyclopedia of Negro Baptists in Alabama *(Birmingham, 1895)*

This church, founded by Reverend T.W. Walker in 1891, grew to become Birmingham's largest church by 1900.

The Reverend Dr. W.R. Pettiford. Courtesy of the Sixteenth Street Baptist Archives

Pettiford was one of the key leaders of the African American community from 1885 to 1915. Among his greatest achievements was the establishment of the Alabama Penny bank.

Sunday Morning worship service, 1940. Courtesy of the Sixteenth Street Baptist Church Archives

Sardis Baptist Church and Pastor Robert L. Alford

The ACMHR was founded at the Sardis Baptist Church, June 5, 1956.

Meeting of the Alabama Christian Movement for Human Rights (ACMHR)

The ACMHR met every Monday in different churches. The mass meetings were full of religious fervor. Above is the picture of the movement meeting, June 23, 1958, East Thomas Baptist Church.

Seventeenth Street AOH Church

St. Luke AME Church

Bethel AME Church

These three Civil Rights churches all had basements. Most black churches built between the 1920's and 1950's were built on this style.

a "Royal Elected Ruler," a "King of All Israel," the potentate of a regal kingdom, or perhaps a god or goddess of a new age.[31]

A third major reason for the attraction of Pentecostal, Holiness, and Spiritualist churches were the opportunities they gave to women. In the mainline churches, women made up the bulk of the membership, organized the activities of the church, and assumed the major financial responsibility for its maintenance. Despite these important roles, women could not become pastors. In some Methodist denominations they could preach, but Baptist pastors were adamant in their objection to women having any ministerial role. Many ambitious women joined churches of the Pentecostal and Holiness movement because it provided them an opportunity to preach and pastor. By 1940 a few women had pastored and founded churches of the Pentecostal and Holiness denominations in Birmingham. In 1939 Mrs. Ophelia Griffin was pastoring the Bessemer Church of God. Allene Dean organized the Birmingham Church of God and served as its first pastor. Mattie Peterson from the Bessemer Church of God was one of three persons who came from the Bessemer Church of God and helped organize the Roosevelt City Church of God. Mrs Hannah Woods established the Church of God on Third Avenue in North Birmingham that was still in existence in 1939. Women were also evangelists in these churches and served in all ministerial capacities. Many women in Spiritualist churches were elders, mediums, and healers. In the churches of the Pentecostal, Holiness, and Spiritualist traditions, there was some prejudice and men still assumed the leading positions, but women had much more opportunity for leadership than in the mainline denominations.[32]

The Pentecostal, Holiness, and Spiritualist movements were diverse, with many different groups and Biblical interpretations. Many of these churches were founded by former Baptists or Methodists who became dissatisfied with those churches. They formed their own churches with their own peculiar Biblical understandings. Some churches were the result of strong charismatic personalities and personality differences. Others emerged over the issue of what was the original religion of African Americans, others over such seemingly trivial issues as what to wear, and still others over doctrine. Doctrinal differences centered on such issues as sanctification, the work of the Holy Spirit, the Trinity, and baptizing only in the name of Jesus. All these differences led to the mushrooming of many different groups, churches, and denominations.[33]

Of the thirty-six African American churches of the Pentecostal, Holiness, and Spiritualist traditions listed in the *Birmingham Directory* of 1940, at least eleven were Spiritualist churches. Most of these churches resembled the Pentecostal and Holiness churches in their belief in justification, sanctification, the baptism of the Holy Spirit, healing, prophecy, hand clapping, and foot stomping. There were, however, two major differences. One was the Spiritualist's belief in seances, communicating with the dead, and entering the spirit world at death. In these churches, ministers and mediums helped members communicate with the spirit world, where messages came from the spirit of deceased relatives or friends. A second difference was the Spiritualist's emphasis on the here and now. While many Pentecostal and Holiness churches had an otherworldly emphasis, Spiritualist churches sought to answer practical questions and provide material success through religious rituals and esoteric knowledge. Through spiritual means, members of these churches sought to acquire wealth, employment, love, or the improvement of a strained relationship. Most Spiritualist churches in Birmingham were very small, with many having less than twenty members. The Spiritualist services and seances were held in private homes and rented halls. Most of these services included a prayer, music, a sermon, and spiritual messages from the dead. As African Americans experienced tough economic times in Birmingham in the 1920s and 1930's, a few gravitated to these churches where they found hope and the possibility of economic success.[34]

Among the denominations of the Pentecostal-Holiness tradition, which tended to be more otherworldly and moralistic than the Spiritualist churches, several established at least one church in Birmingham in the 1920s and 1930s. These included the Emmanuel Holiness Church, the Church of God by Faith, the Church of Jesus Christ, the Holy Church of God, the United Holiness Church of God, and the Apostolic Faith Church. Denominations establishing two or more churches included the Church of the Living God and the Apostolic Overcoming Holy Church of God.[35]

The Reverend William Christian, an African American minister, founded the Church of the Living God in Wrightsville, Arkansas, in 1889. The church emphasized sanctification, speaking in tongues, and the blackness of many Church saints. This denomination formed two churches in Birmingham during the period between the two world wars. In 1921, the Reverend A.D. Dunlap came to Birmingham from Greenville, Alabama, and formed the first Church of the Living God in

Birmingham. His church first met in his house and then moved to a rented storefront. In 1937 a second church began in Ensley with an initial membership of five persons.[36]

The Reverend W.T. Phillips, a former Methodist minister in Mobile, who joined the Holiness movement in 1913, formed the Apostolic Overcoming Holy Church of God in 1916. His own church in Mobile was incorporated in 1920 as the Ethiopian Overcoming Holy Church of God, with "Ethiopian" changed to "Apostolic" in 1927. His church stressed "oneness," a belief that rejected the trinity, and believed in baptizing only "in the name of Jesus." Phillips also emphasized the holiness doctrine of sanctification, perfection, foot washing, and divine healing. The church accepted women in the ministry and allowed them to preach. Services generally were emotional affairs, with participants speaking in tongues and engaging in ecstatic dances. By 1940 fellow believers in Birmingham had established two churches, one on First Avenue South and the other on Fifteenth Avenue South.[37]

The leading church among the Pentecostal and Holiness churches in Birmingham was the Church of God in Christ, which had its headquarters in Memphis, Tennessee. By 1940, there were at least five churches in Birmingham. These churches combined both Pentecostal and Holiness elements. Charles H. Mason, the founder, was a former Baptist minister. One of the driving forces in his life was to recover the religion of the slaves and thereby the original religion of African American. He was soon converted to the doctrine of the second blessing of sanctification, which purged the believer of sin, making him pure. The Baptists regarded the doctrine of Christian perfection as heresy, but Mason made it one of his foundational doctrines and began calling his following the Church of God in Christ. In 1906 Mason visited Azura Street Church in Los Angeles, where he was converted to William Seymour's doctrine of the third blessing — the baptism of the Holy Spirit and fire — which empowered Christians to cast out devils, heal the sick, and speak in tongues. Returning to Memphis, Mason officially completed the organization of his church adding the third blessing as a cardinal doctrine. He called a meeting of all African American ministers in the mid-South who believed in speaking in tongues as proof of the baptism of the Holy Spirit, and at this, the first general assembly of the Church of God in Christ, Mason was elected the chief overseer.[38]

As African Americans migrated into urban areas in the North and South, including Birmingham, lay members and missionaries from the church of God in Christ formed churches of that denomination. For example, in the 1920s the Reverend R.F. Williams came to Birmingham and started the East Birmingham Church of God. By 1930 he had constructed a church and a parsonage. In 1926 the Reverend Joseph King founded a Church of God in Christ in Pratt City after holding a revival meeting. Besides these two churches, other churches of the denomination began in Fairfield, North Birmingham, and South Birmingham. In these churches, worshipers shouted and sang in the African American tradition of the spirituals, improvising lines and receiving responses from the congregation as they marched in time to the music, swaying their bodies from side to side with their arms and eyes raised upward to heaven. In these services, it was not unusual for worshipers to speak in tongues, enter trances, jerk violently, and shake uncontrollably. Worshipers saw these actions as proof that a person had received the baptism of the Holy Ghost and had become perfect.[39]

Worship was the most important activity of the churches of the Pentecostal, Holiness, and Spiritualist traditions. Members gathered several times a week for worship. Services were unusually long, lasting for several hours. Some nights members did not get home from church until eleven o'clock. Spontaneity was a key to these services. Participants prided themselves on being caught up in the spirit and letting the Holy Spirit have his way. Despite this emphasis on spontaneity, most churches divided their services into three parts: a devotional service, the service of the Word, and a closing. This basic three-part worship service remains essentially unchanged to this day.[40]

The devotional service included an opening hymn, scripture reading, requests for prayer, the prayer, a song service in which members would sing several congregational hymns, and a testimony service. In the testimony service each member had an opportunity to participate. Members generally testified to the goodness of God and his power in their lives. The testimony followed a basic pattern. The person testifying acknowledged God and various persons present, recounted God's blessings, which often included deliverance from financial problems, ill health, or spiritual and emotional trials. The testimony then ended with the testifier urging the saints to continue to pray for him or her. Observers of Pentecostal worship services have left examples of some of these testimonies.

> Giving honor to God and all the saints, I'm glad to say this evening, I'm saved, sanctified, and hallelujah [she twists to the side] filled with the marvelous Holy Ghost.

> I'm thanking my God for looking over me and my children one more week, for keeping Satan away, for stepping in when I needed him most. Truly . . . God's been my all in all for without him today children I couldn't have made it thus far. Truly . . . I've learned if God be for you, he's more than the whole world against you and there's reality in serving a true and living God. Truly . . . his Grace is sufficient and all the days of my appointed time I intend to stretch out on his goodness and wait till my change comes. I'm asking you to pray much for me, cause I'm still a motherless child standing in the need of prayer. Amen, glory to God, thank the Lord.[41]

After the devotional service concluded with testifying, the service of the Word began, with the pastor or his assistant taking over. In many churches the deacons, church mother, or a minister would then take the offering. Many churches in Birmingham did not have choirs in the 1920s and 1930s; the music that followed the offering was congregational, accompanied by piano, drums, and tambourines. Hand clapping and foot stomping were an integral part of the singing, as worshipers moved in rhythm. The subject matter of most of the songs was personal victory, with the singers praising God for his deliverance power. Among favorite songs were "Sunrise Always Follows Rain," "The Storm Is Passing Over," "You Can't Make Me Doubt Him," "He Brought Me Out," and "Stand By Me." The sermon followed the music and was the high point of the service. The preaching was highly emotional, including gestures, mannerism, and rhetorical devices that increased the forcefulness of the preaching. The sermon was not an effort solely on the part of the preacher. The preacher received loud responses from the congregation. Depending on the congregation, worshipers even stood and actively exhorted the preacher to "go ahead," "help yourself," "make it right" and so forth. The preacher sought to make the spirit of God real to the participants, to lead people to salvation, and to edify the believers. Following the sermon, the minister made an altar call in which the unsaved received an opportunity to come forth and accept salvation. After a successful altar call the pastor conversed with and prayed for the newly saved persons and gave them an opportunity to testify concerning their salvation.[42]

In some churches there was always a prayer and healing service after the altar call. Other churches restricted such services to the revival.

The pattern for the prayer and healing service was similar to that of the altar call. The minister invited worshipers to come forth for prayer and healing. During the prayer and healing service people came forth to discuss their particular ills and needs with the minister, who laid hands on the supplicant while praying over him or her. Prayers differed in length and fervor depending on the needs of the person. "O God, we come before you this evening; heal your faithful servant, O God. Rebuke this ill, O Lord; deliver her from this affliction. Heal this backache; make her every whit whole. We ask in Jesus' name. Amen."[43]

The third part of the service was the closing. The preacher turned this part of the service over to the presiding minister. The minister gave visitors an opportunity to make remarks. Sometimes these visitors would testify of their salvation and tell how they received a blessing from the service. The church clerk then announced upcoming church events. When everything had been said, the pastor came forth for final remarks and the benediction. The pastor raised his hands or arms, the members of the congregation raised one or both of theirs, and the preacher said: "Grace, mercy, and truth from God the Father, through Jesus Christ, the Son of the Father, with the Holy Spirit, in peace and love, let the church say Amen." This concluded the service. The ministers and congregation gathered around to greet each other, shaking hands and congratulating the speaker or pastor on the sermon. There was often laughter and mirth as people visited and exchanged news. In some churches people would hug and kiss each other in affectionate greeting.[44]

The insecurity and trauma caused by the Great Depression in the African American community of Birmingham caused new political and religious responses to surface. Both pastors and the African American middle class rejected communism as idealistic, atheistic, and emotional. Gospel music and the churches of the Pentecostal, Holiness, and Spiritualist traditions received more favorable responses. Pentecostal, Holiness, and Spiritualist churches grew rapidly in the 1920s and 1930s, providing poor and working class African Americans with religious certainty and security that many did not find in the mainline Baptist and Methodist churches. Through their highly emotional worship services that consisted of tongue speaking, dancing, hand clapping, and gospel music, many African Americans found the fortitude to face life during these harsh times. Gospel music made its way into the city and changed worship patterns in mainline churches. The former emphasis on congregational participation in the music part of the worship gave way to more individualistic performances that included solos and choirs with the worshipers increasingly becoming the audience. These gospel songs emphasized faith and hope, admonishing the hearer to trust in Christ. Gospel music and Pentecostal churches also made a social statement. African Americans during this time of economic insecurity, rampant injustice, and oppression turned to the religion of their forefathers. Although there were elements of otherworldliness, they decided to be themselves and celebrate their religious heritage. In both Pentecostalism and gospel music there was a return to one's roots and an incipient race pride. After World War II Pentecostalism and gospel music would continue to be a part of the religious life in the city as churches and pastors would champion a new militancy calling for the end of segregation and full rights for African Americans.

VII

Rising Militancy and the African American Church from World War II to the Civil Rights Movement

World War II gave rise to a new militancy in the African American community of Birmingham and the nation. African Americans insisted on full rights and freedoms. The African American church and its pastors in Birmingham were an essential part of the new militancy while maintaining their traditional roles as spiritual leaders and builders and preservers of institutions in the community. Reflecting the new militancy, the idea of gradual racial progress gave way among many pastors to a demand for the immediate end of segregation and full. Pastors began to express this newfound militancy during the war years. In the postwar years they became leaders in the fight for full civil rights. They expressed this in sermons and addresses, the activities of ministerial groups, participation in and support of the NAACP, and through personal acts of courage.

Fighting for freedom abroad, African Americans became more conscious of their own lack of freedom at home. This consciousness led to growing protest in both the North and the South during World War II. In the North, there was self-criticism because of past acceptance of certain forms of segregation. In the South, many African Americans began to question Jim Crow openly. The March on Washington movement most typified the new militancy and heightened sense of race consciousness during the war years. In 1941 A. Philip Randolph issued a call for a march on Washington, D.C., to protest job discrimination in the defense industry. His tactic of mass pressure through a demonstration of black power struck a cord among African Americans. The number pledged to march on Washington on July 1, 1941, increased to 50,000, and only President Franklin Roosevelt's agreement to issue an executive order establishing the President's Committee on Fair Employment Practices (FEPC) led to a cancellation of the march.[1]

The formation of the Fair Employment Practices Committee also reflected growing African American political power in the country. During the 1930s, African Americans began to accumulate significant voting strength in northern states like New York, New Jersey, Indiana, and Ohio. The African American vote had become an important element in the new coalition supporting the Democratic Party. While African Americans were becoming more militant and were asserting their political power, whites were becoming more tolerant. Confrontation with Hitler and fascism in World War II forced many white Americans to see the racism that existed in the United States. Many Americans saw for the first time that white supremacy conflicted with the American ideals of liberty and equality. Recognition of this conflict helped create the climate for racial change during World War II and, to some extent, in the postwar decades. Supreme Court decisions in the 1940s were a major part of this new tolerance and more liberal racial climate. The rulings of the Court in education, voting, housing, and labor affirmed the rights of African Americans to guarantees of the Fourteenth and Fifteenth Amendments. African Americans believed they could now look to the Court for protection of their constitutional rights. These factors taken together — the heightened consciousness among African Americans, the expanded power of the northern black electorate, and the more tolerant racial attitude by the Supreme Court and many white Americans — combined to produce a greater sense of militancy.[2]

Awakened by the new sense of militancy on the national level, African Americans in Birmingham began to show more aggressive responses to the discrimination which they faced, and to protest as never before. For example, beginning in 1942 African Americans frequently accused the city bus and streetcar lines of brutality and rudeness, and began to demand that city drivers be thoroughly investigated. Industrial workers complained about discrimination and the indifference of labor unions in Birmingham to Philip Murray, the national president of the United Steelworkers of America. In 1943 fifteen African American workers at the TCI tin mill went on strike after complaining about their lack of seniority and vacation pay, and being refused a wage adjustment.[3]

African Americans formed several organizations to champion their rights in the city. One of these groups began in a church, since churches were often used as meeting places. In 1941 in the basement of the Miller Memorial Presbyterian Church, twenty-one civic groups came together to form the Alabama Federation of Colored Civic Leagues. Groups from

Enon Ridge, South Elyton, Bessemer, Brighton, Fairfield, and North Birmingham were among the civic leagues represented. Besides championing better community services, the federation initiated voter registration efforts and promoted anti-crime programs. From the civic league groups, persons moved to other organizations and became leaders.[4]

Another organization that emerged during the war years in 1943 was the Jefferson County Progressive Democratic Council. It was a partisan political organization that supported Democratic Party candidates. After he failed to qualify as a candidate for the Alabama state legislature in 1942, Arthur Shores, an African American Birmingham attorney, and other leaders realized that to gain a political voice in Alabama they needed to make inroads into the Democratic Party, which controlled the state by virtue of the one-party system that prevailed in the South. According to Shores, the purpose of the organization was "to increase the number of black voters and to educate them about the mechanics of voting and political issues and candidates."[5]

Two of the most militant organizations championing the rights of African American in Birmingham during the early war years were the United Mine Workers of America and the Communist party. In the 1930s the United Mine Workers sent William Mitch into Birmingham. Mitch led a successful organizational drive and eventually won the favor of the NAACP and other African Americans by putting African American miners in leadership positions in local unions and by openly supporting black political rights. Speaking at the Emancipation Day program on January 1, 1949, Mitch insisted that "Elevation of the workers must be equal between the colored and white workers."[6] The local NAACP and organized labor became firmly allied.

The Communist party in Birmingham, taking advantage of the growing dissatisfaction among African American industrial workers, continued to agitate for job advancement for blacks and greater political rights. In 1938 Hosea Hudson and Joseph S. Gelders, a white radical activist, formed a "right to vote" club to register voters before the Democratic primary of May 1938. Among the club's members were Harold Knight of the UMW and Emory Jackson, editor of the *Birmingham World*, the city's main African American newspaper. African Americans' increasing concerns about voter discrimination moved the NAACP to support the work of the Right to Vote Club, and, as Hudson later explained, "we were able to establish a united front.

"Although only about one hundred members of the Right to Vote Club were registered in 1938 and 1939, its activity had suggested the promise of greater black and worker political power, and it brought about an alliance of workers, radicals, and the African American middle class.[7]

The local chapter of the NAACP was the largest and best known voice for African Americans in the city. During the war years the membership greatly increased, from 1,032 in 1940 to a record high of 8,500 in 1946. It addressed many issues during this period. One of its greatest concerns was police brutality. During the 1940s the organization exerted constant pressure to combat that brutality. Its investigations in 1940 and 1941 into the murders of O. Dee Henderson and John Jackson, two African Americans killed while in police custody in the suburban community of Fairfield, resulted in the dismissal of two police officers accused in the incidents. The NAACP was also extremely active in fighting racial inequity in teacher's salaries. When the Supreme Court ruled in the 1940s that racially based discrimination in teachers' salaries was unconstitutional, the NAACP sprang into action. Birmingham branch attorney Arthur Shores and national legal counsel Thurgood Marshall represented William Bolden, a county high school principal, in his suit in federal district court against the Jefferson County Board of Education. Their arguments resulted in a federal court ruling three years later that declared Alabama's system of salaries based on race to be unconstitutional.[8]

Two other issues to which the Birmingham NAACP devoted considerable attention during the war were voting and job discrimination. The Birmingham branch played a leading role in several "right-to-vote" drives and offered legal assistance to those denied the right to vote. During the spring and summer of 1939 several hundred African Americans of the Right to Vote Club attempted to register to vote but were denied. This led to the first suit by the NAACP against the Jefferson County Board of Registrars. Other suits followed in 1940 and 1942. In 1942 Arthur Shores, the NAACP's lawyer, filed suit in federal court. Although none of the suits were successful, the challenge to the disfranchisement of African Americans in Alabama had gone further than at any time since it was established by the Alabama Constitution in 1901. Job discrimination was another issue that inflamed the African American community. Despite the FEPC, African Americans in Birmingham were denied job advancement in major industries. In 1941 Shores filed suit on behalf of Bester William Steele, a black Birmingham man who had been demoted as a fireman for the Louisville and Nashville Railroad. *Steele v. L & N* would become a landmark Supreme Court decision against union and employer discrimination in 1944.[9]

Affected by the unparalleled militancy in the city during World War II, African American clergy in Birmingham expressed a greater sense of militancy. The past calls for fair play and gradualism gave way to demands for the immediate elimination of inequality. Pastors began to support movements, led by laymen, to obtain full rights for African Americans in the city. The reasons for this new militancy among a significant group of pastors were numerous. First, like laymen in the community, pastors felt that the wartime sacrifices and loyalty of African Americans entitled them to full freedom. Second, some African American pastors had been taught in historically black colleges by exponents of the social gospel, who stressed that the church should become involved in changing the evils of society. Some of these college-trained pastors came into Birmingham energized to work to change the system of segregation. Third, unlike past pastoral leaders like William Pettiford and John Goodgame, Sr., who saw no hope of eliminating segregation during the late 1800s and the early 1900s because of the hostile racial climate in the nation, the new tolerance expressed by white intellectuals, the rulings of the Supreme Court, and the success of the March on Washington movement gave many pastors a feeling that now was the time to press for full freedom. Fourth, as they did in Memphis, Tennessee, parishioners in churches began to push their pastors to press for their rights. As leaders of the people who had the freedom to do so because of economic support from their churches, many pastors felt an obligation to express the new militancy of their congregations. All these factors created a more militant group of African American pastors in Birmingham.[10]

The Birmingham Baptist Ministers' Conference, the largest group of ministers in the city, became more active in defending the rights of African Americans in the city during the war. For example, in 1940 the Birmingham Baptist Minister's Conference became involved in the case of Joe Vernon, an African American police informer accused of murder and sentenced to die in the electric chair. Ministers from the conference formed the Joe Vernon Defense Committee and held mass meetings to raise funds for legal fees and to galvanize community support. The conference, along with the NAACP, insisted that the evidence was not sufficient to warrant a conviction and that the death penalty was unjust. The protest was successful in getting a stay of execution for Vernon.

Similarly, the Baptist conference sought an audience with the Birmingham Electric Company to protest the shooting of Steve Edwards by a streetcar operator when he protested having to stand when there were empty seats in the white area of the streetcar. In December 1945 six ministers from the Birmingham conference went to Montgomery to protest the Jim Crow seating laws before the Alabama Public Service Commission.[11]

Some sermons and addresses of pastors during the war years expressed the view that African Americans should have full freedom because of their loyalty and sacrifices. For example, Rev. W.H. Perry, pastor of Ebenezer Baptist Church, delivering the 1943 speech celebrating the signing of the Emancipation Proclamation, maintained that African Americans should enjoy the same freedom that they were fighting for. "Such freedom," he insisted, "was due all Americans." Rev. John W. Goodgame, Jr., made a similar point in one of the most militant and passionate pleas for justice during World War II. At a memorial service for Lieutenant James Holloway, a member of the Sixth Avenue church who was killed in combat, Goodgame denounced segregation and Jim Crow, and insisted that any African American soldier who fights and dies, does so in the hope of freedom, justice, and equality. "Anything less," he maintained, "does not do justice for the blood, sweat, and tears paid into it." He continued "Any man who dies in an army which discriminates against his race dies a hero. The irony of all this is that a Southern Negro can die for democracy but can't always vote for it. It is therefore for us the living to make a democracy as democratic as death. Otherwise we become unworthy of the sacrifices made by our friends who die. My friend Lieutenant James W. Holloway, like other dark-skinned soldiers, died that we might have a chance to drive on toward that goal of full freedom which is the dream of all humankind."[12]

Support for the right to vote was high on the list of concerns for African American clergy during the war years. The Jefferson County Board of Registrars remained adamantly opposed to black voting, allowing only a few African Americans to vote to avoid the appearance of wholesale violation of the law. They were determined, however, to hold the black vote to a minimum. African Americans reacted with forthright challenges to the board's refusal after the Supreme Court outlawed the white primary in 1944. Pastors aided the attempt to vote in several ways. Through their sermons and addresses, pastors urged blacks to register. In 1945 Bishop Shaw of the AME Zion Church appealed to teachers to vote because of the example it would set for other members of the race. In 1944 Rev. James Hargrove, pastor of the Union Bethel Independent Methodist Church and one of the first radio ministers in Birmingham, announced during his radio broadcast that he was going to register to vote. In that same year, ministers from the Birmingham Baptist Ministers' Conference announced that they were going to register. Several pastors held voting clinics at their churches in which they tutored African Americans on how to register to vote. Among these churches were the Forty-fifth Street Baptist Church, Mt. Zion Baptist Church of Zion City, the Macedonia Baptist Church of Ensley, and the Twenty-second Avenue Baptist Church of North Birmingham.[13]

Although lay persons remained the major leaders of the NAACP, a small group of pastors began to move gradually into significant positions of leadership. The Reverend Goodgame, Jr., served as chairman of the membership drive and gave the membership kickoff speech in 1942. In that same year, Goodgame was elected vice-president of the NAACP. In 1944 several ministers were added to the executive committee of the NAACP, including Bishop Nichols of the AME Church, Bishop Shaw of the AME Zion Church, Rev. W.H. Perry of the New Ebenezer Baptist Church, Rev. J. Perry, rector of the St. Mark, and Rev. S.J. Mashaw of the Metropolitan CME Church. In 1945 Rev. W.H. Perry became the organization's vice-president.[14]

Along with the increased militancy of pastors during the war years was the continuation of pastors as spiritual leaders and institutional builders and preservers. Pastors insisted that African American institutions needed to be supported. By continuing their traditional function, pastors strengthened their position as leaders in the community. The most ambitious project undertaken by pastors was an African American hospital. African Americans received the worst medical care in the city. The white hospitals segregated them, and at Hillman Hospital, the largest in the city, the staff placed blacks in the basement in crude conditions. The city hospitals barred Birmingham's thirty African American doctors from performing surgery or caring for their patients in these hospitals because African Americans could not join the Jefferson County Medical Society, a prerequisite for hospital affiliation.[15]

To alleviate the hospital crisis, African American citizens led by pastors banded together to form an organization called the Jefferson County and Birmingham Hospital Association. Bishop Shaw of the AME Zion Church was the leader and chairman of the organization. Born in Mississippi, Shaw was a strong evangelistic preacher and militant opponent of segregation. He resided in Birmingham, although his presiding bishoprics were in Georgia and North Carolina. Appalled by the lack of sufficient medical and hospital facilities, Shaw founded the organization in order to raise funds to build a 100-bed African American hospital in Birmingham. Rev. M.L. Thornton, pastor of the St. James Baptist Church, served as treasurer. Two influential pastors, Rev. Luke Beard of the Sixteenth Street Baptist Church and Rev. H.M. Gipson of the Saint Paul Methodist Church, served on the organization's executive committee. After Bishop Shaw's death, Rev. C.H. George, pastor of the Regular Missionary Baptist Church, became the chairman. Although the efforts of these ministers failed, they were not completely in vain. In 1954 the interracial committee of Birmingham, seeing the need and noting the prior effort, led the way in building Holy Family Hospital for African Americans in the city.[16]

Two concerns that had always claimed the attention of pastors and church leaders in Birmingham continued to do so during and after the war: preserving educational institutions and supporting African American businesses. Baptist associations and Methodist conferences gave the largest share of their funds for the support of their schools. The Baptists continued to operate Birmingham Baptist College, which offered a Bible certificate, a Bible diploma, and a Bachelor of Theology. It also offered a high school education and conducted day and night classes. The night classes were intended for bivocational pastors who had to work during the day. Daniel Payne College discontinued its high school program in 1941 to concentrate on its junior college program and School of Religion. Miles College had suspended its high school program in 1933 and during this period offered four-year terminal degrees. The Catholic church operated two high schools for African Americans: Immaculata High School and Holy Family High School. Because of their educational institutions, the Catholic church attracted several hundred African Americans during this period.[17]

Churches and pastors remained strong supporters of African American businesses in segregated Birmingham. Black businesses in Birmingham were located mainly on Fourth Avenue, but they could also be found scattered throughout the African American areas. The leading African American business in the community was the Booker T. Washington Insurance Company, which had been started with the support of pastors. As he had done before the war, Arthur G. Gaston, its founder, built a close working relationship with pastors and churches. Celebrating its eighteenth anniversary, the company reported that in its eighteen years it had made donations of $45,000 to area churches. These gifts were one way the company advertised itself through the churches.[18]

Although opposition to the militancy of African Americans began during the war years, after the war this opposition intensified. White political leaders in the city and state of Alabama began to plot ways of destroying African American political aspirations. One means was the Boswell Amendment. Passed by the Alabama Legislature and approved by state voters in 1946, this amendment to the Alabama Constitution required that prospective voters be able to "understand and explain" any section of the United States Constitution. By giving local boards of registrars broad powers to approve or disapprove of an individual's interpretation of the Constitution, the amendment seriously threatened the voting rights of African Americans and poor whites. The Boswell Amendment received strong support from white industrial workers in Birmingham who were convinced that the maintenance of segregation was necessary for them to maintain their job superiority. In addition to political measures, resistance took the form of residential bombings, the reemergence of the Ku Klux Klan, and the aggressive defense of segregation by Birmingham city officials. All of these measures caused support for militancy to dwindle in the African American community. The NAACP's membership declined from 8,500 members in 1946 to 2,444 in 1949 and would continue to decrease in the 1950s. Despite this setback in membership, the NAACP continued to challenge Jim Crow in the city through the courts and other legal means.[19]

In these circumstances, pastors with their newfound militancy intact and with the economic freedom that many laymen did not have asserted leadership greater than in the war years. Two laymen who were strong community activists testified to the importance of ministers during this period. At the installation of Rev. R.L. Alford as president of the Birmingham branch of the NAACP, W.C. Patton, president of the state chapters of the NAACP, stated that if it had not been for the churches, the organization would have lost ground. Similarly, Emory O. Jackson, editor of the *Birmingham World*, commenting on the election of R.L. Alford, said ministers were making commendable leaders.[20]

Pastors and their organizations continued to engage in many of the same protest activities as during the war years and intensified these activities. In their sermons and addresses, pastors continued to speak forthrightly against racial injustices and to call for full integration. Rev. C.J. Baker, pastor of Miller Memorial Presbyterian Church, said in his 1947 Emancipation Proclamation speech, that "America needed one standard of citizenship for all its citizens." "African Americans," he pointed out, "had fought in all the wars and should be citizens like everyone else and enjoy its benefits." He also stated that "the church should become more militant, preach a social gospel, and never compromise with injustice." Rev. J.L. Ware, pastor of the Trinity Baptist Church, in a 1950 speech celebrating the signing of the Emancipation Proclamation, called for full emancipation. Alluding principally to the Dixiecrats and the Ku Klux Klan, he said that there were forces designed to keep African Americans in political and economic slavery, to "make sure that our children remain hewers of wood and drawers of water." These forces, he maintained, would stop at nothing to achieve their end. For African American to develop a desire for full freedom they must first develop a desire to be free. He also insisted that there must be unity, especially between the church and fraternal organizations. He concluded with a note of optimism, saying that African Americans would win "because our love of freedom would cause us to persevere and do the impossible."[21]

In some speeches, pastors were highly critical of city officials. In the 1948 Emancipation Proclamation speech, Rev. Calvin Perkins, pastor of the Twenty-third Street Baptist Church, said that "City Hall needed renovating." He strongly suggested that it was the municipal government's insistence on segregation that kept the Freedom Train out of Birmingham. Like other pastors of his time, Perkins insisted that African Americans were due full rights because of the blood they had shed in World War II and other wars.[22]

African American pastors continued to insist on the right to vote in their sermons and addresses. In 1945 Bishop B.G. Shaw of the AME Zion Church urged teachers to vote because of the example they would set for other members of the race. Rev. R.L. Alford, pastor of Sardis Baptist Church, in a speech supporting the NAACP in 1948, insisted that the ballot and freedom are one in a democracy. "Who is not a voter," he maintained, "is not free." In a 1952 meeting of the Alabama Baptist State Convention in Lanett, Alabama, Rev. M.W. Whitt, pastor of the Harmony Street Baptist Church of Birmingham and one of the most forceful preachers against segregation and discrimination in the city, insisted that all forms of discrimination, including disfranchisement, should cease. In the same speech, with city officials and several white pastors in the audience, Whitt lashed out against segregated churches. He made it clear that "any church that denied people the right to attend it because of race was not really a Christian church."[23]

Several other concerns led African American pastors to issue strong condemnations from their pulpits. In 1946, when a white mob lynched two African American men and their wives in Monroe, Georgia, local police did not respond. The case became a cause celebre and brought condemnation from around the nation. Three pastors in Birmingham used their pulpits on the first Sunday in August to condemn the lynching: Pastor Goodgame, Rev. J.L. Ware of Trinity Baptist Church, and Rev. E.W. Williams of First Baptist Church, Fairfield. The Reverend Ware was also successful in getting the Alabama Baptist Sunday School and Baptist Training Union Congress to issue a resolution condemning the lynching. In 1948 after southern segregationists formed the States Rights Party to thwart the civil rights platform of President Harry S. Truman and the Democratic Party, Pastor Goodgame of the Sixth Avenue Baptist Church announced that he would preach on "The Appeal of Right."[24]

Ministerial conferences continued to take a militant stance after World War II. Several such groups existed in the Birmingham community, including the Birmingham Baptist Ministers' Conference, the Central Baptist Minister's Conference, the Methodist Minister's Alliance, and the Interdenominational Ministers' Alliance. With a membership of approximately two hundred pastors, the Birmingham Baptist Ministers' Conference was by far the largest and most influential of these groups. It size and strength came from the approximately four hundred African American Baptist churches that were in the area.[25]

One of the reasons for the militant stance of the Birmingham Baptist Ministers' Conference after the war was the leadership of the Reverend Ware, one of the most militant pastors in Birmingham during the World War II era. Born in abject poverty in a sharecropper's cabin near Wetumpka, Alabama, Ware at an early age developed an abhorrence of the segregation and injustice that African Americans faced. Called into the ministry, he studied for a brief period at Selma University. After pastoring several churches in rural Alabama, he came to Birmingham in 1941 to pastor the Trinity Baptist Church. He immediately became involved in activities to eliminate segregation and racial injustice in the city. In 1949 he became president of the Birmingham Baptist Ministers' Conference. It was in this position and as president of the Emancipation Proclamation Association that he exerted his influence in the city.[26]

Although the Birmingham Baptist Ministers' Conference had spoken out against racism during the war, under Ware's leadership it assumed an even more activist role. In 1947 the Birmingham Baptist Ministers' Conference refused an invitation to participate with the white pastors' conference in a Festival of Faith Rally at Legion Field when they discovered that the rally would be a segregated affair. Two years later the conference opposed participation of African Americans in the Christmas Festival Parade on a segregated basis. In 1950, it objected to going to the National Baptist Convention on the Pennsylvania-Southern Railroad when members discovered that a curtain would segregate white and African American passengers. Ware's ministerial group, along with other groups in the city, opposed an Easter egg hunt sponsored by a white company in a segregated park in 1953. He said that those African Americans who supported the event were "Tomming for a mess of eggs."[27]

In the early 1950s pastors were the exclusive leaders of the Emancipation Association Committee, which issued resolutions against segregation and injustice. The association sponsored a special community program on New Year's Day celebrating the signing of the Emancipation Proclamation. The association's officers were Rev. J.L. Ware, pastor of Trinity Baptist Church, president; Rev. G.W. McMurray, pastor of Metropolitan AME Zion Church, vice president; Rev. Prince Vaughn, pastor of Tabernacle Baptist Church, secretary; and Rev. C.H. George, pastor of Regular Missionary Baptist Church, treasurer. In 1955 the association issued a resolution opposing a plan for a segregated ball at the inauguration of Governor Jim Folsom. It condemned the ball as an attempt to cut new patterns of segregation. The resolution stated:

> The Greater Emancipation Program reaffirms its position of full freedom and the principle of first class citizenship for all citizens regardless of race, creed, or color.
>
> We denounce the "separate but equal" doctrine and vigorously oppose all forms of compulsory segregation based on race, creed, or color.
>
> The organization commends all persons and organizations which have expressed opposition to segregation and committed themselves to eliminate such segregation from American life.[28]

Ministerial groups, as they had done during the war, pressured city officials for African American rights. A committee of the Interdenominational Ministerial Alliance headed by Rev. W.L. Varnado, pastor of the Tabernacle Baptist Church, and Rev. J. Clyde Perry, pastor of the Miller Memorial Presbyterian Church, went to City Hall in 1947 to confer with the city commission on the hiring of African American police officers and the need for better protection from crime on Fourth Avenue.[29]

Ministerial groups, led by the Birmingham Baptist Ministers' Conference, also opposed any of its members or groups in the community who supported segregation. One such group was the Southern Negro Improvement Association, which was formed in 1954. Its leaders opposed integration and warned fellow African Americans that to try to force integration would rekindle race hatred and set the race back twenty-five years or more. Instead of agitation, they counseled that African Americans should improve themselves and stay decent, and that eventually they would receive the rights accorded other citizens.[30]

Among this group were some African American ministers who opposed any mingling of religion with politics. They insisted that pursuing issues like racial equality would diminish the gospel truth. One member of the Southern Negro Improvement Association was Dr. Collier P. Clay, who operated a school to train ministers at the First Baptist Church of Fairfield and was former president of Easonian Baptist Seminary. In January 1955 he made a speech in Notasulga, Alabama, in which he endorsed segregation. Word of the speech reached Birmingham and members of the Birmingham Baptist Ministers' Conference responded with a barrage of criticism. The conference set a date for dealing with Clay and other ministers who belonged to the Southern Negro Improvement Association. In February 1955 the conference voted sixty-three to two to expel Clay and Rev. C.J. Glaze, another member of the association.[31]

Some pastors and ministers showed their growing militancy and opposition to the denial of full rights through personal example, especially in the area of voting rights. African Americans in Birmingham often suffered reprisals when they attempted to register to vote. To help African Americans overcome their fears of registering to vote, ministers on several occasions announced publicly that they were going to the courthouse to register. Usually pastors were allowed to register on such occasions because of fear that refusing to register them would lead to court action.[32]

When the NAACP brought legal action against the city and state, African American ministers were among those who allowed their names to be used in test cases. One major attack of African American groups was the Boswell Amendment. After being thwarted in its attempt to defeat the amendment at the polls, the NAACP decided to take legal action. Rev. Eugene Otis Braxter, pastor of the Allen Temple AME Church, agreed to have his case used to test the constitutionality of the Boswell Amendment, although his did not prove to be the test case.[33]

No pastor showed more endurance and consistency in individual courage than J.L. Ware. Emory Jackson in 1950 in commenting on Ware referred to him as the "people's pastor", and the "city's most dependable advocate of equality." Between 1941 and 1956 Ware was concerned with all the major issues involving segregation and racial injustice in the city. Among these were the Joe Vernon case, the Jim Crow showing of the Freedom Train, unequal teacher's salary protest, protest in the relocation of African American on the Southside to build a hospital complex, and the integration of the University of Alabama. Ware's participation usually involved presiding at mass rallies, making speeches, raising funds, and testifying before city and other governmental agencies. An example of Ware's involvement and courage is seen in the attempt to integrate the University of Alabama. In 1952 Ware accompanied Arthurine Lucy and Polly Myers to the University of Alabama after their initial acceptance. After their rejection, he called a community mass meeting in support of their readmission. In 1955 Ware delayed going to the National Baptist Sunday School Congress to serve as a witness for the NAACP in its suit to have Lucy readmitted. The result of the case was a permanent injunction forbidding the University of Alabama from denying admission to any student because of race.[34]

The Reverend Prince Vaughn, pastor of Tabernacle Baptist Church and an active worker for the NAACP, acted courageously when he opposed the relocation of the Birmingham hospital. Because of the city's decision to place the university hospital complex on the Southside, many African Americans would be evicted. The interracial committee, of which Vaughn was a member, sanctioned the city's decision, but the plan met with general disapproval in the African American community. When Vaughn received word of the interracial committee's action, he resigned. In a letter to Bishop C.J. Carpenter, chair of the committee, a letter that Vaughn made public by publishing it in the *Birmingham World,* Vaughn listed three reasons for his resignation. First, he stated that the committee issued a statement without his knowledge. Second, he maintained that the committee was set up merely to pacify African American demands. Third, he claimed the interracial committee was afraid to express itself. Vaughn's public actions brought him disfavor from many influential whites and some African Americans but served to highlight the relocation issue and show the timidity of the interracial committee.[35]

No one in the African American community showed greater personal courage during this era than the Reverend George Rudolph. Harboring a deep resentment against segregation and appalled that the Birmingham police department refused to hire African American officers, Rudolph led a one-man crusade to secure the hiring of African American police officers. He explained that he was not afraid to act alone because he believed that God would protect him. In November 1954 he went to City Hall and made a personal plea to the city council. In June 1955 he returned to the council and renewed his request for African American police officers. A few months later, he went before the city's personnel board to continue his push. Rudolph's persistence was symbolic of the new militancy and activism that was emerging in the ministerial community.[36]

Although his major work would be the formation of the Alabama Christian Movement for Human Rights in 1956, Rev. Fred Shuttlesworth showed unusual personal courage during this period. Like Rudolph, the lack of African American police officers in Birmingham enraged Shuttlesworth. In 1955 he formed the Interdenominational Ministerial Association to push for African American officers. During the month of July he attended the meeting of the Birmingham Baptist Ministers' Conference and persuaded seventy-seven ministers to sign a petition to be given to the city commission urging the city to hire African American police officers. Ministers from the other ministerial groups in the city also signed the petition that Shuttlesworth presented to the city council. The petition gave the following reasons for hiring African American as police officers:

> They have a normal and civic right.
>
> It would greatly reduce the crime rate, in many cases preventing crime from happening.

They have already proved themselves worthy and capable in many cities further south than Birmingham; in fact, in many cities in Alabama.

The Age and Hour call for and demand that they (Negroes) help shoulder responsibility of not only paying taxes, but also helping to protect Life and Property, especially within their sphere.

Not withstanding the loyalty, fidelity, and trustworthiness of others, no one would be more willing, more ready, or more proud to protect Negro Life and Property than Negroes themselves.[37]

After the city council rejected this petition, Shuttlesworth presented a petition with 3,500 signatures asking for African American police officers. Again turned down, Shuttlesworth and his ministerial group went before the city council for a third time in October 1955. The council again rejected their request.[38]

Another way ministers showed their growing militancy was by assuming greater leadership in the Birmingham NAACP. Many lay persons faced the threat of violence and economic pressure after the war, which caused them to abdicate leadership and leave the organization. A substantial group of ministers throughout the city stepped into the gap. Four ministers were elected president of the NAACP's Birmingham branch after the war: J.L. Ware, R.L. Alford, Prince Vaughn, and R.R. Harden. Two of these pastors did not serve. The Reverend Ware was elected president in December 1952, but in January 1953 announced that he would not continue his duties, giving no explanation. The Reverend Vaughn was elected president in December 1954, but had to resign after he accepted a pastorate in Rockford, Massachusetts, in January 1955. The Reverend Alford, pastor of the Sardis Baptist Church, was elected president in 1950 and served for two years. The Reverend Hayden served as president for one year. All four of these pastors were elected to the presidency of the Birmingham NAACP after 1948, when the group began to decline in membership. One motive in electing a pastor president was to attract the working class to the organization. Because pastors were close to the people, it was felt they could attract new members better than others.[39]

Pastors served in various other capacities, including membership on the executive board of the NAACP. Rev. J. King Chandler, a minister and president of Daniel Payne College, was chairman of the executive committee in 1952. Several pastors served as vice-president, including J.L. Ware in 1948. Some pastors served as presidents of local suburban chapters; among these were Rev. G.W. Dickerson of the Kingston chapter and Rev. G.W. Gipson of the Fairfield chapter. Pastors also served on key committees. Rev. Prince Vaughn was chairman of the education committee, which sought to upgrade African American schools in the city and to raise funds to integrate the University of Alabama. Rev. Hiram Scruggs, pastor of the Thankful Baptist Church, and Rev. R.L. Alford served on the relocation committee, which sought to stop the building of a medical center on the Southside.[40]

On many occasions, African American pastors spoke at NAACP programs, especially during its membership drives. In 1947 Rev. E.W. Williams, in a membership drive speech, urged African Americans to join the organization, maintaining that through the NAACP African Americans could help themselves. He warned that freedom was costly and that the race should be prepared to pay the price for it. Rev. M.W. Whitt in 1954, and Fred Shuttlesworth in 1956 gave similar speeches.[41]

Another way pastors backed the NAACP was through financial support. The NAACP called on the churches to support efforts such as the equalization of teacher salaries and the defeat of the Boswell Amendment. By 1947 the Birmingham branch had instituted NAACP Sunday in the city's churches to build awareness of the organization and to raise funds. On the NAACP Sunday in 1949, at least twenty-six churches reported funds to the local branch. In 1952 the Sixteenth Street Baptist Church placed the NAACP in its church budget. Occasionally, churches in a local community came together for a mass meeting to support the NAACP, as happened in 1951 in the Enon Ridge community, when seven churches came together to raise funds for the educational efforts of the organization.[42]

Responding to the militancy that emerged in Birmingham during World War II, pastors joined lay leadership by supporting the call for the immediate end to segregation and racial discrimination. After the war, pastors assumed greater leadership in civil rights activities in an atmosphere of greater resistance. Through their sermons and speeches, activities in minister's conferences, and participation in the NAACP, a group of pastors worked for the elimination of Jim Crow. Many showed personal courage by leading voter registration campaigns and petitioning city officials for equal justice. Pastors did all of this while maintaining the church's traditional functions of providing worship, sponsoring education, and boosting black-owned businesses. By 1956, with its traditional roles intact, its new found militancy, and the emergence of pastors with more aggressive methods of protest, the African American church was set to lead a mass-based civil rights movement in Birmingham. The struggle in Birmingham for equal rights would become a significant part of the success of the civil rights movement in the nation.

VIII

The African American Church and the Civil Rights Movement

Between 1956 and 1963 the African American church in Birmingham initiated a movement to free blacks from the rigid segregation that existed in the city. Led by one courageous pastor and buttressed by their unique Christianity, ministers started a movement that ended long-entrenched forms of segregation in the city and gained broader rights for African Americans. The movement mirrored the African American church in every respect. Using direct action and confrontation rather than simply the usual methods of petition and legal recourse, the movement struggled to eliminate segregation in Birmingham. In 1963 the movement brought Martin Luther King, Jr., to the city and organized massive demonstrations that captured the attention of the nation and led to the passage of the 1964 Civil Rights Act.

In spite of growing militancy and activism on the part of pastors and others in the African American community during and after World War II, Birmingham remained in 1956 a citadel of segregation and racial discrimination. Some observers called it the most segregated city in the South. Others referred to it as the Johannesburg of the nation. African Americans in the city lived in a segregated world. Being African American meant being born in a segregated hospital to parents who lived in a segregated neighborhood. It meant attending an all-African American school that was vastly inferior to white schools in physical facilities. Being an African American child meant playing mainly in the streets because parks for African Americans were abysmally inadequate. Being African American also meant that you rode in a certain section of the street car, used special elevators in public buildings, and drank from water fountains marked "colored."[1]

Besides social oppression, African Americans faced economic and political exploitation. The 1950 census revealed that African Americans in Birmingham earned an average annual income of $1,087, compared to $2,274 earned by whites. In 1960 the median income for African Americans was still less than one half that of whites. The wide gap existed because of the limited job opportunities available to African Americans, who were primarily menial and domestic workers. Despite the presence of labor unions in major Birmingham industries, white workers thwarted any major improvements in African American job elevation. Because of segregation and discriminatory hiring practices, there were no African American police officers, bus operators, or fire fighters in the city. None of the city's banks or white-owned supermarkets employed African Americans as cashiers or clerks. The city essentially disfranchised African Americans, with only 3,650 of the eligible African American voters in Birmingham registered to vote by 1952, a figure that would show only a slight increase by 1956.[2]

A consensus for segregation had existed in Birmingham almost from the city's founding. White industrial workers fought to maintain segregation as a way of maintaining their job superiority. This consensus was strengthened partly because of the massive resistance that emerged in the South after 1954 when the Supreme Court ruled in *Brown v. Board of Education* that segregation in public schools was unconstitutional. Although African Americans did not immediately begin an onslaught against segregation, the optimism created by the *Brown* decision caused a more vigorous push to end segregation. In August 1955 the Birmingham NAACP petitioned the city's board of education to desegregate schools. A few months later the Montgomery bus boycott began, led by Martin Luther King. July 1955 the United States District Court ruled that the University of Alabama could not deny Arthurine Lucy and other African Americans admission to the University of Alabama because of race. These three events more than any others brought about massive resistance from whites. This resistance led to anti-integration legislation and the formation of white citizen councils and other groups. Even Birmingham's elite shared in this resistance. The emergence of black activism frightened white industrial workers who supported the Boutwell Amendment and the Dixiecrat Party in an attempt to maintain their job supremacy. Even Birmingham's elite shared in this resistance. Many of them saw maintenance of segregation as the best way to keep peace in the community.[3]

The major beneficiary of this resistance and the strong consensus for segregation in Birmingham was Eugene "Bull" Connor. A former sports announcer, Connor was elected as public safety commissioner in 1937 as a defender of the people with no ties to the elite. In his campaign, he championed tax reform, fiscal responsibility, and the use of civil service examinations. In 1951 Connor left office after he was convicted on charges of moral turpitude. After a hiatus of six years, he made a comeback. Basing his campaign on the maintenance of segregation, and amassing large majorities in the blue collar districts such as Ensley, West End, and East Lake, Connor regained his old post as commissioner of public safety. Although he won by only 103 votes, Connor interpreted his election as a mandate for the defense of segregation. Even before assuming office, he issued a strong warning against all attempts at integration. In his inaugural speech he declared that "until they are removed from the ordinance books," he would enforce Birmingham's segregation laws "to the utmost of my ability and by all lawful means." Connor, however, went beyond lawful means, arresting and fingerprinting protestors, tapping their phones, and confiscating their personal property with or without a warrant. Local leaders offered no objections to Connor's methods, and up to 1961 the newspapers supported him. Connor became the most visible symbol, especially in the African American community, of segregation and racial injustice.[4]

The NAACP offered the most formidable opposition to such a strong segregationist consensus in Birmingham. The Birmingham NAACP, however, was primarily middle-class in leadership and was weak because of pressure from the white community and internecine conflict over the most effective ways to attract a larger membership. In 1949 in a letter of resignation as executive secretary of the Birmingham branch, Jackson accused the leadership of the organization of becoming dispirited and depleted because of resistance from the white community. He called for a return to the militancy of the early 1940s, when there was "solid-front leadership on which the Birmingham branch fashioned its great legal victories and built up a substantial membership." In 1951 Emory Jackson, in an editorial in his paper the *Birmingham World*, criticized the local branch for using a black Greek-letter fraternity to conduct its membership drive. He urged them to perform their duties of fighting for liberty and equality, rather than seeking to "hold on to prestige." In retaliation for his editorial, William Shortridge, chairman of the executive committee, wrote a letter to Jackson, reminding him that the NAACP was a "national organization and not owned or controlled by one individual." Such internal disputes and white opposition robbed the organization of the dynamic that had made it militant and aggressive during the war years. The local organization continued to decline in the

1950s, with its membership falling below one thousand. Nevertheless, the Birmingham NAACP with occasional support from ministerial groups, continued to provide the only organized and consistent opposition to segregation in Birmingham.[5]

By 1956 the African American churches and their pastors were in the best position to project a mass-based movement. The church touched every segment of the African American community, the masses and the middle-class alike. There was also a common church culture. For example, all African American churches sang similar songs: spirituals, meter hymns, congregational hymns, and gospel songs. Long and fervent prayers were part of all church services in practically all churches. The minister was a charismatic figure whom parishioners expected to preach with emotion and power, and elicit a loud chorus of "amens." It was also through their churches that African Americans recognized the importance of cooperation and giving to worthy causes. By 1956 there were at least four hundred African American churches in Birmingham and Jefferson County, located in every African American community. People in the black community generally respected ministers, and ministers had a history of leadership in the community. These clergy had developed ministerial and denominational organizations that allowed cooperation on common issues. These factors provided the features necessary to mobilize large numbers of persons.[6]

The outlawing of the NAACP in Alabama was the spark that set off a mass-based civil rights movement in Birmingham. The NAACP had been the chief organization in promoting school integration and other antisegregation practices in the state after the *Brown* decision of 1954. Alabama Attorney General John Patterson felt that the elimination of the NAACP would thwart black activism. Inspired by Louisiana Attorney General Jack Gremillion, who won an injunction in that state that prohibited the NAACP from operating until it complied with Louisiana's registration requirements, Patterson took the offensive by seeking a similar injunction in Alabama in 1956.[7]

One person perturbed by the ban of the NAACP was Rev. Fred Shuttlesworth, pastor of the Bethel Baptist Church. Shortly after moving to Birmingham, Shuttlesworth had joined the NAACP because he saw it as the only organization in the city which was attempting to destroy segregation and racial injustice in any significant way. As chairman of the membership committee of the NAACP's Birmingham branch, Shuttlesworth had striven hard to enlarge the branch's membership and make it a more broad-based organization. In the major speech at the installation of the new president of the Birmingham branch, E.B. Colvin, in 1956 Shuttlesworth had urged the group to launch a program to reach the masses. The NAACP, he insisted, "must not live in the treetops or in a maze of grandiose phrases. Its goals and principles must be made clear" to the African Americans of Birmingham. Demoralized by the court's action in banning the NAACP, Shuttlesworth asked NAACP attorney Arthur Shores what could be done. Shores replied that "nothing could be done." Early in the morning of June 2, 1956, a distraught Shuttlesworth felt God talking with him saying: "They are trying to kill hope, but you can't kill people's hope." He awoke with the scripture "You shall know the truth and the truth shall make you free" (John 8:32) ringing in his head. Shuttlesworth interpreted this scripture to mean that the "people had to know the truth, that the state was saying to them you cannot be free and you cannot even fight to be free."[8] This experience moved Shuttlesworth to action.

Shortly afterward, Shuttlesworth proposed a mass meeting to see if African Americans in Birmingham wanted to organize to fight for their rights. He convinced four pastors — N.H. Smith, Jr., G.E. Pruitt, T.L. Lane, and R.L. Alford — to join him in the call. They announced the rally over the radio and in the newspaper, scheduling the meeting for June 5, 1956, at the Sardis Baptist Church. Shuttlesworth called a strategy meeting on June 4, 1956, at the Smith and Gaston Funeral Home to plan the meeting. Shuttlesworth and the group drafted a "Declaration of Principles" that described the group's Christian philosophy and its allegiance to the United States, while setting forth the group's civil rights objectives. The group recommended that the name of the new organization be the Alabama Christian Movement for Human Rights (ACMHR).[9]

Tuesday evening, June 5, 1956, more than one thousand people overflowed the Sardis Baptist Church. The meeting resembled a tent revival, with Shuttlesworth the "featured evangelist." "The action of the Attorney General makes it more necessary that Negroes come together in their own interest and plan together for the furtherance of their cause," Shuttlesworth maintained. He warned the audience that the "citizen's councils won't like this, but then, I don't like a lot of things they do." "Our citizens," Shuttlesworth continued, "are restive under the yoke of segregation . . . The only thing we are interested in is uniting our people in seeing that the laws of the land are upheld according to the Constitution of the United States." The crowd responded with "Amen,"

"That's right," and "Yes, yes," as if they were in an African American revival.[10]

Although a few ministers who had been longtime leaders in the community spoke against the formation of the organization, the audience voted three times to adopt the recommendations of the Shuttlesworth group and form the ACMHR. Shuttlesworth was elected president, Alford first vice-president, Smith secretary, and W.E. Shortridge, a layman and former officer of the NAACP, treasurer. For the next sixteen years, the ACMHR met every Monday night. Members adopted the slogan, "The movement is moving." A mass-based civil rights movement had started in Birmingham.[11]

Despite the fervor of the new organization, it faced some opposition in the African American community which limited its effectiveness. In addition to the ministers who had spoken against the new organization at the first meeting, others refused to join. Several reasons were given. Some pastors, especially those of the larger and more prestigious churches, felt that they and not Shuttlesworth should be the leader, since Shuttlesworth was a newcomer and they had been in the city much longer. The Reverend J.L. Ware, president of the powerful Birmingham Baptist Ministers' Conference, had been the spokesman for the ministerial community for many years. He believed that Shuttlesworth was attempting to usurp his role and he spoke openly against the methods of the ACMHR. A second reason was the autocratic methods employed by Shuttlesworth. He considered himself the leader of the movement and did not respond well to criticism or outside advice. The Reverend John Porter, pastor of the largest Baptist church in the city, recalled that Shuttlesworth once told him that this was his movement and that he or nobody else "was going to take it over." Another reason was fear. Some bivocational pastors who depended on white employers for their livelihood felt that they might lose their jobs if they joined the ACMHR. Also the presence of white extremist groups and the history of bombings in the city led some pastors to fear reprisals against them if they joined the movement.[12]

The lack of a substantial group of professionals in the movement also hampered the ACMHR's effectiveness. Unlike movements in other cities, such as Montgomery, Baton Rouge, and Tallahassee, where the initial thrust came from secular organizations that included middle-class and professional African Americans and traditional leaders who asked pastors of prestigious churches to assume the leadership, in Birmingham working-class blacks who were dedicated Christians almost completely composed the membership of the movement. Other reasons also accounted for the lack of middle-class participation. A major reason was disagreement over tactics. Emory Jackson, editor of Birmingham's largest African American newspaper, the *Birmingham World*, and Arthur G. Gaston, president of the Booker T. Washington Insurance Company and the wealthiest black man in the city, believed that the movement should employ legal methods and not the confrontational tactics of the ACMHR. Other professional blacks could not accept the autocratic leadership style of Fred Shuttlesworth. Still others could not adjust to the intense religious emotionalism of the ACMHR. Accustomed to a more structured and less emotional religious experience, they refused to participate in the organization.[13] Despite these limitations, the ACMHR became the most militant and active civil rights organization in the community between 1956 to 1963.

An important feature of the Birmingham movement and the ACMHR was the central role of Fred Shuttlesworth. Born on March 19, 1922, in Mount Meigs, Alabama, Shuttlesworth came to Birmingham at age three when his mother married Tom Shuttlesworth, an unemployed miner suffering from silicosis. During the depression the family lived on welfare while residing in the mining camp community of Oxmoor. After he finished high school, Shuttlesworth married. In 1943 he moved to Mobile where he worked in the defense industry at Brookley Field Air Force Base. Called to the ministry, Shuttlesworth sought to prepare himself by attending Selma University, a Baptist college operated by the all-black Alabama Baptist State Convention in Selma, Alabama. In the summer of 1948, he pastored two small rural churches before assuming the pastorate of the First Baptist Church of Selma. He moved to Birmingham in 1953 and afterward joined the NAACP and became its membership chairman. The 1954 *Brown* decision that outlawed segregated schools inspired Shuttlesworth to believe that African American freedom was possible and propelled him into increased involvement in civil rights. He attended meetings of the Montgomery bus boycott and communicated with its leadership. When the NAACP was outlawed in Alabama, Shuttlesworth sprang into action and formed the ACMHR.[14]

Shuttlesworth possessed a stubborn will, indomitable faith, and a sense of divine compulsion and destiny. He felt that God had called him to be the leader of his church. While pastoring the First Baptist Church in Selma, Shuttlesworth had refused to allow the deacon board of the church to make major decisions for the church without his participation.

He succeeded in getting the church to stand with him over the objection of the deacons. Shuttlesworth brought the same determination and sense of divine commission with him to the civil rights movement. In December 1956, less than six months after the formation of the ACMHR, Shuttlesworth's home was bombed. The bomb exploded underneath the room where he was talking to a deacon. The force of the explosion threw Shuttlesworth into the air and destroyed the box springs of the bed on which he was sitting, but miraculously he escaped any harm. Shuttlesworth and his followers interpreted his survival as a sign that God has ordained him to lead the movement. "He's all right," shouted a woman from among the crowd of five hundred persons who had assembled at his bombed house, and "he is going to be all right." Some one else cried out, "God saved the reverend to lead the movement." Shuttlesworth said on more than one occasion that this event convinced him that God would protect him and give him the victory over segregation in Birmingham. **More than any other event, the bombing galvanized the movement and gave** Shuttlesworth a **personal following.**[15]

A core of approximately fifteen pastors surrounded Shuttlesworth, forming the ACMHR's inner circle. They supported the movement financially and with their attendance, served on the board of directors, and were dedicated to Shuttlesworth's leadership. Among them were Edward Gardner, Abraham Woods, Nelson Smith, Jr., Calvin Woods, J.S. Phiffer, L.O. Lane, L.J. Rogers, and Herman Stone. They drew strength from Shuttlesworth's courage and believed that he was God's man for the task of destroying segregation in Birmingham. They could identify with the religious militancy of the ACMHR more than with the style of the NAACP or other organizations in Birmingham. Like Shuttlesworth, these ministers had deeply resented the segregation and oppression of African Americans in the city. Several of these ministers were inspired by the Montgomery movement and believed that it was possible to duplicate its success in Birmingham.[16]

Next to Shuttlesworth, the key person in the movement was the Reverend Edward Gardner. Born in 1907 in Lowndes County, Alabama, to sharecropping parents, Gardner moved to Birmingham with his mother at age nine shortly after his father had died. His mother moved with her family of eight children seeking better economic opportunities for herself and her children. Gardner attended Parker High School and then Birmingham Baptist college, where he received a high school diploma and a degree in theology in 1954. Following graduation he became pastor of the Mt. Olive Baptist Church in Birmingham.[17]

Growing up in Birmingham, Gardner became incensed over the segregation and oppression in the city. Visiting other cities where there were African American police officers and where whites treated African Americans with more courtesy, increased his resentment. The experience of having to ride the freight elevator in Hillman Hospital was one incident that struck out in Gardner's mind and further strengthened his displeasure and anger. To attack the Jim Crow system in Birmingham, Gardner joined the NAACP in 1954 because it was the only organization that was seeking to destroy segregation. In 1956 he joined the ACMHR and became its first vice-president. When Shuttlesworth accepted a pastorate in Cincinnati in 1961, it was Gardner who held the local movement together. Tremendously loyal to Shuttlesworth, whose courage Gardner admired and whom he saw as the God-sent leader of the movement, Gardner insisted that Shuttlesworth was the leader and not himself.[18]

The Reverend Abraham Woods, Jr., was a key member of the inner circle and leadership of the ACMHR. Born in Birmingham, Woods was the oldest of eleven children. His father was a local minister and industrial worker. Woods maintained that three things were important in his decision to join the ACMHR. The first was the growing emergence of racial consciousness through his education. He recalled that as a student at Parker High School in the 1940s, he read a book by Carter G. Woodson on great African Americans that made him aware of the outstanding black Americans in history and created in him a sense of race pride. While he was a student at Morehouse College in Atlanta, which he attended for one year, Woods was inspired by the chapel addresses by President Benjamin Mays, especially when he urged students to resist Jim Crow. As a student at Birmingham Baptist College, Woods represented the school at the 1953 Emancipation Day program. In his speech he urged the churches and pastors to take a stand against segregation. Besides his growing racial consciousness through his education, he had a growing disgust with the Jim Crow system in Birmingham resulting from bitter personal experiences, especially in his early years. Woods recalled how upset he became, seeing his father humiliated by a white grocer when he sought to purchase food on credit for his large family. He remembered that when he was a boy, white boys had urged their dogs to attack him in a neighborhood close to where he lived. A third influence for Woods was the 1954 school desegregation decision of the Supreme Court. With the *Brown* ruling Woods felt African Americans finally had a chance to gain full and equal rights. Woods was a charter member of the ACMHR. For him, the organization offered the best opportunity to attack the segregation and discrimination that existed in Birmingham. Woods became second vice-president of the ACMHR.[19]

The Reverend **Calvin Woods** followed his older brother into the inner circle of the ACMHR. As a student at Parker High School, Woods became president of the current events club. His interest in history and current events sensitized him to the plight of African Americans in the nation. He began to attend meetings of the NAACP and began to see the need for aggressive action to overcome the segregation and discrimination against African Americans in the city. Entering the ministry, Woods studied at Birmingham Baptist College and became pastor of the East End Baptist Church. He joined the ACMHR soon after its formation and saw the organization as the best way to fight injustice in the city. When the group decided to promote a bus boycott Woods became very active in urging African Americans not to ride the buses. The police arrested him for promoting the boycott, which created quite a stir in the African American community. **Woods served on the ACMHR's executive committee and headed several important committees.**[20]

The Reverend Nelson Smith, Jr. served as secretary of the ACMHR. Smith was born in Monroe County, Alabama. His father was a farmer and a rural pastor. After finishing the local Baptist academy, Monroe County Baptist Academy, he attended Selma University, where he received his bachelor's degree. After pastoring several rural churches, Smith came to Birmingham in 1953 to become pastor of the New Pilgrim Baptist Church, where he soon garnered the reputation of "fireball" because of his preaching ability. While pastoring in Birmingham, Smith became increasingly infuriated with the complete segregation in the city. The segregation of elevators, which meant African Americans had to ride on freight elevators, especially angered him. On several occasions, he and Shuttlesworth, who had been classmates at Selma University, talked about the oppression of African Americans in the city. When the NAACP was outlawed, Smith joined Shuttlesworth in forming the ACMHR. He was elected secretary at the initial meeting of the organization and continued to serve in that capacity until the early 1970s. Proclamations, petitions, and demands from the

ACMHR to the city to end segregation practices usually bore his signature along with that of Shuttlesworth.[21]

The Reverend L.J. Rogers served on the executive board. He was born in 1902 in Montgomery County. His parents were sharecroppers who eventually succeeded in buying their own land. In 1918 at the age of sixteen, Rogers moved to Birmingham to work in the coal mines. At age 40 he entered the ministry, attended Easonian Baptist Seminary, and became pastor of Shady Grove Baptist Church in North Birmingham. Upon his assumption of the pastorate of the Shady Grove church, he left the coal mines and became an independent contractor specializing in brick masonry work. Like other pastors of the inner circle, his personal experiences caused him to resent increasingly the segregation that African Americans faced in the city of Birmingham. When Shuttlesworth came to the Baptist Minister's Conference seeking ministers to sign a partition demanding that the city hire African American police officers, Rodgers signed immediately and became active in the campaign. In 1955 Rogers wrote a letter to the personnel board insisting on African American police officers. When Shuttlesworth formed the ACMHR, Rogers quickly joined. He never went to jail, as did most of the pastors of the inner circle but was a strong financial supporter, attended the meetings, and encouraged members of his church to support the organization.[22]

Beyond their growing disgust with the system of segregation and their devotion to Shuttlesworth, members of the inner circle had several other things in common. All were from poor economic backgrounds and had witnesses first hand the oppression of segregation; most of those born in the Black Belt of Alabama had been part of sharecropping families. Second, the pastors of the inner circle had a freedom that most African Americans did not have. Those who had secular jobs had the type of jobs where they were not dependent on whites. In addition, most were Baptist pastors, which meant they were free from bishops and other denominational restrictions. Third, they were primarily pastors of small churches and were not the traditional religious leaders in African American community. As Emory Jackson, editor of the *Birmingham World*, rightly observed in 1956 "Shuttlesworth had helped to spotlight and bring to the front lesser known ministers who were quietly but solidly working to advance the group toward full employment of the blessing and promises of democracy." Fourth, and most important, these pastors had the religious conviction that God would enable them to defeat the sin of segregation, which they saw as the real enemy. With

Shuttlesworth and these pastors a new type of leadership had emerged in Birmingham. More militant than the NAACP and made up of religious leaders who had faith in the righteousness of their cause and the power of God to redeem Birmingham from the dark forces of segregation and discrimination. The militancy of Shuttlesworth, centered in religious faith, appealed to them more than the secular orientation of the NAACP. They were convinced that a more aggressive approach was needed than merely the legal approach of the NAACP. These pastors urged their members to join the ACMHR, most of whom were working-class persons. In Birmingham the pulpit had become linked to a religious and mass-based movement for first class citizenship.[23]

In almost every way the ACMHR mirrored the African American church. Its leader was a charismatic figure in a pastoral mode who believed God had called him for the task. His followers also believed in his divine calling and would show their esteem for his leadership by standing and applauding as he entered the mass meetings. The ACMHR's board of directors resembled a board of deacons. They met infrequently, at Shuttlesworth's request, and essentially he made the decisions. The group raised funds through its membership dues, but also as in most African American churches, it raised money by taking offerings at mass meetings and special events such as suppers, teas, musicals, and candy and bake sales. Each year the ACMHR observed an anniversary celebration which resembled the anniversary celebrations that were common in African American churches. It was a way of fund raising and celebrating the achievements of the organization, with President Shuttlesworth giving his yearly report.[24]

In addition to the charismatic leadership of Shuttlesworth and pastors, the movement had an influential group of laymen. The most influential was Shortridge. A former officer of the Birmingham NAACP, Shortridge was one of the few leaders of the NAACP to join the ACMHR. A funeral home director and president of a burial society in Ensley, Shortridge served as secretary of the movement. He was aggressive in his attempt to collect funds from African American business people and professionals, often assailing those who did not give to the ACMHR. At the regular meetings of the ACMHR, Shortridge led in taking the collection. At several meetings he told those in the audience who did not plan to give to get up and "let someone else have their seat." Shuttlesworth and the other members of the ACMHR greatly respected Shortridge because of his honesty and aggressiveness.[25]

Laymen performed three basic functions in the movement: leading devotion at the mass meetings, taking up the offering, and serving as bodyguards for Shuttlesworth and other leaders. The first two functions were common activities of laymen in African American churches. Several laymen also served on the executive and advisory board. Among these were J.J. Ryles, E.H. Murphy, H.N. Guin, James Armstrong, Shortridge, and George Price.[26]

As in every African American church, the ACMHR had its own choir and ushers. Twenty-three members of the organization formed the ACMHR choir in July 1960 at the Forty-sixth Street Baptist Church. W. E. Shortridge, treasurer of the ACMHR, and Mrs. Georgia Price, an active laywoman, inspired its formation. Shortridge saw it as a way of enhancing the spirituality of the Monday night meetings. Its first organist was Nathaniel Lee, but in 1960 Professor Carlton Reese became the director, song arranger, writer, and organist for the group. The ACMHR choir combined freedom songs with gospel music to produce a charismatic style of music unique in the civil rights struggle. The use of gospel music was a characteristic of the urban African American church and Birmingham had a strong gospel music tradition. Thus, the ACMHR choir's use of gospel music emphasized the ACMHR's cultural and religious ties to the African American community and the indigenous nature of the Birmingham movement. In the ACMHR's mass meetings, singers allowed their emotions to take over, and on many occasions ushers had to restrain them. One choir member remarked that "the choir sings with faith in God, knowing that his power works through their songs and gives them courage to keep singing while struggling for freedom." One of the favorite songs of the choir was "Ninety-nine and a Half Won't Do." Composed by Reese, the song expressed the need for total commitment to the cause. Other songs, such as "God Will Make a Way," expressed absolute faith in God who would give them the power to overcome the pro-segregation forces in the city.[27]

Highly personal, gospel music differed from other forms of African American music in that the soloists presented individual testimonials instead of expressing communal suffering. Bernice Johnson Reagon has shown the contrast in the two styles of music by contrasting Birmingham gospel soprano Cleo Kennedy and the a cappella performance of Mississippi activist Fannie Lou Hamer on the album *Voices of the Civil Rights Movement*. She suggests that whereas Hamer's traditional singing of "Walk with Me Lord" could have occurred in any rural southern community, Kennedy's gospel interpretation of "A City Called Heaven" suggested an atomized urban experience and a transcendent or otherworldly emphasis. Through this kind of gospel singing the ACMHR choir heightened the movement's religious intensity.[28]

The ACMHR formed an usher's group shortly after the movement began. In churches, ushers provided an opportunity for people to gain a sense of worth and importance. Although one was a maid or janitor in the secular world, one could put on an usher's uniform or badge and be very visible in church. Most church ushers were females, and this was also true of the ACMHR ushers. Coming from different churches and under the direction of Rev. Charles Billups, ACMHR ushers met persons at the door, welcomed them into the church sanctuary, kept order, and restrained those who became overly emotional. The ushers saw themselves as providing a service and assisting an organization that was creating change for African Americans in Birmingham.[29]

Women were indispensable to the ACMHR. As in African American churches, **they made up the majority of ACMHR members, 61.7 percent in 1959.** Although men made the major decisions, women were the chief fund raisers. Women almost exclusively directed candy and bake sales, socials, and dinners. Women organized special occasions like the annual anniversary. They made up most of the choir and ushers. Key women included Lucinda Roby, a school principal, who directed the youth division of the movement, and Georgia Price, who assisted her husband in coordinating the voting emphasis of the movement. Women serving on the advisory and executive board included Mrs. Price, Daisy Jeffries, Lola Hendricks, Altha Stallworth, Josephine Jones, Rella Williams, Mrs. Roby, Myrtice Dowdell, and Dester Brooks.[30]

The influence of the African American church and its peculiar culture on the ACMHR stands out most vividly in the organization's weekly mass meetings. These meetings were essentially African American worship services. The meetings began with a thirty-minute devotional service made up of prayers, spirituals, and meter hymns, followed by singing by the ACMHR choir. The presider, usually vice-president Edward Gardner, offered brief remarks, a local supporting pastor delivered a sermon. President Shuttlesworth then made some remarks and the ushers took up the offering. The meetings were very emotional with much shouting. For example, at the meeting of January 23, 1961, the Reverend Oscar Herron, a local pastor, preached. The result was that a dozen women became so emotional that ushers had to remove them from the church. Fellow ministers and ushers had to restrain the Reverend Herron from continuing his sermon for fear that the meeting would break into pandemonium or a stampede. At the meeting of April 17, 1961, in which there was unusual emotional fervor and shouting, Shuttlesworth had to remind the audience that this was not a church but a movement with business to take care of. The emotionalism of the mass meetings, as in an African American church, provided not only emotional release but also the courage to fight the forces of segregation in a hostile environment.[31]

A 1959 study of the membership of the ACMHR by sociologist Jacqueline Clarke, who polled 254 members, showed a striking similarity between the ACMHR and the typical African American church. Lower middle-class persons who were upwardly mobile composed the majority of the organization's membership. Ninety-eight percent were church members, with 87.3 percent of that figure being Baptists. Most were working-class people, with 50 percent being semiskilled or unskilled. But in spite of their relatively low occupational status, more than 40 percent owned their own homes and 67 percent were registered voters. They were new to civil rights activity, with less than 1 percent having been members of the NAACP or affiliated with a socially active group or organization. Many saw in the ACMHR a chance to open new opportunities for themselves and their children.[32]

Like the pastors, the women and laymen were militant Christians. What separated them from the rest of the African Americans in Birmingham was the belief that God would give them the victory over the forces of segregation. In his second anniversary address, Shuttlesworth compared the ACMHR to a religious crusade. "We will win," he insisted, "because we are using the weapons of spiritual warfare."[33]

Spurred on by their leader, Fred Shuttlesworth, the ACMHR also relied on a new strategy that combined direct action and legal redress. The group would break segregation laws and then challenge them through the courts. Shuttlesworth led the group in breaking segregation laws, sometimes acting alone, going to jail, and then filing court action. This approach represented a radical departure from prior civil rights activity in Birmingham in which groups would petition the city or go to court. The causes that the ACMHR championed were numerous: the hiring of African American police officers, bus integration, integration in waiting rooms and restaurants, integration of public parks and other public facilities, voting rights, school integration, and equity in hiring.[34]

The hiring of African American police officers was the initial thrust of the movement and an early concern of Shuttlesworth. Before organizing the ACMHR, Shuttlesworth had formed a group of ministers called the Interdenominational Ministers Association that petitioned the city commission and personnel board to hire African American police officers. In July 1956, one month after the formation of the ACMHR, Shuttlesworth appeared before the city commission with several other ACMHR members with another request that the city of Birmingham hire African American police officers. Public Safety Commissioner Robert E. Lindberg flatly turned the group away, maintaining that the time was not right to hire African American police officers because African Americans could not perform police duties. The ACMHR, instead of drafting more petitions, recruited two African Americans to take the city's civil service examination for police officers. Accompanied by Shuttlesworth, George Johnson and Clyde Jones went to City Hall on August 20, 1956, where Ray Mullins, director of personnel, informed them that the test stipulated for "whites only." The ACMHR went to court to force the board to allow African Americans to take the test. Officials held a secret meeting at which time they opted to delete the "whites only" qualification. Meanwhile, the Englander Company fired Clyde Jones from his job in August 1956, and in August 1958 George Johnson removed his name from the application process. Despite continued agitation, the ACMHR was not able to break the gridlock and succeed in causing the city to hire African American police officers.[35]

Inspired by the Montgomery bus boycott, the ACMHR made bus integration one of its prime objectives from the beginning. After its first meeting, the movement appointed a transportation committee, which petitioned the Birmingham Transit Authority to begin a "first seated" policy on the city buses. The city commission ignored the request. When the U. S. Supreme Court ruled that the law mandating segregated buses in Montgomery was unconstitutional, Shuttlesworth and Nelson Smith wrote the Birmingham Transit Authority and city officials requesting compliance with the Montgomery ruling, maintaining that if the city refused to rescind the order the ACMHR would ride in a desegregated fashion anyway.[36]

In December 1956, shortly after his house was bombed, Shuttlesworth led 250 African Americans in riding in the front of the buses. Once aware of the confrontation, Birmingham police officers arrested twenty-one ACMHR members for violating the segregated seating ordinance. After Judge Ralph Parker convicted the twenty-one, the ACMHR filed an appeal. In the fall of 1957, the case reached federal court. Aware that the judge would rule Birmingham's segregation ordinance invalid, the city commission substituted a new law that authorized the transit company to decide the seating of the bus passengers. The company formulated a new policy that gave bus drivers the authority to regulate seating with African Americans sitting from the rear and whites from the front of the bus. When the ACMHR challenged the law, police arrested Shuttlesworth and the Reverend J.S. Phifer along with twelve other members of the organization. The group was convicted and sentenced to ninety days in jail and a fine for their integrationist effort.[37] Shuttlesworth then proposed a boycott of the buses, which received support from J.L. Ware and the Jefferson County Betterment League. The boycott failed, primarily because of a news blackout by the white media and lack of support from various elements in the African American community. Fear also contributed to the failure of the boycott. In an attempt to suppress the boycott by silencing the preachers, Bull Conner charged Calvin Woods, pastor of the East End Baptist Church, with violating the state anti-boycott law after Woods encouraged his congregation to stay off the buses. Finally in December 1959, the bus integration challenge reached United States District Judge H.H. Crooms, who ruled as unconstitutional the city's ordinance that authorized bus drivers to enforce segregated seating. The ACMHR had won a great victory.[38]

Segregation in bus and train terminals for interstate passengers came to the attention of Shuttlesworth when police officers arrested an African American couple in 1956 for going into the "white waiting room" at the train terminal. On March 5, 1957, United States Judge Seyburn Lynne ruled that the state of Alabama could not compel "interstate Negro passengers to occupy waiting rooms designated colored." This ruling prompted Shuttlesworth to challenge the segregated seating at Terminal Station. Announcing his action over the local radio stations, Shuttlesworth entered the white waiting room and purchased a ticket for Atlanta. While in the station, a local white lay minister, Rev. Lamar Weaver, sat with him. Police officers protected Shuttlesworth from pro-segregation whites who had assembled at the station. A mob of some fifty whites attacked Weaver as he left the train station. The police had done nothing to protect Weaver, who shortly afterward left Birmingham. Despite Shuttlesworth's successful venture and later the removal of signs at Terminal Station, Birmingham continued to practice segregation in its terminals.[39]

In 1957 the Little Rock school integration case inspired Shuttlesworth and the ACMHR to challenge Birmingham's failure to integrate its school system. With eight other families, most of them members of the ACMHR, Shuttlesworth petitioned the school board to admit their children to integrated schools. Impatient at what he saw as stalling by the school board, Shuttlesworth decided to take matters into his own hands by direct action and informed the newspapers and the police of his intention to enroll four children in all-white Phillips High School. Shuttlesworth went to Phillips on September 9, 1957, accompanied by his wife and the Reverend J.S. Phifer, a waiting mob armed with chains and brass knuckles beat Shuttlesworth as he arrived at the school. Having stumbled and struggled to stay conscious, Shuttlesworth testified that he heard God's voice tell him, "You can't die. Get up. I got a job for you to do." By this time several police officers arrived on the scene, which allowed Shuttlesworth to break free and get to his car. Before the car escaped, several members of the mob smashed windows and hit the body of the car. Despite Shuttlesworth's bravery and despite court litigation, schools in Birmingham remained segregated.[40]

The ACMHR also pushed to integrate city parks and other public recreational facilities. As far back as 1958, the ACMHR began to petition the city to desegregate city parks. In October 1959, the movement filed suit in the United States District Court to desegregate the parks. Finally, on October 24, 1961, United States District Court Judge H.H. Grooms ordered Birmingham to desegregate its sixty-seven parks, thirty-eight playgrounds, eight swimming pools, four golf courses, zoo, art museum, state fair, municipal auditorium, and Legion Field by January 15, 1962. The city commission chose to close these facilities rather than integrate them. Several groups in the city, including the Birmingham Ministerial Association, and the Young Men's Business Club voiced opposition to that move. Both newspapers, the *Birmingham News* and *Post Herald*, criticized the closing of the parks. The city commission's decision did much to create a split in the segregation consensus among the decision makers in the city. The closing of the parks, along with Bull Connor's poor handling of the Freedom Rides, led a group of citizens to initiate a move to change the form of government to a mayor-council form that eventually led to Connor being voted out of office. Yet parks remained closed during this period in Birmingham.[41]

The activities of the ACMHR in the area of voter registration were not as spectacular as its other forms of action but constituted an integral part of the work of the movement. The city of Birmingham generally denied African Americans in the city the ballot through such restrictions as the poll tax and literacy test. The ACMHR sought to address this injustice in two ways. At practically every meeting of the movement, leaders urged those present to register and vote. George Price usually gave instructions on how to go about qualifying. In many meetings Shuttlesworth stressed voting. At the meeting of January 12, 1961, he urged everyone present to pay their poll taxes for the coming election of the city commissioners. At the March 27 meeting of the same year, Shuttlesworth told the group that the only way to defeat Bull Conner was to vote him out. "Last time," he maintained, "only 14,000 Negroes voted." Second, the ACMHR occasionally undertook special voting rights projects. For example, in 1958 the group launched the "Double the Vote Campaign" in Birmingham, which was a part of a national campaign by the Southern Christian Leadership Conference. The group held voting clinics in churches as a part of the campaign. Yet African Americans remained a small percentage of the voting population in Birmingham, less than 6 percent throughout the 1950s.[42]

In 1962 the ACMHR joined with students from African American colleges in the city in an effort to desegregate eating facilities in department stores and to upgrade job opportunities for African Americans. Impatient with the pace of integration in Birmingham, students at Miles College and Daniel Payne College formed the Anti-Justice Committee. Informing Shuttlesworth, who supported them, students planned to begin demonstrations. In May 1962 students initiated a "selective buying campaign" with the support of the ACMHR. Feeling the squeeze because of the boycott, Birmingham's merchants nevertheless refused to desegregate their store facilities or upgrade black employment. The boycott lost steam, but the momentum of the student-led boycott prompted Shuttlesworth to invite Martin Luther King to come to Birmingham to help end discrimination and segregation in the city.[43]

In 1962 the ACMHR made some temporary headway in integrating facilities in the department stores in the city. In that year, Shuttlesworth announced that the annual convention of the Southern Christian Leadership Conference would be in Birmingham and spread rumors of protest marches during the convention. This threat convinced the Chamber of Commerce to organize a group called the Senior Citizens Committee in an effort to thwart the demonstrations. Meeting in September 1962 with Shuttlesworth, the leading merchants of Birmingham agreed to remove the "whites only" signs from water fountains. On the basis of that promise, Shuttlesworth called off the scheduled demonstrations. The stores painted over the Jim Crow signs. When the SCLC Convention was over, Bull Connor sent building inspectors into the downtown stores that had voluntarily removed the Jim Crow signs and harassed the stores into putting up the signs they had removed or painted over. Except for Blach's Department Store, Jim Crow signs returned. The ACMHR and the Miles College students resumed the boycott. The breach between the white business community and the African American civil rights leadership widened because of this event.[44]

The struggle of the ACMHR through 1962 had brought only limited gains. The movement had succeeded in integrating the buses and the train and bus terminals, but despite numerous jailings, beatings, and other attacks, schools remained segregated, the city had hired no black police officers, public accommodations were still segregated, and there had been no elevation of black employment. The city government, led by Commissioner Connor had simply refused to make concessions. Realizing that he needed additional help if African Americans were to bring an end to segregation in Birmingham, Shuttlesworth again invited Martin Luther King and SCLC to come to Birmingham and assist the movement. "The only way this city was ever going to change," he told King, "was for their two organizations to join forces and do battle with sin and darkness here.[45]

At the urging of the ACMHR, King made the decision to come to Birmingham. His major reason was to assist the ACMHR achieve its goals in the city. King called a meeting of his SCLC staff at Dorchester, Georgia, to plan the Birmingham campaign. The defeat at Albany inspired King to make more thorough preparation. Two important assets that King brought to the ACMHR led movement in Birmingham were his national reputation and his ability to attract the national media, assets that observers and scholars have documented well. But King's success in broadening the base of support of the movement and enhancing the church culture that had sustained the ACMHR movement was equally significant.[46]

Some segments of the African American community had not responded to Shuttlesworth's leadership, including pastors of some of the largest churches and leading professionals. King was successful in attracting many of these persons. Some professionals joined because of their friendship with King. For example, prominent businessman John Drew and his wife, who had been active in the NAACP and voting rights organizations, joined the movement because of their longtime friendship with King and invited him to stay at their home. King also formed an advisory committee composed of professional blacks that gave them a voice in decision making. This move brought support from some in this group and served to neutralize others. Similarly, King brought several key pastors with large church buildings and congregations into the movement. John Porter had served as King's assistant pastor while a student in Montgomery. When King came to Birmingham, Porter readily joined the movement. King convinced John Cross, pastor of the Sixteenth Street Baptist Church, the oldest African American church in the city, to join the movement when King made an appeal before the Birmingham Baptist Minister's conference. The churches pastored by Cross and Porter became headquarter churches for the movement.[47]

King's arrival enhanced the religious dimension of the ACMHR and its church culture. With King's involvement, the ACMHR held meetings every night, instead of just Monday mights. The meetings were highly spiritual and emotional. Crowds were larger. It was necessary to hold meetings in the larger churches. King, Shuttlesworth, and Abernathy took center stage. It was at these meetings that persons willing to go to jail came down front after the appeal, just as persons might come down the aisle to join African American churches after the ministers had preached a sermon and asked new believers to join the church. In addition, King's activities in Birmingham took on religious symbolism. He was arrested on Good Friday, the day of the celebration of the Christ's crucifixion. While in jail in Birmingham, he wrote a letter to a group of white clergymen, a letter similar to the prison epistles of Paul.[48]

The climax of the movement in Birmingham began with the decision to intensify the demonstrations using children, and Police Commissioner Bull Conner's use of dogs and hoses, events that historians of the civil rights movement have well documented. On May 10, 1963, the white business community and the civil rights leaders reached a truce which was interpreted by the African American community as a victory. According to the agreement, within ninety days lunch counters, restrooms, fitting rooms, and drinking fountains in the downtown stores would be desegregated. Within sixty days, African Americans would be hired as sales persons and clerks in stores. With two weeks a biracial committee would be established to improve communications between whites and blacks in the city. For many civil rights historians and scholars, Birmingham was the turning point of the civil rights movement that made possible the Civil Rights Act of 1964 and rehabilitated the leadership of Martin Luther King.[49]

The Birmingham movement showed clearly the importance, power, and central role of the African American church in the civil rights movement. The church in Birmingham provided the leadership, charisma, funding, and organization for initiating the masses. Fred Shuttlesworth was the acknowledged leader and set the tone, direction, and strategy for the movement. Most of all, the African American church provided the common religious culture that sustained the movement. Blacks in Birmingham could identify with the church more than the NAACP and other organizations led by middle-class blacks. Martin Luther King brought to the Birmingham movement a national reputation and the attention of the national mass media, but equally as important, he helped build a broader base of support for the movement. He also identified with and enhanced the common church culture that made the Birmingham civil rights movement possible.

Conclusion

From the time that slaves first arrived in the area in 1815 to the time that the civil rights movement peaked in the city of Birmingham in 1963, religion and the church played a significant role among African Americans. In Birmingham the African American church boosted businesses, sponsored education, fostered moral discipline, promoted values, dispensed benevolence, and led the civil rights movement in the city. Most of all, the church was a spiritual fortress and served as a shelter in the midst of the racist environment that sought to dehumanize blacks. Through their church, African Americans gained hope and self-esteem in the segregated society in which blacks were forced to live.

Scholars continue to debate the nature of African American religion and the African American church. Some have suggested that it was primarily conservative, compensatory, and otherworldly. Others have insisted that African American religion and the church was essentially radical, this worldly, and militant. Still others have maintained that it was both compensatory and militant.[1]

The Birmingham experience validates the latter view, which holds that the African American church possessed elements of compensation and militancy. In the sense of helping blacks cope with their oppression by being a refuge in a hostile environment, the church performed a compensatory function. It consoled and supported African Americans who suffered from the ravages of segregation and discrimination. It was otherworldly in that it held that this life was not the end, nor the full measure of existence. The compensatory function of the African American church in Birmingham can also be seen during the depression with the emergence of gospel music and the growth of churches of the Pentecostal, Holiness, and Spiritualist tradition. Gospel music tended to be more otherworldly than the spirituals or meter hymns. In Birmingham in the 1920s and 1930s, Pentecostal, Holiness, and Spiritualists churches gave blacks spiritual solutions by focusing attention on religious purity and rituals rather than confronting the social and political situation. Although both gospel music and churches of the Pentecostal, Holiness, and Spiritual tradition possessed a strong otherworldly element, they also helped blacks face life in their day to day existence.

On the other hand, the church in Birmingham had a radical or prophetic dimension. In the period before World War I, pastors spoke out against what they saw as the abuses of segregation. After World War II, pastors begin to insist on the elimination of segregation and full rights for African- Americans. The civil rights movement brought the protest tradition of the church to fruition with the breaking of laws, marches, sit-ins, and other confrontational protest.

The African American church in its broadest perspective must be seen as the central institution in the African American community. After the period of slavery, the church was the first institution which African Americans formed. Denied access to political and economic institutions, the church played several roles in the lives of African Americans. These roles were both spiritual and secular, with the church not only providing spiritual solace but also forming institutions to serve the African American community.

The history of the African American church in Birmingham also shows that self-help was an essential feature of the African American church tradition. After the period of slavery, ex-slaves through their churches developed a theology, strategies, and institutions for the uplift of African Americans. These strategies were often different at various times, but with a consistency of religious and often middle-class values such as self-discipline, morality, and education. Migrants who moved into Birmingham found in their churches, hope and values to sustain themselves in the racist storm they found in the city. These churches in the 1950s and 1960s led African Americans in Birmingham in protesting for the overthrow of Jim Crow and in providing greater freedom and opportunity.

NOTES

Chapter I: Slavery, Religion, and African American Churches

1. Malcolm C. McMillian, *Yesterday's Birmingham* (Miami: E.A.Seaman Publishing, Inc., 1957), pp. 9-10; William Sumner Rutledge, "An Economic and Social History of AnteBellum Jefferson County, Alabama" (Unpublished Masters Thesis: University of Alabama, (1939), p.7; Leah Atkins, *The Valley and the Hills: An Illustrated History of Birmingham and Jefferson County* (Woodland Hills, California: Windsor Publications, Inc. 1981), pp.16-23

2. Birmingfind, [Robert J. Norrell]. *The Other Side,* no. pg,: Rutledge, "Economic and Social History," pp.40, 52-53; Virginia Rolunds Brown and Janice Porters Nabors (ed), *Mary Gordon Duffee's Sketches of Alabama* (University, Alabama: University Alabama Press, 1970), pp. 20-30.

3. Atkins, *Valley and Hills,* pp. 20-22; Rutledge, "Economic and Social History," pp. 100-105.

4. Anson West, *History of Methodism in Alabama (*Spartanburg, South Carolina: The Reprint Company, Publisher, 1983), p. 293; Unpublished History of First Methodist Church, Tarrant, Alabama; Unpublished History of Pleasant Hill United Methodist Church, McCalla, Alabama.

5. Interview with Lee N. Allen, Alabama Baptist Historian, October 20, 1992; Hosea Holcombe, *A History of the Rise and Progress of the Baptists of Alabama* (Philadelphia: King and Baird, 1840), pp. 41-42; W.D. Holladay, "Camp Meetings in Alabama" (A.B. Thesis: Howard College, 1929), pp. 40, 228.

6. Charles A. Johnson, *The Frontier Camp Meeting* (Dallas: Southern Methodist University Press, 1955), pp. 114-118; Milton C. Sernett, *Black Religion and American Evangelicalism: White Protestants Plantation Missions, and the Flowering of Negro Christianity,* 1787-1865 (Metuchev, N.J.: The Scarecrow Press, 1978), pp.103-104.

7. Minutes of the Annual Conference of the Methodist Church, South (Nashville: Southern Methodist Publishing House, 1870) p.70; Thomas Leonard Williams, "The Methodist Mission to the Slaves," (Unpublished Dissertation: Yale University, 1943), pp. 229-235.

8. Unpublished History of Mt. Joy Baptist Church; History of Mt. Joy Baptist Church found in WPA Files in Alabama archives.

9. Unpublished History of the Oak Grove Baptist Church in Alabama Baptist Historical Society Archives, Samford University, hereafter cited as ABHS.

10. Julius C. Greene, " Reminiscence of Julius C. Greene," a paper located in the archives of the Southern History Section of the Birmingham Public Library; Robert Nichols, "Life in Jefferson County Prior to the Civil War," (B.A. Thesis: Samford University, 1928), p.15; Harold A.Carter, The Prayer tradition of Black People (Baltimore: Gateway Press Inc. 1982), pp. 31-32. Glover Moore, *William Jemison Mims: Soldier and Squire* (Birmingham: Birmingham Publishing Company, 1966), p. 80.

11. Genovese, *Roll, Jordan, Roll: The World the Slaves Made* (New York: Random House, Inc.,1972), p. 216; Frederick Law Olmstead, *The Cotton Kingdom, 2 vols.*(New York, 1861), pp. 312-313; William E. Montgomery, *Under their Own Vine and Fig Tree: The African American Church in the South, 1815-1900* (Baton Rouge: Louisiana State University Press, 1993), pp. 263-264; Clarence Walker, Jr., *A Rock in a Weary Land: The African Methodist Episcopal Church During the Civil War and Reconstruction* (Baton Rouge: Louisiana State University Press, 1982), pp.23-24; Joe M. Richardson, *Christian Reconstruction, The American Missionary Association and Southern Blacks, 1861-1890* (New York: Pilgrim Press), pp. 154-155; Leon F. Litwack, *Been in the Storm So Long: The Aftermath of Slavery* (New York: Random House, Inc., 1979), p. 461.

12. Charlotte Forten, "Life on the Sea Islands," *Atlantic Monthly*, XIII (1864), 593-94; Rose, *Rehearsal for Reconstruction*, p. 92; William Wells Brown, *My Southern Home or the South and its People* (Boston: A.G. Brown and Co., Publishers, 1880), pp. 188-193; Daniel Payne, *Recollections of Seventy Years* (Nashville: AME Publishing Board, 1888), p. 254; Walker, *Rock in a Weary Land*, p.58.

13. Albert Raboteau, *Slave Religion: The Invisible Institution in the Antebellum South* (New York: Oxford University Press, 1978), pp. 3-43; Sernett, *Black Religion and American Evangelicalism*, pp. 83-86; William E. Montgomery, *Under Their Own Vine and Fig Tree: the*

African-American church in the South, 1865-1900 (Baton Rouge: Louisiana University Press, 1992), pp. 1-37; Charles Joyner, *Down by the Riverside: A South Carolina Slave Community* (Chicago: University of Chicago Press, 1984), pp. 141-171; George Rawick, *From Sundown to Sunup: The Making of the Black Community* (Westport, Connecticut: Greenwood Publishing Company, 1972), pp. 30-53.

14. Clifton H. Johnson, ed., *God Struck Me Dead,* (Cleveland, Ohio: The Pilgram Press, 1993) pp. 60, 64, 77; George Parrinder, *African Traditional Religion* (London, 1954), pp. 70-94, 90-100, 102-103; Margaret Washington Creel, *"A Peculiar People":Slave Religion and Community-Culture Among the Gullahs* (New York: New York University Press, 1988), pp. 285-295.

15. Donald G. Matthews, *Religion in the Old South* (Chicago: University of Chicago Press, 1977), pp. 185-236; Miller, *Voice of Deliverance,* pp. 13-28.

16. Lawrence Levine, *Black Culture and Black Consciousness: Afro-American Folk Thought from Slavery to Freedom.* (New York: Oxford University Press 1977), pp. 3-35; Sernett, *Black Religion and American Evangelicalism,* pp. 105-109; Raboteau, *Slave Religion,* pp. 250-265.

17. Blassingame, *Slave Community,* p. 70.

18. Matthews, *Religion in the Old South,* pp. 218-236; Carter, *Prayer Tradition of Black People,* p. 21; John B. Boles, *Black Southerners,* 1619-1869 (Lexington: University of Kentucky Press, 1983), pp. 157-158.

19. Simon J. Smith and Fanna K. Bee, *Canaan-Garden Spot By the Cuttachoee* (Bessemer: Canaan Baptist Church, 1972), p. 57; Lee N. Allen and Fanna K. Bee, *Sesquicentennial History of Ruhama Baptist Church, 1818-1969* (Birmingham: Oxmoor Press, 1969), p. 5; *Leeds...Her Story* (Anniston, Alabama: Higginbotham Publishing Company, 1964) pp. 143-144; Katherine Hale Hanlin, *The Steeple Beckons: A Narrative History of the First Baptist Church, Trussville, Alabama, 1821-1971* (Trussville: First Baptist Church, 1971), p. 35.

20. Unpublished History of the Bethlehem United Methodist Church; Unpublished History of the Pleasant Hill United Methodist; West, *Methodism in Alabama,* p. 293.

21. *Records of St. John Parish, Elyton, Alabama,* transcribed by the WPA, 1938, and found in the Southern History Department of the Birmingham Public Library; Mabel Ponder Wilson, Dorothy Youngblood Woodyerd, Rosa Lee Busby, (Compilers) *Some Early Alabama Churches* (Birmingham: Parchment Press, 1973), p. 79.

22. James H. Walker, Jr., *Roupes Valley: A History of the Pioneer Settlement of Roupes Valley which is located in Tuscaloosa and Jefferson Counties, Alabama* (Bessemer, Alabama: Montezuma Press, 1871), pp. 12-13; Wilson, *Early Alabama Churches*, p. 78.

23. Holcombe, *Baptists in Alabama*, p. 243; Atkins, *Valley and Hills* p. 22; Grace, "Autobiography", pp. 331-348.

24. Nancy Claiborne Roberson, "The Negro and Baptists of Antebellum Alabama," (Unpublished Thesis: University of Alabama, 1954), p. 54.

25. Beulah Brunson, "Reconstruction in Jefferson County," (B.A. Thesis: Samford University, 1928), p. 2; Moore, *William Mims*, p. 33; Atkins, *Valley and Hills*, pp. 31-36.

26. James Pickett Jones, *Yankee Blitzkrieg: Wilson's Raid through Alabama and Georgia* (Athens: University of Georgia Press, 1976), pp. 57-60; C. Robert Watkins, "General Wilson's Raid through Alabama and Georgia in 1865" (M.A. Thesis: Alabama Polytechnic Institute, 1959), pp. 47-48; Moore, *William Mims*, pp. 54-55; Julius C. Greene, *Reminicence of Julius C. Greene*, an unpublished paper found in the archives of the Southern History Department of the Birmingham Public Library.

27. Moore, *William Mims*, pp. 94-95; Brunson, "Reconstruction in Jefferson County," pp. 14-16; Quoted in Atkins, *Valley and Hills*, p. 44.

28. Watkins, "Wilson's Raid," p. 131; Atkins, *Valley and Hills*, p. 43.

29. Norrell, *The Other Side*, no. p.; Montgomery, *Under their Own Vine*, pp. 52-54.

30. B.F. Riley, *A Memorial History of the Baptist of Alabama* (Philadelphia: The Judson Press, 1923), pp. 166-167.

31. Unpublished History of the Canaan Baptist Church, Bessemer, Alabama.

32. Unpublished History of the St. Paul Christian Methodist Episcopal Church.

33. Interview with John Woods, January 5, 1993; Allen and Bee, *History of Ruhama Baptist*, pp. 61-62.

34. Unpublished History of the Mt. Pilgrim Baptist Church, Powderly, Alabama.

35. Unpublished History of the First Baptist Church, Powderly, Alabama.

36. Unpublished History of the Mt. Joy Baptist Church, Trussville, Alabama.

37. Unpublished History of the Shady Grove Baptist Church, Oxmoor, Alabama.

38. *Birmingham Free Speech*, December 28, 1901; Boothe, *Cyclopedia of Colored Baptists*, pp. 214-215.

39. Unpublished History of the Mt. Calvary Baptist Church, Irondale, Alabama; Unpublished History of the Mt. Pleasant Baptist Church, Leeds, Alabama.

40. Unpublished History of the Mt. Pleasant Baptist Church, Leeds, Alabama; Boothe, *Cyclopedia of Colored Baptists*, pp. 214-215.

41. Boothe, *Cyclopedia of Colored Baptists*, p. 74-76.

Chapter II: Migration and the Formation of African American Churches in the New South City of Birmingham

1. The founding of Birmingham is told in several books and publications. Among these are Ethel Armes, *The Story of Coal and Iron in Alabama*, (Birmingham: Birmingham Chamber of Commerce, 1910), pp. 215-237; Leah Atkins, *The Valley and the Hills*, pp. 50-61; Martha Mitchell Bigelow, "Birmingham: Biography of a City of the New South" (Ph.D dissertation, University of Chicago, 1946), pp. 13-54; George M. Cruikshank, *A History of Birmingham and its Environs*, 2 Volumes (Chicago: Lewis Publishing Company,1920), pp. 90-99; Carl V. Harris, *Political Power in Birmingham, 1887-1921* (Knoxville: University of Tennessee Press, 1977), pp. 12-18; Malcolm C. McMillan, *Yesterday's Birmingham*, pp. 9-38; and Marjorie Longenecker White, *The Birmingham District: An Industrial History and Guide* (Birmingham: Birmingham Historical Society, 1981), pp. 42-51.

2. Bigelow, "Biography of a City," pp. 21-22; Caldwell, *History of Elyton Land Company*, p. 12; McMillan, *Yesterday's Birmingham*, pp. 34-38.

3. Peter Kolchin, *First Freedom: The Response of Alabama's Blacks to Emancipation and Reconstruction* (Westport, Connecticut: Greewood Press, 1972), pp. 41-42; Eric Foner, *Reconstruction: America's Unfinished Revolution, 1863-1877* (New York: Harper & Row, Publishers, 1988), pp. 102-110.

4. Wayne Flint, *Poor But Proud: Alabama's Poor Whites* (Tuscaloosa: University of Alabama Press, 1989); Kolchin, *First Freedom*, pp. 45-48.

5. Glen Sisk, "Alabama Black Belt: A Social History, 1875-1917" (Ph.D dissertation: Duke University, 1951), pp. 39, 192, 274, 332, 296, 293.

6. Charles S. Johnson, *Shadow of the Plantation*, pp. 154-156; Kolchin, *First Freedom*, pp. 118-119; Glen Sisk, "Negro Churches in the Alabama Black Belt, 1975-1900," *Journal of Presbyterian Historical Society* XXXIII (June, 1955), 87-88.

7. Johnson, *Shadow of the Plantation*, p. 150; Sisk, "Negro Church in the Black Belt," p. 88; Sisk, "Social History of the Black Belt," pp. 269-270.

8. Kolchin, *First Freedom*, p. 120; Boothe, *Cyclopedia of Colored Baptists*. p. 44; Mixon, *AME Church in Alabama*, pp. 18, 32; Walls, *History of the AME Zion Church*, p. 70.

9. Sisk, "Social History of the Black Belt," p. 269; Keith D. Miller, *Voice of Deliverance: The Language of Martin Luther King, Jr. and its Sources* (New York: The Free Press, 1992), pp. 23-28; Interview with Curtis Maggard, January 2, 1992.

10. *Birmingham Age Herald*, December 8, 1889, *Birmingham News*, June 11, 1909, Quoted in Harris, *Political Power*, pp. 187, 188-189; Carl V. Harris, "Reforms in Government Control of Negroes in Birmingham, Alabama," 1890-1920," *Journal of Southern History* (November, 1972), pp. 567-600.

11. United States Senate, *Report of the Committee upon Relations Between Capital and Labor* (Washington, D.C.: Government Printing Office, 1885), pp. 374-378, 382, 398, 395, 397, 402; Harris, *Political Power*, pp. 172-173.

12. Henry M. McKiven, "Class, Race and Community: Iron and Steel Workers in Birmingham Alabama, 1875-1920" (Ph.D dissertation: Vanderbilt University, 1990), pp. 220-221; W.M. McGrath, "Conservation of Health," found in *Survey* 14 (January 6, 1921), pp. 1506-1514; Harris, *Political Power*, pp. 160-161.

13. McKiven, "Class, Race and Community," p. 85; Paul Worthman, "Black Workers and Labor Unions in Birmingham, Alabama, 1897-1904," *Labor History*, 10 (Summer, 1969), pp. 385-95.

14. Worthman, "Black Workers and Labor Unions", pp. 403-407.

15. Sisk, "Social History of the Black Belt," pp. 221-222; Montgomery, *Under Their Own Vine*, pp. 107-108; Boothe, *Colored Baptist of Alabama*, pp. 74-76.

16. George,V.R. *Segregated Sabbaths: Richard Allen and the Emergence of Independent Black Churches, 1760-1840* (New York:

Oxford University Press, 1973) pp. 21-48; Clarence Walker, Jr., *A Rock in a Weary Land: The African Methodist Episcopal Church During the Civil War and Reconstruction* (Baton Rouge: Louisiana State University Press, 1982), pp. 5, 19-20-51.

17. William J. Walls, *The African Methodist Episcopal Zion Church* (Charlotte, North Carolina: AME Zion Publishing House, 1974), pp. 121, 197-198, 211-212; WPA Church Records in Alabama State Archives, Montgomery, Alabama, Boxes # 44-46.

18. Othal Hawthorne Lackey, *The History of the CME Church* (Memphis: CME Publishing House, 1985), p. 282; WPA Church Records, Box 45-46; Unpublished History of the Thirgood CME Church in author's possession.

19. William B. McClain, *Black People in the Methodist Church* (Cambridge, Massachusetts: Scherkman Publishing Company, Inc., 1984), pp. 65; Chester A. Brown, *Black United Methodist in the North Alabama Conference* (Privately Published), pp. 12-25.

20. Montgomery, *Under their Own Vine*, pp. 350-351; Interview with Curtis Maggard, December 5, 1992.

21. Joe M. Richardson, *Christian Reconstruction, The American Missionary Association and Southern Blacks, 1861-1890* (New York: Pigram Press, 1991), pp. 157-159; Robinowitz, *Race Relations in Urban South*, pp. 202-203; Leon Litwack, *Been In The Storm So Long: The Aftermath of Slavery* (New York: Random House, Inc., 1979), pp. 462-469.

22. WPA Church Records, Boxes 44-46.

23. *Ibid.*

24. Unpublished History of New Hope Baptist Church in the author's possession.

25. Souvernir Journal of the New Ephesus Seventh Day Adventist Chuch, April 19, 1986 in author's possession.

26. WPA Church Records, Boxes 44-46.

27. WPA, Church Records of Jefferson County in Alabama State Archives, Montgomery, Alabama, Boxes 44-46.

28. Ibid.

29. Marlene Hunt Rikard, "An Experiment in Welfare Capitalism: The Health Care Services of the Tennessee Coal, Iron, and Land Company" (Ph.D dissertation: University of Alabama, 1983), p. 70; WPA Church Histories of Jefferson County, Boxes 41-43.

30. Unpublished History of the St. Mark AME Chuch in the author's possession; Interview with Cutis Maggard, January 2, 1992.

31. Mixon, History of the AME Church, pp. 147-150; Histories of the Bethel AME Church and the Woodward Chapel AME Church found in the WPA Church Records.

32. Interview with C.C. Welch, January 3, 1993: Richard Alan Straw, "Birmingham Miner's Struggle for Power, 1894-1908," (Ph.D dissertation: University of Missouri-Columbia, 1981), pp. 164-223; Harold Joseph Goldstein, "Labor Unrest in the Birmingham District, 1871-1894," (M.A. thesis: University of Alabama, 1951), pp. 21-27; Rikard, "Welfare Capitalism," pp. 70-73.

33. WPA Histories of the Sixteenth Street Baptist Church, the St. John AME Church, and the Metropolitan AME Zion Church.

34. Centennial Souvenir Program of the Tabernacle Baptist Church, no. pg.; Centennial Program of the St. James Baptist Church, no. pg.

35. Eighty-Second Anniversary Program of the Sixth Avenue Church, 1881-1963, no. pg.; Dedication Services Program of the Bethel Baptist Church, May 14, 1972, no. pg.; WPA Histories of the Allen Chapel AME Church and Green Liberty Baptist Church.

36. Bigelow, "Biography of a City," p. 59; Montgomery, *African American Church*, pp. 256-264.

37. White, *Birmingham District*, pp. 106-107.

38. White, *Birmingham District*, pp. 106-107; Unpublished History of the Jerusalem Baptist Church in the writer's possession; WPA Histories of the Antioch Baptist Church and New Zion Baptist Church.

39. White, *Birmingham District*, pp. 98-108; Souvenir Program of the Anniversary of the First Baptist Church of Ensley; WPA Church Records of Jefferson County, in Alabama State Archives, Montgomery, Alabama, Boxes 44-46.

40. White, *Birmingham District*, pp. 35-42; Unpublished History of the First Baptist Church, Brighton; interview with C.C. Welch, January 3, 1993.

41. Interviews with Richard Cunningham, July 3, 1992; Interview with Vertis Maggard, January 2, 1992; Interview with C.C. Welch.

42. Interviews with C.C. Welch, Richard Cunningham, and Harry Stewart.

Chapter III: Expansion and African-American Church Life

1. *Birmingham City Directory*, 1900, p. 52-54; *Birmingham City Directory*, 1920, p. 164-165.

2. *Souvenir Booklet of the One Hundredth Anniversary and Homecoming of the Broad Street Baptist Church*, no. pg.; *Pictorial Directory of the Trinity Baptist Church, 1990*, no. pg; Unpublished History of the Twenty-Third Street Baptist Church in author's possession; Date on the Cornerstone of the South Elyton Baptist Church; Diamond Jubilee Plus Souvenir Journal and Program of the Zion Star Baptist Church, 1989, in author's possession.

3. M.L.S. Robinson, Historical Sketch of the Jefferson County Association, privately printed and in the writer's possession; Carrie Tyler Anderson, *Historical Sketch of the Peace Baptist District Association and its auxiliaries,* 1910-1984, privately printed and in the writer's possession.

4. Interview with Reverend Eugene Jones, July 12, 1995; Interview with Mrs. Carrie Hudson, July 12, 1995; Montgomery, *Under their Own Vine*, pp. 111-117.

5. Birmingham City Directory, 1920, p. 164-165; Wesley J. Gaines, *African Methodism in the South:For Twenty-Five Years of Freedom*, Reprint of 1899 edition (Chicago: African-American Press, 1969), pp. 220, 229.

6. Mixon, *History of the AME Church in Alabama*, pp. 17-18; Winfred Mixon's Four Year Journal of the Greensboro District of the African Methodist Episcopal Church for 1892-1895 found in the Winfred Mixon Papers, Duke University Library; Dennis C. Dickerson, "Winfred Henri Mixon: A Pioneer Presiding Elder in Alabama" *The AME Church Review* (April-June, 1990), 18-22.

7. Winfred Mixon Diary, 1897, Winfred Mixon Papers, Duke University Library, May 6, 7; August 8, 14, 1897.

8. Mixon Diary, 1897, September 2, 1897.

9. Walls, *The AME Zion Church*, pp. 188-189, 322-323; Lackey, *History of the CME Church*, p.70.

10. R.H. Walker, Jr. Publisher, 1902), p. 25; William J. Simmons, *Men of Mark, Progresssive and Rising* (New York: Arno Press and New York Times, 1968), p. 464; Centennial Souvenir Booklet of the Sixteenth Street Babtist Church in the author's possession.

11. One Hundredth Anniversary and Homecoming Program of the Broad Street Baptist Church , 1978, in author's possession; Unpublished History of the St. John Baptist Church, Pratt City in the author's possession.

12. Bigelow, "Biography of a city," p. 98; Advertisements of churches found in African-American papers such as *Wide Awake, Hot Shots,* and *The Truth* show this all day pattern.

13. Walter Pitts, *Old Ship of Zion: The Afro-Baptist Ritual in the African Diaspora* (New York: Oxford University Press, 1993), p. 15.

14. Wyatt Tee Walker, *"Somebody's Callin My Name"* Black Music and Social Change (Valley Forge, Pennsylvania: Judson Press, 1979), pp. 70-71: Eileen Southern, *The Music of Black Americans: A History* (New York: W.W. Norton and Company, 1971), pp. 259-260.

15. Interview with Curtis Maggard, January 2, 1992; Clerk's Record of the Sunday Service of the Shiloh Baptist Church, June 14, 1910, in writer's possession.

16. Interview with Marie Jackson, July 3, 1991; Interview with John Douglass, July 3, 1991.

17. Preaching and worship in the post-Reconstruction African-American Churches has been discussed in two important books: William H. Pipes, *Say Amen, Brothers: Old Time Negro Preaching A Study in American Frustration* (Westport, Connecticut: Negro University Press, 1951) and Walter Pitts,*Old Ship of Zion: The Afro-Baptist Ritual in the African Diaspora* (New York: Oxford University Press, 1993).

18. Isabel Dangaix Allen, "Negro Enterprise: An Institutional Church," *Outlook* (September 1904), p. 183.

19. Miller, *Voice of Deliverance,* p. 122; Pitts, *Old Ship of Zion,* p. 23.

20. Pitts, *Old Ship of Zion,* pp. 59-63; Gerald Davis, *I Got The Word in Me and I Can Sing It, You Know: A Study of the Performed African-American Sermon* (Philadelphia: University of Pennsylvania Press, 1985)

21. Bruce A. Rosenberg, *The Art of the African-American Folk Preacher* (New York: Oxford University Press, 1970), pp. 36-49.

22. WPA Church Histories, Boxes 41-43.

23. Interview with AME Church Historian, Dwight Dillard, November 22, 1993; Interview with Sarah Jackson, July 14, 1992.

24. Interview with Eleanor Harris, October 12, 1992; These activities for women were also gleaned from reading histories of churches in Birmingham.

25. Boothe, *Cyclopedia of Colored Baptists,* p. 70.

26. Interview with Eleanor Harris; Montgomery, *Under their Own Vine*, pp. 95-96.

27. Boothe, *Cyclopedia of Colored Baptists*, pp. 77-78; Isabel Dangaix Allen, "Negro Enterprise: An Institutional Church" *Outlook* (September 1904), 181-183.

28. Allen, "Institutional Church," p. 181.

29. *Ibid.*, pp. 181-182.

30. *Ibid.*, pp. 181-183; Interview with Wilson Fallin, Sr., July 14, 1995.

31. Rabinowitz, *Race Relations in Urban South*, pp. 198-199; Interview with Vertis Maggard, January 2, 1992.

32. Birmingfind, [Robert J. Norell], *The New Patrida, The Story of Birmingham's Greeks*, n. pg; Sofia Lafakis Petrou, *A History of Greeks in Birmingham, Alabama* (Privately Printed, 1979), pp. 16-24.

33. Birmingfind, [Robert J. Norell], *The Italians*, no. pg; Theresa Aguglia Beavers, "The Italians of the Birmingham District," (M.A. Thesis: Samford University, 1969), pp. 41-54.

34. Rabinowitz, *Race Relations in the Urban South*, pp. 198-209.

35. Norrell, *The Other Side*, no. pg.

36. Miller, *Voice of Deliverance*, pp. 23-26.

37. *Ibid.*, pp. 22-23.

38. Frazier, *The Negro Church*, pp. 44-46; Interview with J.C. Cockrell, January 2, 1992; Interview with Mrs. Eleanor Harris, December 2, 1993.

39. McKiven, "Class, Race, and Community," p. 76; Rabinowitz, *Race Relations in the Urban South*, p. 199; Bigelow, "Biography of a City," pp. 100, 114-116; WPA Histories of Jefferson County Churches, Boxes 44-46.

40. Interview with Robert Stewart, March 13, 1992; Interview with C.C. Welch, January 12, 1993; Interview with Richard Cunningham, July 3, 1992.

41. Edward L. Wheeler, *Uplifting the Race: The Black Minister in the New South, 1865-1902* (New York: University Press of America, 1982), p. 80.

42. Eric Foner, *Reconstruction: America's Unfinished Revolution* (New York: Harper & Row, Publishers, 1989), pp. 82-88; C. Eric Lincoln and Lawrence H. Mamiya, *The Black Church in the American Experience* (Durham: The Duke University Press, 1990), p. 402-404.

43. William R. Pettiford, *Divinity in Wedlock* (Birmingham: Alabama Publishing Company, 1895), pp. 45-54, 33-43, 31, 62-84.

44. Charles L. Fisher, *Social Evils: A Series of Sermons* (Jackson, Mississippi: Truth Publishing Company, 1899), pp. 23-35.
45. *Ibid.*, pp. 73-88.
46. *Hot Shots*, March 10, 1894; Fisher, *Social Evils*, pp. 49-61.
47. *Ibid.*, pp. 62-72.
48. *Ibid.*, pp. 36-48.
49. *Ibid.*, pp. 73-88, 62-72.
50. James H. Eason, *Sanctification vs. Fanaticism: Pulpit and Platform Efforts* (Nashville, Tennessee: National Baptist Publishing Board, 1899).
51. *Ibid.*, pp. 87-104.

Chapter IV: Leadership, Institution-Building, and the African-American Church in Birmingham

1. Harris, "Reforms in Government Control," p. 571; Corley, "Quest For Racial Harmony," p. 25.
2. Harris, *Political Power*, p. 58; Robin D.G. Kelley, *Hammer and Hoe* (Chapel Hill: University of North Carolina Press, 1990), p. 2; W.M. McGrath, "Conservatism of Health," in *Survey* 14 (January 6, 1912), pp 1506-1514; Harrris, "Stability and Change," pp. 395-398.
3. *The Truth*, March 31, 1906, *The Negro American*, December 24, 1887; Whitted, State Women's Clubs, p.7.
4. *The Churchman of Sixteenth Street Baptist Church*, pp. 3-4; Brown, "Blacks in Jones Valley," p. 10-11; *The Truth*, January 19, 1907; Minutes of the 36th Annual Session of the North Alabama Conference of the AME Church, (Nashville: AME Sunday School Union Printing Company), 1914, pp. 22-26.
5. Bailey, "Birmingham's Weekly Press," pp. 109-111.
6. Theodore Roosevelt King, "The History of Negro Education in Birmingham, Alabama, 1873-1957" (M.A. Thesis: Atlanta University, 1959), pp. 56, 33, 37, 38; Carol W. Hayes, *Report of the Birmingham Public Schools, September 1, 1920 to August 31, 1925* (Birmingham Board of Education, 1926) p. 103; Arthur Howard Parker, *A Dream Comes True*, (Birmingham Industrial High School, n.d.), pp. 34-35; *The Truth*, May 13, 1905; May 23, 1907; February 1, 1908; November 21, 1908.
7. W.E. Burghardt DuBois, *The Negro Church* (Atlanta: Atlanta University Press, 1903), p. 3; Birmingfind, *The Other Side*, no. pg.;

Carter Godson Woodson, "Insurance Business Among Negroes," *Journal of Negro History* 14 (April 1929), p. 203.

8. Brown, "Alabama Blacks in Jones Valley," pp. 70-71; Louis R. Haran, ed. *The Booker T. Washington Papers*, Vol. 1:182, 3:480, 5:393, 6:233, 5:388, 6:269.

9. Simmons, *Men of Mark*, pp. 460-464; Boothe, *Colored Baptists of Alabama*, pp. 183-185.

10. Simmons, *Men of Mark*, p. 464; John Witherspoon DuBose, *Jefferson County and Birmingham, Alabama: Historical and Biographical* Vol I (Birmingham: Teeple and Smith, 1887) p. 242.

11. Pegues, *Our Baptist Ministers*, pp. 384-385; Boothe, *Colored Baptists of Alabama*, pp. 185-186.

12. William R. Pettiford, *Guide of the Representative Council* (Birmingham: Willis Printing Co., no date), pp. 2-6; Brown, "Alabama Blacks in Jones Valley," p. 10; Bigelow, "Biography of a City," p. 160.

13. Brown, "Alabama Blacks in Jones Valley," p. 10; Bigelow, "Biography of a City," p. 160; Arthur H. Parker, *A Dream that Came True: The Autobiography of Arthur Harold Parker* (Birmingham: Industrial High School Printing Department, 1932), n.p.

14. Booker T. Washington, *The Negro in Business* (Boston: Hertel Jenkins and Company, 1907), pp. 113-114; John N. Ingham and Lynne B. Feldman, *African-American Business Leaders: A Biographical Dictionary* (Westport, Conn.: Greenwood Press, 1993), pp. 549-550.

15. Address delivered by Pettiford at the *First Annual Convention of the National Negro Business League*, Boston, 1900; Brown, "Blacks in Jones Valley," pp. 10-11; Arnett G. Lindsay, "Negro in Banking": *Journal of Negro History*, 14 (April 1929), pp. 170-171; *Birmingham City Directory*, 1900, 1905, 1907 and 1911.

16. Clement Richardson, "The Nestor of Negro Bankers," *The Southern Workman* 43 (November 1914), pp. 608-609; Unpublished History of Tabernacle Baptist Church, Birmingham, Alabama in the writer's possession.

17. Brown, "Blacks in Jones Valley," pp. 10-11; *Report of the Seventh Annual Convention of the National Negro Business Lague*, Atlanta, 1906; Richardson, "Nestor of Negro Bankers," pp. 609-610; *Birmingham City Directory*, 1901, 1905, 1908, and 1911.

18. Richardson, "Nestor of Negro Bankers," p. 608; Lyne Feldman, "Black Business in Birmingham" (M.A. Thesis: Florida State University, 1993) p. 137.

19. Simmons, *Men of Mark*, pp. 460-465; *Centennial Booklet of the Sixteenth Street Baptist Church, 1872-1972*, n.p.; *Hampton Negro Conference*, No. VII, July 1903; Meier, *Negro Thought in America*, pp. 125-126.

20. Address delivered before the *Sixth Annual Convention of the National Negro Business League*, New York City, August 15-18, 1905; Address delivered before the *Thirteenth Annual Convention of the National Negro Business League*, Chicago, 1912.

21. Lynne Feldman, "Black Business in Birmingham" (M.A. Thesis: Florida State University, 1993) In her thesis Feldman shows through mortgagae records that the Penny Bank was the leading financer of housing in Smithfield.

22. Lindsay, "Negro in Banking," pp. 170-171; Richardson; "Nestor of Negro Bankers," pp. 610-611.

23. Richardson, "Nestor of Negro Bankers," p. 609.

24. Lindsay, "Negro in Banking," pp. 170-171.

25. Harlan, *Papers of Booker Washington*, Vol. 5, p. 660; Walker, *The Trumpet Blast*, pp. 43-51.

26. Isabel Dangaix Allen, "Negro Enterprise: An Institutional Church" *The Outlook* (September 1904), pp. 179-180; Boothe, *Colored Baptist of Alabama*, pp. 212-213; Brown, "Blacks in Jones Valley," pp. 10-11; Samuel Bacote, *Who's Who Among the Colored Baptists of the United States* (Kansas City, Missouri: Franklin Publishing Company, 1913), pp. 167-169.

27. Boothe, *Colored Baptist of Alabama*, pp. 212-213; Brown, "Blacks in Jones Valley," pp. 10-11; Samuel Bacorte, *Who's Who Among the Colored Baptists of the United States* (Kanses City, Missouri: Franklin Publishing Company, 1913), pp. 167-169.

28. Boothe, *Colored Baptists of Alabama*, pp. 212-213; Robert Walker Jr., *The Trumpet Blast* (Washington, D.C.: The R.H. Walker Publisher, 1902), pp. 43-51; Allen "An Institutional Church", p. 180.

29. Boothe, *Colored Baptists of Alabama*, pp. 212-213.

30. Allen, "Institutional Church," pp. 180-183; Bacote, *Who's Who*, p. 168.

31. Alexa Besson Henderson, *Atlanta Life Insurance Company: Guardian of Black Economic Dignity*, (Tuscaloosa: University of Alabama Press, 1990), pp. 9-11.

32. August Meier, *Negro Thought*, pp. 142-143; Henderson, *Atlanta Life Insurance Company*, pp. 10-11; Norrell, *The Other Side*, n.p.

33. Bailey, "In Their Own Voices," p. 24; Kolchin, *First Freedom*, p. 63; James D. Anderson, *The Education of Blacks in the South, 1860-1935* (Chapel Hill: University of North Carolina Press, 1988), pp. 17-18.

34. Edward L. Wheeler, *Uplifting the Race the Black Minister in the New South*, 1865-1902 (New York: University Press of America, 198), pp. 110; Paul Griffin, *Black Theology as the Foundation of Three Methodist Colleges, The Educational Views and Labors of Daniel Payne, Joseph Price, Issac Lane* (Lanham, Maryland: University Press of America, 1984), pp. 40, 84; *The Truth*, February 1, 1908.

35. Wheeler, *Uplifting the Race*, p. 112: Griffin, *Black Theology as Foundation*, pp. 95-98; Brown, *Secondary Education for Negroes*, p. 90. Issac Lane was the founder of Lane College in Jackson, Tennessee, and J.C. Price founded Livingstone College in Livingstone, North Carolina.

36. Thomas Jesse Jones, *Negro Education: A Study of the Private and Higher Schools for Colored People in the United States Prepared in Cooperation with the Phelps-Stokes Fund under the Direction of Thomas Jesse Jones, Specialist in the Education of Racial Groups, Bureau of Education* Volume II (Washington, D.C.: Government Printing Office, 1917), p. 52.

37. Brown, *Secondary Educating* , pp. 13-14: Jones, *Negro Education*, p. 53.

38. That these were not actually colleges is shown by academic programs that were originally offered.

39. Brown, *Secondary Education*, 18-20; Jones, *Negro Education*, pp. 53-54

40. Booklet and Souvenir Program of the Diamond Jubilee Celebration of the freedom of the American Negro observed by the Four Annual Conferences in the Alabama Colored Methodist Episcopal Church, 1939, no. pg.

41. Brown, *Secondary Education* p. 20; Jones, *Negro Education*, pp. 51-52.

42. Wheeler, *Uplifting the Race*, pp. 103-104.

43. Catalogue of the School of Religion, Birmingham Baptist College, 1967, p. 7; Jones, *Negro Education*, p. 100.

44. *Centennial Souvenir Booklet of the Women's Auxiliary of the Mt. Pilgram District Association*, October 5-7, 1993, in the writers possession.

45. L.L. Berry, *A Century of Missions of the African Methodist Episcopal Church*, 1840-1940 (New York: Gutenberg Printing Company, Inc., p. 284.

46. August Meier, *Negro Thought*, pp. 142-143.

47. Sisk, "Negroes in the Black Belt," p. 369; E. Franklin Frazier, *The Negro Church in America (New York: Shocken Books, 1963)*, p. 36.

48. *Negro American*, March 17, 1894; Brown, "Blacks in Jones Valley," p. 10; Unpublised Histories of Oak Grove, New Zion, Macedonia, and St. Luke Baptist Churches in the author's possession.

49. Bigelow, "Biography of a City," p. 105; *Birmingham News*, December 20, 1895.

50. Horance Mann Bond, *Negro Education in Alabama*, (New York: Octagon Press, 1939), pp. 169-170.

51. *The Negro American*, May 5, 1894.

52. *Birmingham Reporter*, March 25, 26, 30; April 13; June 27, 1918.

Chapter V: The African-American Church Between the World Wars: Continuity and Preservation

1. *Birmingham Reporter*, April 20; May 4, 18, 1918; Dorothy Autrey, "The National Association for the Advancement of Colored People in Alabama, 1913-1952" (Ph.D Dissertation: Notre Dame University, 1985), p. 15.

2. Autrey, NAACP in Alabama," pp. 57-63, 121-123; *Birmingham Reporter*, August 15; October 3, 1931; November 7, 28; December 5, 19, 1931; January 23, 30; March 7; August 26; October 22; November 12, 26, 1932; July 22, October 21, 31, 1933

3. David M. Chalmers, *Hooded Americanism: The History of the Ku Klux Klan* (Durham: Duke University Press, 1978), pp.28-33; Atkins, *Valley and Hills*, p. 113; William Robert Snell, "The Ku Klux Klan in Jefferson County, 1916-1930" (MA Thesis: Samford University, 1967) , pp. 58-60; Autrey, "NAACP in Alabama," pp.66-67; Richard A Straw, "The United Mine Workers of America and the 1920 Coal Strike in Alabama" *The Alabama Review* (April 1975), pp. 107, 116-128.

4. Brownwell, "New South City," pp. 29-30; Harris *Political Power*, pp. 34-35; Edward S. LaMonte, "Politics and Welfare in Birmingham, 1900-1975" (Ph.D Dissertation: University of Chicago, 1976), pp. 32-34; Corley, " Quest for Racial Harmony," pp. 24-25; Autrey, NAACP in Alabama," p. 138; Glen Thomas Eskew, But for Birmingham: The Local and National Movements in the Civil Rights Struggle" (Ph.D Dissertation: University of Georgia, 1993) p. 22.

5. Charles S. Johnson, *Shadow of the Plantation* (Chicago: University of Chicago Press, 1969), pp. 1-29; 103-119; Barbara Nunn, compiler,

Like it Ain't Never Passed: Remembering Sloss Quarters (Birmingham: Sloss Furnaces National Historical Commision, 1985) pp. 3-4, 16-17; *Birmingham Reporter*, January 22, 1921.

6. WPA Report of Churches in Birmingham and Jefferson County in Alabama State Archives, Mongomery, Alabama.

7. History of the Twenty-Third Street Baptist Church, Ensley, and the New Kingdom Baptist Church found in the WPA church files located in the Alabama State Archives, Montgomery, Alabama, Boxes 41-44.

8. *Ibid*. Interviews with C.C. Welch and J.D. Rodgers.

9. Benjamin Elijah Mays and John William Nicholson, *The Negro's Church* (New York: Arno Press, 1993), pp. 210-211; *Birmingham Reporter*, January, 1930.

10. Norrell, *The Other Side*, no. pg.; Johnson, *Shadow of the Plantation*, pp. 150-162; Interview with J.C. Cockrell.

11. Mays and Nicholson, *Negro's Church*, p. 206.

12. Interviews with C.C. Welch, L.J. Rogers, Mrs. Mary Elsaw.

13. Mt. Pigrim Baptist District Association Minute of 1940, no pg.; WPA Study of Churches in Birmingham and Jefferson County, Boxes 41-44.

14. Interview with C.C. Welch and Mrs. Eleanor Harris.

15. Mays and Nicholson, *Negro's Church*, pp. 287-288.

16. *Birmingham Reporter*, March 31, November 3, 1930; Unpublished History of the Sixth Avenue Baptist Church by Levi Williams in the author's possession.

17. *Birmingham Reporter*, March 31, November 3, 1930; Centennial Memoirs of the Sixteenth Street Baptist Church, no pg.; Interview with Levi Williams.

18. *Birmingham Reporter*, December 18, 1920.

19. Interviews with Rev. Dwight Dillard, J.C. Cockrell, and Mrs. S.J. Jackson; Moorman, *Colored Leaders*, p. 88.

20. *Birmingham Reporter*, February 2, 1929; Interview with Mrs. S.J. Jackson.

21. William E. Montgomery, *Under Their Own Vine*, pp. 256-259; Richardson, *Christian Reconstruction*, pp. 141-159; Thomas Holt, *Black Over White: Negro Political Leadership in South Carolina During Reconstruction* (Urbana: University of Illinois Press, 1979), p. 59.

22. W.E.B. DuBois, "The Negro in the Black Belt," Bulletin of the Department of Labor, No. 22, May, 1899, pp. 411-413 found in Sisk, "Alabama Black Belt," pp. 275-277.

23. Williard B. Gatewood, Jr., *Aristocrats of Color: The Black Elite, 1880-1920* (Bloomington: University of Indiana Press, 1990), pp. 69-95; Williard B. Gatewood, Jr., "Aristocrats of Color South and North: The Black Elite, 1880-1920,"Journal of Southern History, LIV (1988), 3-20.

24. Gatewood, "Aristocrats of Color," pp. 3-20.

25. *The Other Side*, no pg.; Bigelow, *Biography of a City*, 116-120.

26. Barbara Smith, *St. Mark's Academic and Industrial School, 1892-1940* (Birmingham: Privately Printed, 1976), p. 1-6; Unpublished History of the Miller Memorial Presbyterian Church in writer's possession.

27. Centennial Yearbook of First Congregational Christian Church, 1882-1982. Privately Printed and in writer's possession.

28. Interviews with James L. Meyers and J. Mason Davis.

29. Centennial Yearbook of First Congregational Church, no pg.

30. Interviews with James L. Meyers and J. Mason Davis.

31. Unpublished histories of St. Paul AME Church, Metropolitan AME Zion Church, Thirgood CME Church, and St. John AME Church-all in writer's possession; Interviews with A.G. Gaston, Chester Brown, and Dwight Dillard.

32. Peques, *Our Baptist Ministers and Schools*, pp. 381-385; Simmons, *Men of Mark*, pp. 463-465.

33. Bacote, *Who's Who Among Colored Baptist*, pp. 241-243; Cantennial Memoirs of Sixteenth Street Baptist Church, no pg.; Moorman, *Colored Leaders*, p. 19.

34. Centennial Memoirs, no pg.

35. *Birmingham Reporter*, December 25, 1920; Moorman, *Colored Leaders*, pp. 92, 96; Autrey, "NAACP in Alabama," pp. 71-73.

36. *Birmingham Reporter*, August 7, 1926; April 3, 1926; July 26, 1926; February 19, 1927.

37. *Birmingham Reporter*, July 10, 1926; July 10, 1920; January 6, 1923; May 8, 1926; February 12, 1921; January 7, 1928; January 20, 1923.

38. *Birmingham Reporter*, December 22, 1923, January 6, 1923; January 8, 1930; September 8, 1923; October 13, 1923.

39. Arthur George Gaston, *Green Power: The Successful Way of A.G. Gaston*, (Troy, Alabama: Troy State University Press, 1968), pp. 48-59.

40. *Ibid.*, Interview with A.G. Gaston.

41. *Ibid.*, pp. 67-71. Interview with Donald Solomon and A.G.Gaston.

42. Catalog of Birmingham Baptist College, 1968-1970, pp. 12-13.

43. Catalog of Daniel Payne College, 1970, p. 2; *Birmingham Reporter*, July 25, 1930.

44. *Birmingham Reporter*, August 25, 1928; January 25, 1930; October 31, 1931. Booklet and Souvenir Program of the Diamond Jubilee Celebration of the Emancipation from Slavery sponsored by the CME Church of Alabama, pp. 5-10.

45. Moorman, *Colored Leaders*, p. 18.

46. *Birmingham Reporter*, December 7, 1929; Moorman, *Colored Leaders*, p. 92.

47. *Birmingham Reporter*, November 13, 1920; March 6, 1926; February 5, 1927.

48. *Birmingham Reporter*, December 18, 1920; October 6, 1928.

49. *Birmingham Reporter*, November 20, 1920; Interview with Levi Williams, July 2, 1994.

50. John W. Goodgame, *A Collection of Sermons and Addresses by Rev. John W. Goodgame, D.D., Pastor of Sixth Avenue Baptist Church* (Birmingham Privately Printed, no date), pp. 18-22.

51. *Birmingham Reporter*, January 20, 1923; Interview with Levi Williams and John Porter.

52. Goodgame, *Collection of Sermons*, p. 22.

53. Interview with Levi Williams, July 2, 1994; Catalog of Birmingham Baptist College, 1968.

Chapter VI: The African-American Church Between the World Wars: Communism and New Religious Responses

1. Eskew, "But for Birmingham," pp. 23-24; Lamonte, "Welfare in Birmingham," pp. 160-200; George R. Leighton, "Birmingham, Alabama: The City of Perpetual Promise," *Harper's Magazine* 175: 8 (August 1937), p. 230.

2. Corley, "Quest for Racial Justice," p. 31.

3. Kelley, *Hammer and Hoe*, pp. 19-20; Hudson, *Black Worker*, pp. 51-52; Interview with Johnny Battle, April 5, 1993.

4. Kelley, *Hammer and Hoe*, pp. 10-33; The best book on the Scottsboro Case is Dan T. Carter, *Scottsboro: A Tragedy of the American South* (Baton Rouge: Louisiana University Press, 1979)

5. Hudson, *Black Worker in the South*, pp. 1-44; Kelley, *Hammer and Hoe*, pp. 24-30; Nell Irvin Painter, *The Narrative of Hosea Hudson: His Life as a Negro Communist in the South* (Cambridge, Massachusetts: Harvard University Press, 1979), pp. 75-95.

6. Painter, *Narrative of Hosea Hudson*, pp. 75-80; 269-270.

7. *Birmingham Reporter*, August 1, 15, 1931; Kelley, *Hammer and Hoe*, pp. 108-116; *Commission on Interracial Cooperation Report on Radical Activities in Alabama*, 1931, found in the Archives of the Robert F. Woodruff Library of the Atlanta University Center; Interview with A.G. Gaston; Interview with W.C. Patton; Interview with C.C. Welch.

8. Kelley, *Hammer and Hoe*, pp. 111-112; Papers of the Commission on Interracial Cooperation located in the Archives of the Woodruff Library in Atlanta, Georgia; Unpublished History of the Jackson Street Baptist Church in the writer's possession.

9. Kelley, *Hammer and Hoe*, pp. 115-116; Unpublished History of the Bethel Baptist Church, Collegeville, in the writer's possession.

10. Interview with Dwight Dillard; Interview with Levi Williams; Interview with James Crutcher.

11. Wyatt T. Walker, *"Somebody's Calling My Name" Black Sacred Music and Social Change* (Valley Forge: Judson Press, 1979), pp. 127-151; Eileen Southern, *The Music of Black Americans: A History* Second Edition (New York: W.W. Norton and Company, 1938), pp. 444-456; Lawrence Levine, *Black Culture and Black Consciousness: Afro-American Folk Thought from Slavery to Freedom* (New York: Oxford University Press, 1977), pp. 174-189; J. Wemdall Mapson, *The Ministry of Music in the Black Church* (Valley Forge: Judson Press, 1984), pp. 38-39.

12. Southern, *The Music of Black Americans*, pp. 450-451; C. Eric Lincoln and Lawrence H. Mamiya, *The Black Church in the African American Experience* Durham: Duke University Press, 1990, pp. 360-361; Walker, *Somebody's Calling My Name*, pp.70-71; Vic Broughton, *Black Gospel: An Illustration History of the Gospel Sound.* (London: Blacford Press, 1985), pp. 37-39.

13. *Gospel Pearls* (ed) Willla A. Townsend and others. (Nashville: Sunday School Publishing Board, National Baptist Convention, 1921) Harris, pp. 68, 151-152; Interview with J.H. Calloway, June 2, 1992.

14. Southern, *The Music of Black Americans*, pp. 450-451; Lincoln, The Black Church, pp. 362-363.

15. Interviews with J.H. Calloway, Mary Elsaw, Donald Solomon, Cecil McNear, and Dwight Dillard.

16. Brenda McCallum, *Birmingham Boys: Quartet Singing in Birmingham and Jefferson County*, n.p.; Doug Seroff, *Birmingham: Quartet Scrapbook: A Quartet Reunion in Jefferson County* (Birmingham: Published by Alabama State Council on the Arts And

Humanities, 1980), p.3.

17. Doug Seroff, "Gospel Quartet Singing," in Stephen H. Martin (ed.) *Alabama Folklife: Collected Essays* (Birmingham: Alabama Folklife Association, 1989), pp. 57-59; Serof, *Quartet Scrapbook*, p. 4.

18. McCallum, *Birmingham Boys*, n. p.

19. Seroff, Gospel quartet Singing," p. 59.

20. Seroff, Scrapbook, pp.4-5.

21. McCallum, *Birmingham Boys*, n.p.

22. McCallum, *Birmingham Boys*, no. pg.

23. McCallum, *Birmingham Boys*, no. pg.

24. Ibid., n.p.

25. Seroff, *Birmingham Boys*, n.p.

26. Seroff, "Gospel Quartet Singing," pp. 59-60; *Scrapbook*, pp.5-7.

27. Seroff, "Gospel Quartet Singing," pp. 60-61; McCallum, *Birmingham Boys*, n.p.; Kip Lornell, *Happy in the Service of the Lord*, (Chicago: University of Illinois Press, 1988), p.48.

28. Birmingham City Directory, 1940, pp. 1533-1537.

29. Elaine J. Lawless, *God's Perciliar People: Women Vocies and Folk Tradition in a Pentecostal Church* (Lexington: University of Kentucky Press, 1988), pp.41; Ida Roussea Mukenge, *The Black Church in Urban America: A Case Study in Political Economy* (Lanham, Maryland: University Press of America, Inc., 1983), pp. 62-64.

30. Hans A. Baer, *The Black Spiritual Movement: A Religious Response to Racism* (Knoxville: University of Tennessee Press, 1948), p. 163; Lovett, *"Black Holiness-Pentecostalism,"* p. 77; Washington, *Black Sects and Cults*, pp.73-77.

31.Ibid., p.166; Washington, *Blacks Sects and Cults*, p. 80 Synan, *Holiness-Pentecostal Movement*, pp. 177-178.

32. Lawless, *God's Perculiar People*, 77-109: Synan, *Holiness-Pentecostal Movement*, pp.188-189; Histories of Church of God congregations in Jefferson County in WPA Files, Alabama Department of Archives, Montgomery, Alabama.

33. Leonard Lovett, *"Black Holiness-*Pentecostalism" in Stanley M. BurgessAnd Gary B. McGhee (eds), *Dictionary of the Pentecostal and Charismatic Movement* (Grand Rapids, Michigan: Zondervan Publishing House, 1988), pp.77-82

34. *Birmingham Directory,* 1940, pp. 1533-1537; Hans A. Baer, *"Black Spiritualists Churches:* A Neglected Socoi-Religious Institute", *Phylon: Atlanta University Journal of Race and Culture*, 42 (September 1981), pp. 217-219.

35. *Birmingham Directory*, 1940, pp. 1533-1537.

36. Lovett, *"Black Holiness-Pentecostal,"* p. 79.

37. Frank Mead, (ed) " *Handbook of Denominations in the United States,"* Revised by Samuel S. Hill (Nashville: Abingdon Press, 1990), p.31; Leonard Lovett, *"Black Holiness-Pentecostilm,"* p. 81; Interview with Mrs. Juanita Arrington; Interview with F.D. Parker.

38. David M. Tucker, " *Black Pastors and Leaders:Memphis, Tennessee,* 1819-1972 (Memphis Memphis State University Press, 1975), pp. 88-100; Iain MacRoberts, " *Black Roots and White Racism in the USA* (New York: St. Martin's Press, 1988), pp. 56-58; Vinson Synan, " *The Holiness-Pentecostal Movement in the United States,"* (Grand Rapids, Michigan: William B. Eerdman's Publishing Company, 1971(, pp. 136-137.

39. *Ibid.*, pp. 88-100; Birmingham Reporter, May 24, 1930; Birmingham Directory, p. 1535.

40. Arthur E. Paris, *Black Pentecostalism: Southern Religion in an Urban World* (Amherst: The University of Massachusetts Press, 1892), p 54; Interview with Mrs. Ora Foster; Interview with O.L. Meadows.

41. Anthony Heilbut, *The Gospel Sound: Good News and Bad Times*(New York: Limelight Editions, 1985), p 179.

42. Paris, *Black Pentecostalism*, pp 61-69; Interview with Mrs. Ora Foster.

43. *Ibid.*, pp 67-69.

44. Interview with Mrs. Ora Foster; Interview with O.L. Meadows.

Chapter VII: Rising Militancy and the African-American Church from World War II to the Civil Rights Movement, 1941-1965

1. Autrey, "NAACP in Alabama," pp. 183-184; Mydral, *An American Dilemma*, pp 851-852; Richard M. Dalfiume, "The Forgotten Years of the Negro Revolution," *Journal of American History*, 55 (June 1968), pp. 90-97.

2. Autrey, "NAACP in Alabama," pp. 184-185; Gunner Myral, *An American Dilemma; The Negro Problem and Modern Democracy* (New York: Harper & Row, Publishers, 1942), pp 1008-1115; Robert J. Norrell, "One Thing We Did Right: Protest, History, and the Civil Rights Movement," in Armstead L. Robinson and Patricia Sullivan, eds.,

New Directions in Civil Rights Studies (Charlottesville: University Press of Virginia, 1991), pp. 68-69.

3. Norrell, "Caste in Steel," p. 681; *Birmingham News*, June 25, 1943; *Birmingham World*, August 21, 1942.

4. *Birmingham World*, March 14, 1941; January 30, 1945; July 21,1953; November 10, 1942.

5. Lynda Dempsey Cochran, "Arthur Davis Shores: Advocate for Freedom," (M.A. thesis: Georgia Southern College, 1977), p.126.

6. Norrell, Labor at the Ballot Box," pp. 204-205; *Birmingham World*, January 2, 1942.

7. Norrell, "Labor at the Ballot Box," pp. 205-206; Painter, *Narrative of Hosea Hudson*, pp. 256-263.

8. Autrey, "NAACP in Alabama," pp. 202-211; *Birmingham World* April 18; May 6,9, 1941.

9. Autrey, "NAACP in Alabama," pp. 203-204; *Birmingham World*, April 18; May 6, 9, 1941; Robert J. Norrell, "Labor at the Ballot Box: Alabama Politics from the New Deal to the Dixiecrat Movement," *Journal of Southern History* 57 (May 1991), 224-225; Robert Norrell, "Caste in Steel: Jim Crow: Careers in Birmingham, Alabama," *Journal of American History* 73 (December 1986), 680-681.

10. Interviews with R.C. Cunningham, Abraham Woods, and Rodgers; Tucker, *Pastors and Leaders in Memphis*, p. 70.

11. *Birmingham World*, March 7, 1941, February 17, May 1, 1942, June 25, 1943, December 28, 1945.

12. *Birmingham World*, November 3, 1944.

13. *Birmingham World*, January 30, 1945; October 6, 1944; July 17, 1945.

14. *Birmingham World*, February 10, December 8, 1941; February 15, 1944; January 5, 1945.

15. Corley, *"Quest for Racial Harmony,"* p. 67; *Facts Behind the Facts About the Birmingham and Jefferson County Negro Hospital Association,* (Birmingham: Published by the Jefferson County Negro Hospital Association, n.d.), pp. 3-8; *"Birmingahm World,"* April 4, 1944.

16. *Birmingham World*, April 4, 1944; August 14, 1945; *"Birmingham News,"* November 15, 1953; January 11, 1954.

17. Geraldine Moore, *"Behind the Ebony Mask"* (Birmingham: Southern University, 1961), p. 66; *Birmingham World*, May 30, 1941; Brown, *Secondary Education*, pp. 20-25.

18. *Birmingham World*, July 24, 1942.

19. Autrey, *NAACP in Alabama,"* p. 217.

20. *Birmingham World,* January 12, 1952.

21. *Birmingham World,* January 3, 1947, January 6, 1950.

22. *Birmingham World,* January 9, 1948.

23 *Birmingham World,* January 30, 1945; July 27, 1948; May 21, 1952; Interview with James Cotton.

24. *Birmingham World,* January 30, 1945 July 27 1948; May 21, 1952; Interview with James Cotton.

25. Interview with R.C. Cunningham.

26. *Birmingham World,* July 11, 1941; Interview with Mrs. S.J. Jackson; Interview with Wilson Fallin, Sr.

27. *Birmingham World,* October 31 1947; November 11, 1947; August 15, 1950; April 3, 1953.

28. *Birmingham World,* January 4, 1955.

29. *Birmingham World,* February 17, 1942; May 1, 1942; October 6 1944; January 3, 1947.

30. Corley, "Quest for Racial Harmony," p. 87; *Birmingham News,* July 15, 1959.

31. *Birmingham World,* January 25, 1955, January 3, 1955, February 11, 1955, February 18, 1955.

32. *Birmingham World,* June 13, October 6, 1944; July 17, 1945; September 9, 1952, September 12, 1952; December 18, 1953.

33. Barnard, *Dixiecrats and Democrats,* pp. 59-63; *Birmingham Post Herald,* October 31, 1946; Brittain, Negro Suffrage," pp. 189-192.

34. *Birmingham World,* January 17, 1950; December 12, 26, 1947; May 20, 30,1947; August 7, October 9, 1953; September 23, 1952; July 1, 1955.

35. *Birmingham World,* August 14, 1953.

36. *Birmingham World,* November 5, 1954; June 24, 1955, August 16, 1995.

37. *Birmingham World,* July 29, 1955, August 2, 1955.

38. *Birmingham World,* October 4, 1955.

39. *Birmingham World,* January 13, 1953; January 21, 25, 1955; December 19, 1950; October 12, 1954; Interview with W.C. Patton.

40. *Birmingham World,* February 1, 1952; January 5, 1945; January 16, 1951; January 6, 1953, June 3, 1953.

41. *Birmingham World,* March 21, 1947; February 10, 1942; May 9, 1954; January 10, 1956.

42. *Birmingham World,* March 21, 1947; February 27, 1948; March 6,22, 1949; December 23, 1952; August 31, 1951.

Chapter VIII: The African-American Church and the Civil Rights Movement

1. Lee E. Bains, Jr. "Birmingham, 1963: Confrontation Over Civil Rights," in David J. Garrow, ed., *Birmingham, Alabama, 1956-1963: The Black Struggle for Civil Rights* (Brooklyn, New York: Carlson Publishing, Inc., 1989), p. 165; Martin Luther King, Jr., *Why We Can't Wait* (New York: Harper & Row, Publishers, 1964), pp. 39-43.

2. *Seventeenth Census of the United States*, 1950 Volume Two, General Characteristics of the Population, Alabama, Part 2, Detailed Characteristics Tables 77, 87; Baines, "Confrontation Over Civil Rights," pp. 165-167; Jeraldine Moore, *Behind the Ebony Mask*, p. 211; Donald S. Strong, *Registration of Voters in Alabama* (Birmingham: Birmingham Publishing Company, pp. 48-74; Eskew,"But for Birmingham," p. 141.

3. J. Tyra Harris, "Alabama Reaction to the Brown Decision, 1954-1956: A Study in Early Massive Resistance" (Ph.D dissertation: Middle Tennessee State University, 1978), pp. 251-296: Robert J. Norrell, "Caste in Steel," pp. 683.

4. Eskew, "But for Birmingham." pp. 154-173; *Birmingham Post Herald*, November 5, 1957; The best biography on Eugene "Bull" Conner is William A. Nunnelley, *Bull Conner* (Tuscaloosa: University of Alabama Press, 1991)

5. National Association for the Advancement of Colored People papers, Birmingham Branch File, Microfilm, BPL DAM; *Birmingham Post Herald*, April 24, 1952; Autrey, "NAACP in Alabama," pp. 217-218, 253-254; *Birmingham World*, April 11.

6. Aldon Morris, *The Origin of the Civil Rights Movement: Black Communities Organizing for Change* (New York: The Free Press, 1984), pp. 1-76. The figure of four hundred churches was gained from Baptist associations and Methodist conference records. The city directory was also helpful, but did not include all African American churches in the Birmingham area.

7. Harris, "Massive Resistance," pp. 296-303; Fred Shuttlesworth, "An Account of the Alabama Christian Movement for Human Rights," in Jacqueline Johnson Clarke, *These Rights They Seek: The Comparison of the Goals and Techniques of Local Civil Rights Organization* (Washington, D.C.: Public Affairs Press, 1962), pp. 135-139; Glen Thomas Eskew, "The Alabama Christian Movement & the Birmingham

Struggle, 1956-1963" (M.A. thesis: University of Georgia, 1987), pp. 5-9.

8. *Birmingham World*, January 27, 1956; Lewis L. Jones, "Fred Shuttlesworth: Indigeous Leader," in David J. Garrow, ed., *Birmingham, Alabama, 1956-1963: The Black Struggle for Civil Rights* (Brooklyn, New York: Carlson Publishing Inc., 1989), p. 134; Shuttlesworth, "An Account of the Alabama Christian Movement," p. 136; Interview with Fred Shuttlesworth, January 22, 1993; Anne Braden, "The History That We Made: Birmingham, Alabama, 1956-1979" *Southern Exposure* 7:2 (Summer 1979), pp. 48-54.

9. Shuttlesworth, "An Account of the ACMHR," pp. 136-139; Braden, "Birmingham," pp. 50-51.

10. *Birmingham News*, June 6, 1956; Shuttlesworth, "An Account of the ACMHR," pp. 139-140.

11. *Birmingham News*, June 8, 1956; Shuttlesworth, "An Account of the ACMHR," p. 140.

12. Interview with the following pastors: John Porter, Edward Gardner, Wilson Fallin, Sr., Solomon Crenshaw, J.H. Calloway, and A.H. Felder.

13. Interview with the following professional blacks: A.G. Gaston, Donald Solomon, Louis Willie: Morris, *Origins of the Civil Rights Movement*, p. 45; Eskew, "ACMHR," p. 103; Shuttlesworth, "Account of the ACMHR," p. 146.

14. Clarke, "Goals and Techniques," pp. 163-173; Jones, "Fred Shuttlesworth," pp. 132-135.

15. Stephen B Oates, *Let the Trumpet Sound: The Life of Martin Luther King, Jr.* (New York: Mentor Printing Company, 1985), p. 202; Interview with Fred Shuttlesworth, January 25, 1993.

16. Eskew, "ACMHR," p. 70; Interview with Fred Shuttlesworth, January 25, 1993.

17. Interview with Edward Gardner, September 10, 1993.

18. Ibid., Howard Raines, *My Soul Rested: The Story of the Civil Rights Movement in the Deep South* (New York: G.P. Putman's Sons, 1977), pp. 139-145; *Birmingham World*, June 10, 1959.

19. Interview with Abraham Woods, August 1, 1993: Recorded Interview with Abraham Woods by Addie Pugh of the University of Alabama in Birmingham, October 28, 1975.

20. Interview with Calvin Woods, January 10, 1994; *Birmingham World, November* November 20, 1958.

21. Interview with Nelson Smith, Jr., July 31, 1993.

22. Interview with L.J. Rogers, January 3, 1994.

23. *Birmingham World*, November 10, 1956; Morris, *Origins of the Civil Rights Movement*, pp. 7-10; Shuttlesworth, "An Account of the ACMHR," p. 137; Eskew, "ACMHR," p. 69; Eskew, "But for Birmingham," p. 195.

24. Eskew, "ACMHR," p. 69; Clarke, *These Rights They Seek*, p. 34. Corley, "Quest for Racial Harmony," p. 130.

25. Interview with Mrs. Pinkie Shortridge, December 10, 1993; Eskew, "ACMHR," p. 69.

26. Interview with Stone Johnson, December 4, 1993; *Birmingham World*, July 30, 1958.

27. Interview with Carlton Reese, February 13, 1994; Eskew, "ACMHR," p. 65; Eskew, "But for Birmingham," pp. 196-197.

28. Eskew, "But for Birmingham," pp. 197-198; Bernice Reagon, "Songs of the Civil Rights Movement, 1955-1965: A Study of Cultural History" (Ph.D dissertation: Howard University, 1975).

29. Interview with Fannie Nelson, September 5, 1994; Eskew, "ACMHR," p. 68.

30. Interview with Daisy Jeffries, September 14, 1994; Interview with Lola Hendrix, September 15, 1994.

31. Birmingham Police Report of the ACMHR found in the Southern History Archives of the Birmingham Public Library for January 23, 1961 and April 17, 1961.

32. Clarke, "Goals and Techniques," pp. 163-173.

33. *Birmingham World*, July 15, 1968.

34. Eskew, "But for Birmingham," p. 174; Clarke, *These Rights They Seek*, pp. 54-56; Baines, "Confrontation Over Civil Rights," p. 95.

35. *Birmingham News*, August 20, 2, 27, 1956; Corley, "Quest for Racial Harmony," pp. 73-77; Shuttlesworth, "Account of ACMHR," pp. 148-149.

36. *Birmingham News*, December 20, 21, 1956; *Birmingham World*, December 26, 29, 1956; Shuttlesworth, "An Account of the ACMHR," p. 149.

37. Eskew, "ACMHR," pp. 36-37; *Birmingham News*, October 24, 26, 28, 1958.

38. *Birmingham News*, November 13, December 2, 1958; November 23, December 29, 1959; Interview with Calvin Woods, January 29, 1994.

39. Eskew, "ACMHR," pp. 28-30; *Birmingham World*, March 9, 1947.

40. Corley, "Quest for Racial Harmony," pp. 138-139; Manis, "Religious Experience, Religious Knowledge, and Civil Rights Leadership: The Case of Birmingham's Reverend Fred Shuttlesworth" in Charles Reagan Wilson (ed.) *Cultural Perspectives on the American South, Volume 5* (New York: Gordon and Breach, 1991), pp. 148-149.

41. Eskew, "But for Birmingham," pp. 246-248; *People in Motion: The Story of the Alabama Christian Movement for Human Rights* (Birmingham: Published by Alabama Christian Movement for Human Rights, n.d.), n.p.

42. *Birmingham World*, February 1, 12, 1958, March 5, 1958.

43. Eskew, "But for Birmingham," pp. 269-273; Kelvin Anderson Cassady, "Black Leadership and the Civil Rights Struggle in Birmingham, Alabama, 1960-10-964" (B.A. thesis: Georgetown University, 1986), pp. 33-41.

44. David J. Garrow, *Bearing the Cross: Martin Luther King, Jr. and the Southern Christian Leadership Conference* (New York: William Morrow and Company, 1968), pp. 198-199; Nichols, "Cities Are What Men Make Them," pp. 176-177; Raines, *My Soul is Rested*, pp. 169-170; Cassady, "Black Leadership," pp. 41-44.

45. Stephen B. Oates, *Let the Trumpet Sound: The Life of Martin Luther King, Jr.* (New York: Mentor Printing Company, 1985), p. 202.

46. Eskew, "But for Birmingham," p. 296; Cassady, "Black Leadership," pp. 49-50; Morris, *Origins of the Civil Rights Movement*, pp. 250-253.

47. Eskew, "ACMHR," pp. 101-105; Interview with John Porter; Eskew, "But for Birmingham", pp. 311-312.

48. Fairclough, *To Redeem the Soul of America: The Southern Christian Leadership Conference and Martin Luther King, Jr.* (Athens: University of Georgia Press, 1987), p. 120. Oates, *Let the Trumpet Sound*, pp. 211-222; Malinda Snow, "Martin King's "Letter from the Birmingham Jail" as Pauline Epistle" in David J. Garrow, (ed.), *Martin Luther King, Jr. Civil Rights Leader, Theologian, Orator* (Brooklyn, New York: Carlson Publishing Company, Inc., 1989), pp. 857-873.

49. The climax of the Birmingham Movement and the agreement reached between the businessmen and the civil rights leaders have been recorded in several books. Among these are Oates, *Let the Trumpet Sound*, pp. 224-233; Ralph David Abernathy, *And the Walls Come Tumbling Down: Ralph David Abernathy An Autobiography* (New York: Harper & Row Publishers, 1989), pp. 262-269; Fairclough, *To Redeem America*, pp. 125-129; Garrow, *Bearing the Cross*, pp. 246-259.

Conclusion

1. The debate about African American religion is found in several books and articales: Raboteau, *Slave Religion*; Sernett, *Black Religion and American Evangelicalism*; Cone, *Black Religion and Black Power*; Joseph R. Washington, Jr., *Black Religion* (Boston: Beacon Press, 1964; Gary T. Marx, "Religion: Opiate or Inspiration of Civil Rights Militancy Among Negroes?" *Sociological Review* 32 (Febuary, 1967), 64-72 and Vincent Harding, "Religion and Resistance Among Antebellum Negroes, 1800-1860," in *The Making of Black America*, edited by August Meier and Elliott, 2 vols (New York: Antheneum Press, 1969).

BIBLIOGRAPHY

Manuscript Sources

Alabama Baptist Historical Society Papers. Samford University, Birmingham, Alabama. [Hereafter referred to as *ABHS*.]
Alabama Methodist Historical Society Papers. Birmingham Southern College, Birmingham, Alabama. [Hereafter referred to as *AMHS*.]
Birmingfind Collection. Birmingham Public Library Department of Archives and History, Birmingham Public Library, Birmingham, Alabama. [Hereafter referred to as BPLDAM.]
Birmingham City Directories. BPLDAM
Commission on Interracial Cooperation Papers. Archives of Robert F. Woodruff Library, Atlanta University, Atlanta, Georgia.
T. Eugene "Bull" Connor Papers. BPLDAM.
Emory O. Jackson Papers. BPLDAM.
Martin Luther King, Jr. Papers. Martin Luther King, Jr., Center for Nonviolent Social Change, Inc., Archives. Atlanta, Georgia. [Hereafter referred to as King Center.]
Winfred Henri Mixon Papers. Archives of Duke University Library, Durham, North Carolina.
National Association for the Advancement of Colored People Papers. Birmingham Branch File. Microfilm. BPLDAM.
Police Surveillance Papers. BPLDAM.
Fred Shuttlesworth Papers. King Center.
Work Progress Association Papers. Alabama State Department of Archives and History, Montgomery, Alabama. [Hereafter referred to as ADAH.]

Newspapers

Birmingham *Age-Herald*
Birmingham *Blade*
Birmingham *Free Speech*
Birmingham *Mirror*
Birmingham *News*
Birmingham *Post-Herald*

Birmingham *Reporter*
Birmingham *World*
Christian *Hope*
Hot Shots
The *Negro American*
The *Truth*
Wide Awake

Interviews

Lee N. Allen, October 22, 1992
Johnny Battle, April 5, 1993
Chester Brown, February 4, 1993
Joseph H. Calloway, June 2, 1992
J. C. Cockrell, January 1, 1993
James Cotton, June 4, 1992
James Crutcher, April 1, 1994
Richard Cunningham, July 3, 1992
J. Mason Davis, March 3, 1994
Dwight Dillard, November 22, 1993
John Douglass, July 3, 1991
Mary Elsaw, January 11, 1993
Wilson Fallin, Sr., July 14, 1995
A. H. Felder, December 11, 1992
Ora Foster, January 20, 1995
Edward Gardner, September 10, 1993
Arthur G. Gaston, February 5, 1994
Eleanor Harris, October 12, 1992
Lola Hendrix, September 15, 1994
Carrie Hudson, July 12, 1955
Marie Jackson, July 3, 1991
Sarah J Jackson, July 14, 1992
Daisy Jeffries, September 14, 1994
Stone Johnson, December 4, 1993
Eugene Jones, July 12, 1995
Curtis Maggard, December 5, 1992
James L. Meyers, March 2, 1994
Cecil J McNear, August 13, 1993
Fannie Nelson, September 5, 1994
WC Patton, March 1, 1995
John Porter, February 2, 1993

Carlton Reese, February 13, 1994
LJ Rogers, January 3, 1994
Pinkie Shortridge, December 10, 1993
Fred Shuttlesworth, January 25, 1993
Nelson Smith, Jr July 31, 1993
Donald Solomon, January 30, 1994
Harry Stewart, December 11, 1991
Robert Stewart, March 13, 1992
CC Welch, January 3, 1993
Levi Williams, July 2, 1994
Abraham Woods, August 31, 1993
Calvin Woods, January 10, 1994

Films, Transcripts, Recordings

"Birmingham Boys:" Jubilee Gospel Quartets from Jefferson County, Alabama. Alabama Traditions, 101.

"No Easy Walk, 1961-1963." *Eyes on the Prize*. Boston, Mass.: Blackside, Inc., 1986.

Unpublished Sources

Anderson, Carrie Tyler, Historical Sketch of the Peace Baptist Association and its Auxiliaries.

Booklet and Souvenir Program of the Diamond Jubilee Celebration of the Freedom of the American Negro observed by the Four Annual Conferences in the Alabama Colored Methodist Episcopal Church, 1939.

Catalog of the School of Religion, Birmingham Baptist College, 1967.

Centennial Booklet of the Sixteenth Street Baptist Church, 1872-1972, Birmingham, Alabama.

Centennial Souvenir Booklet of the Women's Auxiliary of the Mt. Pilgrim District Association, October 5-7, 1993.

Centennial Souvenir Program of the Tabernacle Baptist Church, Birmingham, Alabama.

Centennial Souvenir Program of the St. James Baptist Church, Birmingham, Alabama.

Centennial Yearbook of First Congregational Christian Church, 1882-1982, Birmingham, Alabama.

Diamond Jubilee Plus Souvenir Journal of the Zion Star Baptist Church, 1989, Birmingham, Alabama.

Eighty-Second Anniversary Program of the Sixth Avenue Baptist Church, 1881-1963, Birmingham, Alabama.

Greene, Julius C. "Reminiscence of Julius C. Greene." BPLDAM.

McCallum, Brenda. Birmingham Boys: Quartet Singing in Birmingham and Jefferson County, n.p.

Pictorial Directory and History of the Trinity Baptist Church, 1990, Birmingham, Alabama.

Robinson, M.L.S. Historical Sketch of the Jefferson County District Association

Smith, Barbara. *St. Mark's Academic and Industrial School, 1892-1940*. Birmingham, 1976.

Souvenir Booklet of the One Hundredth Anniversary and Homecoming of the Broad Street Baptist Church, Birmingham, Alabama.

Souvenir Journal of the New Ephesus Seventh Day Adventist Church, Birmingham, Alabama.

Vann, David J. Speech. Duard LeGrand Conference, 15 November 1978, Birmingham, Alabama.

Reports

U.S. Congress. Senate. *Report of the Committee upon Relations Between Capital and Labor.* Washington, D.C. : Government Printing Office, 1885.

Hayes, Carol W. *Report of the Birmingham Public Schools, September 1, 1920 to August 31, 1925.* Birmingham: Birmingham Board of Education, 1926.

Jones, Thomas Jesse. *Negro Education A Study of the Private and Higher Schools for Colored People in the United States Prepared in Cooperation with the Phelps-Stokes Fund under the Direction of Thomas Jesse Jones, Specialist in the Education of Racial Groups, Bureau of Education.* Volume II. Washington, D.C., Government Printing Office, 1917.

Proceedings of the National Negro Business League, Hampton University.

Theses and Dissertations

Autrey, Dorothy. "The National Association for the Advancement of Colored People in Alabama, 1913-1952." Ph.D. diss., Notre Dame University, 1985.
Bell, Robert. "Reconstruction in Tuscaloosa, Alabama." Master's thesis, University of Alabama, 1933.
Brunson, Beulah. "Reconstruction in Jefferson County." Bachleor's thesis: Samford University, 1928.
Clarke, Jacquelyne Johnson. "Goals and Techniques in Three Civil Rights Organizations in Alabama." Ph.D. diss., Ohio State University, 1960.
Cochran, Lynda Dempsey. "Arthur Davis Shores: Apostle for Freedom." Master's thesis, Georgia Southern College, 1977.
Corley, Robert Gaines. "The Quest for Racial Harmony: Race Relations in Birmingham, Alabama, 1947-1963." Ph.D. diss., University of Virginia, 1979.
Feldman, Lynne. "Black Business in Birmingham, Alabama." Master's thesis, Florida State University, 1993.
Fuller, Justin. "History of Tennessee Coal, Iron, and Railroad Company, 1852-1907." Ph.D.diss., University of North Carolina, 1966.
Goldstein, Harold Joseph. "Labor Unrest in the Birmingham District, 1871-1899. "Master's thesis, University of Alabama, 1951.
Harris, Tyra J. "Alabama Reaction to the Brown Decision, 1954-1956: A Study in Early Massive Resistance." Ph.D. diss., Middle Tennessee State University, 1978.
Harrison, Mary Phyllis. "A Change in the Government of the City of Birmingham, 1962-1963." Master's thesis, University of Montevallo, 1974
Huntley, Horace. "Iron Ore Miners and Mine Mill in Alabama, 1935-1952." Ph.D. diss., University of Pittsburgh, 1977.
King, Jere C. Jr. "The Formation of Greater Birmingham." Master's thesis, University of Alabama, 1936.
King, Roosevelt. "The History of Negro Education in Birmingham, Alabama, 1873-1957." Master's thesis, Atlanta University, 1959.
LaMonte, Edward Shannon. "Politics and Welfare in Birmingham, Alabama, 1900-1975." Ph.D. diss., University of Chicago, 1976.

Leavy, Oliver W. "Zoning Ordinances in Relation to Segregated Negro Housing in Birmingham, Alabama." Master's thesis, Indiana University, 1951.

McKiven, Henry M. "Class, Race and Community: Iron and Steel Workers in Birmingham, Alabama, 1875-1920." Ph.D. diss., Vanderbilt University, 1990.

Mitchell, Martha Carolyn. "Birmingham: Biography of a City of the New South." Ph.D. diss., University of Chicago, 1946.

Nichols, Michael Cooper. "Cities Are What Men Make Them: Birmingham, Alabama Faces the Civil Rights Movement, 1963." Senior honors thesis, Brown University, 1974.

Reagon, Bernice Johnson. "Songs of the Civil Rights Movement, 1955-1965: A Study in Cultural History." Ph.D. diss., Howard University, 1975.

Rikard, Marlene. "An Experiment in Welfare Capitalism: The Health Care Services of the Tennessee Coal, Iron and Railroad Company." Ph.D. diss., University of Alabama, 1983.

Roberson, Nancy Clairborne. "The Negro and Baptists of Antebellum Alabama." Master's thesis, University of Alabama, 1954.

Rutledge, Sumner. "An Economic and Social History of Antebellum Jefferson County, Alabama." Master's thesis, University of Alabama, 1939.

Sisk, Glenn N. "Alabama Black Belt: A Social History, 1875-1917." Ph.D. diss., Duke University, 1950.

Snell, William Robert. "The Ku Klux Klan in Jefferson County, Alabama, 1916-1930." Master's thesis, Samford University, 1967.

Sterne, Ellin. "Prostitution in Alabama, 1890-1925." Master's thesis, Samford University, 1977.

Stewart, George R. "Birmingham's Reaction to the 1954 Desegregation Decision." Master's thesis, Samford University, 1967.

Straw, Richard Alan. "This Is Not a Strike. It Is Simply a Revolution: Birmingham Miners Struggle for Power, 1894-1908." Ph.D. diss., University of Missouri-Columbia, 1980.

Vick, Mary-Helen. "A Survey of the Governing Body of Birmingham, Alabama, 1910-1964." Master's thesis, Alabama College, 1965.

Watkins, Robert C. "General Wilson's Raid through Alabama and Georgia in 1865." Alabama Polytechnic Institute, 1959.

Articles

Allen, Isabel Dangaix. "Negro Enterprise: An Institutional Church." *Outlook* 88 (September 17, 1904): 181-85.

Atkins, Leah. "Senator James A. Simpson and Birmingham Politics of the 1930s: His Fight Against the Spoilsmen and Pie-Men." *Alabama Review* 41:1 (January 1988): 3-29.

———. "Feuds, Factions, and Reform: Politics in Early Birmingham." *Alabama Heritage* (Summer 1986): 22-33.

Baer, Hans A. "Black Spiritualist Churches: A Neglected Socio-Religious Institution." *Phylon: Atlanta University Journal of Race and Culture* 42 (September 1981): 21-27.

Barnard, William D. "George Huddleston, Sr. and the Political Tradition of Birmingham." *Alabama Review* 36 (October 1983): 234-58.

Bass, S. Jonathan. "Bishop C.C.J. Carpenter: From Segregation to Integration." *Alabama Review* 45:3 (July 1992): 184-215.

Bigelow, Martha. "Birmingham's Carnival of Crime, 1871-1910." *Alabama Review* 3 (April 1950):123-33.

Braden, Anne. "The History That We Made: Birmingham, 1956-1979."*Southern Exposure* 7:2 (Summer 1979): 48-54.

Brown, Charles A. "Alabama Blacks in Jones Valley." *The Mirror* (February 9, 16, 1975): 10-11.

Brownell, Blaine A. "Birmingham, Alabama: New South City in the 1920s." *Journal of Southern History* 38:1 (February 1972): 21-48.

Dalfiume, Richard M. "The Forgotten Years of the Negro Revolution." *Journal of American History*. 55 (June 1968): 90

Dickerson, Dennis C. "Winfred Henri Mixon: A Pioneer Presiding Elder in Alabama." *The AME Church Review* (April-June, 1990): 18-22.

DuBois, W.E.B. "The Negro in the Black Belt." *Bulletin of the Department of Labor* 22 (May 1899): 405-415.

Fell, Charles A. "The Crash and the Moratorium." *Journal of the Birmingham Historical Society* 1:1 (January 1960) : 7-10.

Flynt, Wayne. "Religion in the Urban South: The Divided Religious Mind of Birmingham, 1900-1930." *Alabama Review* 30:2 (April 1977): 108-134.

Forten, Charlotte. "Life on the Sea Islands." *Atlantic Monthly* 13 (1864): 587-596.

Fuller, Justin. "Henry DeBardeleben, Industrialist of the New South." *Alabama Review* 39:1 (January 1986): 3-18.

Gatewood, Williard B. "Aristocrats of Color, North and South: The Black Elite, 1880-1920." *Journal of Southern History* 54 (1988): 3-20.

Harris, Carl V. "Reforms in Government Control of Negroes in Birmingham, Alabama, 1890-1920. *Journal of Southern History* (November 1972): 567-600.

Harris, Carl V. "Stability and Change in Discrimination Against Black Public Schools: Birmingham, Alabama, 1871-1931." *Journal of Southern History* 51:3 (August 1985) 375-416.

Huntley, Horace. "The Rise of Mine Mill in Alabama: The Status Quo Against Industrial Unionism", 1933-1949." *Journal of the Birmingham Historical Society* 6:1 (January 1979): 5-13.

Leighton, George R. "Birmingham, Alabama: The City of Perpetual Promise." *Harper's Magazine* 175:8 (August 1937): 225-242.

Lindsay, Arnett G. "Negro in Banking." *Journal of Negro History* 14 (April 1929): 156-201.

McCallum, Brenda. "Songs of Work and Songs of Worship: Sanctifying Black Unionism in the Southern City of Steel." *New York Folklore* 14 (1988): 1-2.

McGrath, W. M. "Conservation in Health." *Survey* 14 (January 6, 1921): 1506-1514.

Norrell, Robert J. "Caste in Steel: Jim Crow Careers in Birmingham, Alabama." *Journal of American History* 73:3 (December 1986): 669-94.

"Labor at the Ballot Box: Alabama Politics from the New Deal to the Dixiecrat Movement." *Journal of Southern History* 57:2 (May 1991): 201-34.

Owen, Blaine."Night Ride in Birmingham." *New Republic* 84 (August 28, 1935): 65-67.

Richardson, Clement. "The Nestor of Negro Bankers." *The Southern Workman* 43 (November 1914): 607-611.

Rikard, Marlene. "George Gordan Crawford: Man of the New South." *Alabama Review* 31 (July 1978): 163-181.

Sisk, Glen. "Negro Churches in the Alabama Black Belt, 1875-1900." *Journal of Presbyterian Historical Society*. 33 (June 1955): 87-98.

Thomas, Rebecca L. "John J. Eagan and Industrial Democracy at ACIPCO." *Alabama Review* 43:4 (October 1990): 270-88.

Woodson, Carter G. "Insurance Business Among Negroes." *Journal of Negro History* 14 (April 1929): 202-226.

Worthman, Paul. "Black Workers and Labor Unions in Birmingham, Alabama, 1897-1904." *Labor History* 10 (Summer 1969): 385-95.

Chapters and Sections of Books

Bains, Lee E. "Birmingham, 1963: Confrontation over Civil Rights." In *Birmingham, Alabama, 1956-1963: The Black Struggle for Civil Rights* edited by David J. Garrow. Brooklyn, New York: Carlson Publishing Company, 1989.

Eskew, Glenn T. "The Alabama Christian Movement for Human Rights, 1956-1963." In *Birmingham, Alabama, 1956-1963* edited by David J. Garrow. Brooklyn, New York: Carlson Publishing Company, 1989.

Jones, Lewis W. "Fred L. Shuttlesworth, Indigenous Leader" In *Birmingham, Alabama, 1956-1963* edited by David J. Garrow. Brooklyn, New York: Carlson Publishing Company, 1989.

Lovett, Leonard. "Black Holiness-Pentecostal." In *Dictionary of Pentecostal and Charismatic Movement*. Edited by Stanley Burgess and Gary B. McGhee. Grand Rapids: Zondervan Publishing House, 1988.

Manis, Andrew Michael. "Religious Experience, Religious Authority, and Civil Rights Leadership: The Case of Birmingham's Reverend Fred Shuttlesworth." In *Cultural Perspectives on the American South Volume 5*. Edited by Charles Reagan Wilson. New York: Gordon & Breach, 1991.

Norrell, Robert J. "One Thing We Did Right: Reflections on the Movement." In *New Directions in Civil Rights Studies*. Edited by Armistead L. Robinson and Patricia Sullivan. Charlottesville and London: University Press of Virginia, 1991.

Painter, Nell Irvin. "Hosea Hudson and the Progressive Party in Birmingham." In *Perspectives on the American South, Volume One*. Edited by Merle Black and John Shelton Reed. New York: Gordon and Breach, 1981.

Seroff, Doug. "Gospel Quartet Singing." In *Alabama Folklife:Collected Essays*. Edited by Stephen H. Martin. Birmingham: Alabama Folklife Association, 1989.

Snow, Malinda. "Martin Luther King's 'Letter From Birmingham Jail' as Pauline Epistle." In *Martin Luther King, Jr.: Civil Rights Leader, Theologian, Orator*. Edited by David J. Garrow. Brooklyn, N.Y.: Carlson Publishing, Inc., 1989.

Worthman, Paul W. "Black Workers and Labor Unions in Birmingham, 1897-1914." In *Black Labor in America*. Edited by Milton Cantor, Westport, Connecticut: Negro University Press, 1969.

"Working Class Mobility in Birmingham, Alabama, 1880-1914." In *Anonymous Americans: Explorations in Nineteenth Century Social History*. Edited by Tamara K. Hareven. Englewood Cliffs, New Jersey: Prentice Hall, 1971.

Books

Abernathy, Ralph David. *And the Walls Come Tumbling Down: Ralph Abernathy An Autobiography*. New York: Harper & Row, 1989.

Allen, Lee N. and Bee, Fanna K. *Sesquicentennial History of Ruhama Baptist Church, 1818-1969*. Birmingham: Oxmoor Press, 1969.

Anderson, James D. *The Education of Blacks in the South, 1860-1935*. Chapel Hill: University of North Carolina Press, 1988.

Armes, Ethel. *The Story of Coal and Iron in Alabama*. Cambridge, Massachusetts: The University Press, 1910.

Atkins, Leah Rawls. *The Valley and the Hills: An Illustrated History of Birmingham and Jefferson County*. Woodland Hills, California: Windsor Publications, 1981.

Bacote, Samuel. *Who's Who Among the Colored Baptists of the United States*. Kansas City: Franklin Hudson Publishing Company, 1913.

Baer, Hans A. The Black Spiritual Movement: *A Religious Response to Racism*. Knoxville: University of Tennessee Press, 1948.

Barefield, Marilyn Davis. *Bessemer, Yesterday and Today, 1887-1888*. Birmingham: Southern University Press, 1986.

Barnard, William D. *Dixiecrats and Democrats: Alabama Politics: Alabama Politics, 1942-1950*. Tuscaloosa: University of Alabama Press, 1985.

Bartley, Numan V. *The Rise of Massive Resistance: Race and Politics in the South During the 1950s*. Baton Rouge: Louisiana State University Press, 1969.

Bennett, Lerone Jr. *What Manner of Man: A Biography of Martin Luther King, Jr*. Chicago: Johnson Publishing Company, Inc., 1968.

Berry, L.L. *A Century of Missions of the African Methodist Episcopal Church,* 1840-1940. New York: Gutenberg Printing Company, Inc. 1950.

Blassingame, John. *The Slave Community: Plantation Life in the Antebellum South.* New York: Oxford University Press, 1972.

Boles, John B. *Black Southerners, 1619-1869.* Lexington: University of Kentucky Press, 1983.

Bond, Horace Mann. *Negro Education in Alabama: A Study in Cotton and Steel.* Washington, D.C.: Associated Publishers, 1939.

Boothe, C. O. *Cyclopedia of Negro Baptists in Alabama Birmingham:* Alabama Publishing Company, 1895.

Branch, Taylor. *Parting the Waters: America in the King Years.* New York: Simon and Schuster, 1988.

Broughton, Vic. *Black Gospel: An Illustrated History of the Gospel Sound.* London: Blancford Press, 1985.

Brown, Charles A. *Secondary Education for Negroes in Birmingham, Alabama.* Birmingham: Forniss Printing Company, 1972.

Brown, Chester A. *Black United Methodist in the North Alabama Conference.* Birmingham: North Alabama Conference, n.d.

Brown, Virginia Pounds and Nabors, Janice Porters. ed. *Mary Gordon Duffee's Sketches of Alabama.* Tuscaloosa: University of Alabama Press, 1970.

Brown, William Wells. *My Southern Home or the South and its People.* Boston: A.G. Brown and Company, Publishers, 1880.

Caldwell, H. M. *History of Elyton Land Company and Birmingham, Alabama.* Reprint. Birmingham: Birmingham Publishing Company, 1972.

Carson, Clayborne. *In Struggle: SNCC and the Black Awakening of the 1960s.* Cambridge, Massachusetts: Harvard University Press, 1981.

Carter, Dan T. *Scottsboro: A Tragedy of the American South.* Baton Rouge: Louisiana State University Press, 1979.

Carawan, Guy and Candice ed. *Sing for Freedom: The Story of the Civil Rights Movement* Through Its Songs. Bethelehem, Pennsylvania: A Sing Out Publication, 1990.

Carter, Harold A. *The Prayer Tradition of Black People.* Baltimore: Gateway Press, Inc., 1982.

Chalmers, David M. *Hooded Americanism: The First Century of the Ku Klux Klan,* 1865-1965. New York: Doubleday & Company, Inc., 1965.

Creel, Margaret Washington. *"A Peculiar People": Slave Religion and Community-Culture Among the Gullahs.* New York: New York University Press, 1988.

Davis, Gerald. *I Got the Word in Me and I can Sing It, You Know: A Study of the Performed African American Sermon.* Philadelphia: University of Pennsylvania Press, 1985.

DuBois, W. E. Burghardt. *The Negro Church: Report of a Social Study made under the direction of Atlanta University; together with the Proceedings of the Eighth Conference for the Study of Negro Problems, held at Atlanta University, May 26th, 1903.* Atlanta: Atlanta University Press, 1903.

DuBose, John A. Witherspoon. *Jefferson County and Birmingham, Alabama: Historical and Biographical.* Easley, South Carolina: Southern Historical Press, 1887.

Eagles, Charles W. ed. *The Civil Rights Movement in America.* Jackson: University of Mississippi Press, 1987.

Eason, James H. *Sanctification vs. Fanaticism: Pulpit and Platform Efforts.* Nashville: National Baptist Publishing Board, 1899.

Fairclough, Adam. *To Redeem the Soul of America: The Southern Christian Leadership Conference and Martin Luther King, Jr.,* Athens: University of Georgia Press, 1978.

Fisher, Charles L. *Social Evils: A Series of Sermons.* Jackson: Truth Publishing Company, 1899.

Flynt, Wayne. *Poor But Proud: Alabama's Poor Whites.* Tuscaloosa: University of Alabama Press, 1989.

Foner, Eric. *Reconstruction: America's Unfinished Revolution, 1863-1877* New York: Harper & Row, Publishers, 1988.

Franklin, Jimmie Lewis. *Back to Birmingham: Richard Arrington, Jr., and His Times.* Tuscaloosa: University of Alabama Press, 1989.

Frazier, E. Franklin. *The Negro Church in America.* New York: Schocken Books, 1963.

Gaines, Wesley J. *African Methodism in the South: Or Twenty-Five Years of Freedom.* Reprint of 1899 Edition. Chicago: African American Press, 1696.

Garrow, David J. *Bearing the Cross: Martin Luther King Jr., and the Southern Christian Leadership Conference.* New York: William Morrow and Company, Inc., 1968.

ed. *Birmingham, Alabama, 1956-1963: The Black Struggle for Civil Rights.* Brooklyn, New York: Carlson Publishing Inc., 1989.

Garrow, David J. ed. *Martin Luther King, Jr.,: Civil Rights Leader, Theologian, Orator.* Brooklyn, New York: Carlson Publishing Company, Inc., 1989.

George, V. R. *Segregated Sabbaths: Richard Allen and the Emergence of Independent Black Churches, 1760-1840.* New York: Oxford University Press, 1973.

Gaston, Arthur George. *Green Power: The Successful Way of A. G. Gaston.* Reprint. Troy, Alabama: Troy State University Press, 1977.

Gatewood, Williard B. Jr. *Aristocrats of Color: The Black Elite, 1880-1920.* Bloomington: University of Indiana Press, 1990.

Genovese, Eugene. *Roll, Jordan, Roll: The World the Slaves Made.* New York: Vintage Books, 1976.

Goodgame, John W. *A Collection of Sermons and Addresses by Rev. John W. Goodgame.* Birmingham: Privately Printed, n.d.

Griffin, Paul. *Black Theology as the Foundation of three Methodist Colleges, The Educational Views and Labors of Daniel Payne, Joseph Price, Issac Lane.* Lanham: University Press of America, 1984.

Hanlin, Katherine Hale. *The Steeple Beckons: A Narrative History of the First Baptist Church, Trussville, Alabama.* Trussville: First Baptist Church, 1971.

Harris, Carl V. *Political Power in Birmingham, 1871-1921.* Knoxville: University of Tennessee Press, 1977.

Harris, Michael W. *The Rise of Gospel Blues: The Music of Thomas Andrew Dorsey in the Urban Church.* New York: Oxford University Press, 1992.

Heilbut, Arthur E. *The Gospel Sound: Good News and Bad Times.* New York: Limelight Editions, 1958.

Henderson, Alexa Besson. *Atlanta Life Insurance Company:Guardian of Black Economic Dignity.* Tuscaloosa: University of Alabama Press, 1990.

Holcombe, Hosea. *A History of the Rise and Progress of the Baptists of Alabama.* Philadelphia: King and Baird, 1840.

Holt, Thomas. *White Over Black: Negro Political Leadership in South Carolina During Reconstruction.* Urbana: University of Illinois Press, 1979.

Hornady, John R. *The Book of Birmingham.* New York: Dodd, Mead and Company, 1921.

Ingham, John N. and Feldman, Lynne B. *African-American Business Leaders: A Biographical Dictionary.* Westport: Greenwood Press, 1993.

Johnson, Clifton. ed. *God Struck Me Dead.* Cleveland: The Pilgrim Press, 1993

Johnson, Charles. *Shadow of the Plantation.* Chicago: University of Chicago Press, 1969.

Johnson, Charles A. *The Frontier Camp Meeting.* Dallas: Southern Methodist University Press, 1955.

Jones, James P. *Yankee Blitzkrieg: Wilson's Raid Through Alabama and Georgia.* Athens: University of Georgia Press, 1976.

Joyner, Charles. *Down by the Riverside: A South Carolina Slave Community.* Urbana: University of Illinois Press, 1984.

Kelley, Robin D.G. *Hammer and Hoe: Alabama Communists During the Great Depression.* Chapel Hill: University of North Carolina Press, 1990.

King, Martin Luther, Jr., *Why We Can't Wait.* New York: Mentor Press, 1963.

Kolchin, Peter. *First Freedom: The Responses of Alabama's Blacks to Emancipation and Reconstruction.* Westport: Greenwood Press, 1972.

Lackey, Othal Hawthorne. *The History of the CME Church.* Memphis: CME Publishing House, 1985.

LaMonte, Edward S. *George B. Ward: Birmingham's Urban Statesman.* Birmingham:Oxmoor Press, 1974.

Lawless, Elaine J. *God's Peculiar People: Women Voices and Folk Tradition in a Pentecostal Church.* Lexington: University of Kentucky Press, 1988.

Leeds . . . Her Story. Anniston: Higginbotham Publishing Company, 1964.

Levine, Lawrence. *Black Culture and Black Consciousness: Afro-American Folk Thought from Slavery to Freedom.* New York: Oxford University Press, 1977.

Lincoln, C. Eric and Mamiya, Lawrence H. *The Black Church in the African American Experience.* Durhan: Duke University Press, 1990.

Litwack, Leon. *Been in the Storm So Long: The Aftermath of Slavery.* New York: Alfred A. Knopf, Inc., 1979.

Lornell, Kip. *Happy in the Service of the Lord.* Chicago: University of Illinois Press, 1988.

Matthews, Donald G. *Religion in the Old South*. Chicago: University of Chicago Press, 1977.

McClain, William B. *Black People in the Methodist Church*. Cambridge: Scherkman Publishing House, Inc., 1984.

McMillan, Malcolm C. *Yesterday's Birmingham*. Miami:E. A. Seeman Publishing Co., 1975.

MacRoberts, Iain. *Black Roots and White Racism in the USA*. New York: St. Martin's Press, 1988.

Mapson, Wendall J. *The Ministry of Music in the Black Church*. Valley Forge: Judson Press, 1984.

Mays, Benjamin E. and Nicholson, John William. *The Negro's Church*. New York: Institute of Social and Religious Research, 1933.

Mead, Frank. ed. *Handbook of Denominations in the United States*. Revised by Samuel S. Hill. Nashville: Abingdon Press, 1990.

Meier, August. *Negro Thought in America, 1880-1915* Ann Arbor:The University of Michigan Press, 1966.

Miller, Keith D. *Voices of Deliverance: The Language of Martin Luther King, Jr., and Its Sources*. New York: The Free Press, 1992.

Mixon, Winfred H. *History of the African Methodist Episcopal Church in Alabama,with Biographical Sketches*. Nashville: AME Church Sunday School Union, 1902.

Moore, Geraldine. *Behind the Ebony Mask*. Birmingham: Southern University Press, 1961.

Moorman, J. H. and Barrett, E. L. *Leaders of the Colored Race in Alabama*. Mobile: The News Publishing Company, Inc., 1928.

Morris, Aldon. D. *The Origins of the Civil Rights Movement: Black Communities Organizing for Change*. New York: The Free Press, 1984.

Mukenge, Ida Rousseau. *The Black Church in Urban America: A Case Study in Political Economy*. Lanham: University Press of America, Inc., 1983.

Myrdal Gunnar. *An American Dilemma: The Negro Problem and American Democracy*. Two Volumes. New York: Harper and Brothers, 1944.

Norrell, Robert J. *James Bowron: The Autobiography of a New South Industrialist*. Chapel Hill: University of North Carolina Press, 1991.

[Robert J. Norrell] *The Italians:From Bisacquino to Birmingham*. [Birmingham: n.d.]

Norrell, Robert J. *The Other Side: The Story of Birmingham's Black Community.* [Birmingham: n.d.]

Birmingham's Lebanese: "The Earth Turned To Gold". [Birmingham: n.d.]

The New Patrida: The Story of Birmingham's Greeks. [Birmingham: n.d.]

Norton, Bertha Bendall. *Birmingham's First Magic Century: Were You There?* Birmingham: Lakeshore Press, 1970.

Nunn, Barbara. Compiler. *Like It Ain't Never Passed: Remembering Sloss Quarters.* Birmingham: Sloss Furnaces National Historical Commission, 1985.

Nunnelley, William A. *Bull Connor.* Tuscaloosa: University of Alabama Press, 1991.

Oates, Stephen B. Let the Trumpet Sound: *The Life of Martin Luther King, Jr.* New York: Mentor Printing Company, 1985.

Olmstead, Frederick Law. *The Cotton Kingdom: A Traveller's Observations on Cotton and Slavery in the American Slave States.* New York, 1865.

Painter, Nell Irvin. *The Narrative of Hosea Hudson: His Life as a Negro Communist in the South.* Cambridge: Harvard University Press, 1979.

Parker, Arthur H. *A Dream that Came True: The Autobiography of Arthur Harold Parker.* Birmingham: Industrial High School Printing Department, 1932.

Paris, Arthur E. *Black Pentecostalism: Southern Religion in an Urban World.* Amherst: University of Massachusetts Press, 1982.

Parrinder George. *African Traditional Religion.* London: Hutchinson University Library, 1954.

Payne, Daniel. *Recollections of Seventy Years.* Nashville: AME Publishing Board, 1880.

Pegues, A.W. *Our Baptist Ministers and Schools.* Springfield, Massachusetts: Springfield Printing and Binding Company, 1892.

Petrou, Sofia Lafakis. *A History of Greeks in Birmingham in Birmingham, Alabama.* Birmingham: Privately Printed, 1979.

Pettiford, William R. *Divinity in Wedlock.* Birmingham: Alabama Publishing Company, 1895.

Pettiford, William R. *Guide to the Representative Council.* Birmingham: Willis Printing Co., n.d.

Pipes, William H. *Say Amen, Brother! Old-Time Negro Preaching: A Study in American Frustration.* Detroit: Wayne State University Press, 1992.

Pitts, Walter F. *Old Ship of Zion: The Afro-Baptist Ritual in the African Diaspora.* New York: Oxford University Press, 1993.

Rabinowitz, Howard N. *Race Relations in the Urban South, 1865-1890.* Urbana: University of Illinois Press, 1980.

Raboteau, Albert. *Slave Religion:The Invisible Institution in the Antebellum South.* New York: Oxford University Press, 1978.

Raines, Howard. *My Soul is Rested: Movement Days in the Deep South Remembered.* New York: Bantam Press, 1978.

Rawick, George. *From Sundown to Sunup: The Making of the Black Community.* Westport: Greenwood Publishing Company, 1972.

Richardson, Joe M. *Christian Reconstruction, The American Missionary Association and Southern Blacks, 1861-1890.* New York: Pilgrim Press, 1991.

Riley, B.F. *A Memorial History of the Baptists of Alabama.* Philadelphia: The Judson Press, 1923.

Rosenberg, Bruce A. *The Art of the American Folk Preacher.* New York: Oxford University Press, 1970.

Sernett, Milton C. *Black Religion and American Evangelicalism: White Protestants, Missions, and the Flowering of Negro Christianity, 1787-1865.* Metuchev, New Jersey: The Scarecrow Press, 1978.

Seroff, Doug. *Birmingham Quartet Scrapbook: A Quartet Reunion in Jefferson County.* Birmingham: Published by Alabama State Council on the Arts and Humanities, 1980.

Sitkoff, Harvard. *The Struggle for Black Equality, 1954-1980.* New York: Hill and Wang, 1981.

Simmons, William J. *Men of Mark, Progressive and Rising.* Reprint. New York: Arno Press and New York Times, 1968.

Smith, Simon J. and Bee, Fanna K. *Canaan-Garden Spot By the Cuttachoee.* Bessemer: Canaan Baptist Church, 1972.

Southern, Eileen. *The Music of Black Americans: A History.* New York: W. W. Norton and Company, 1971.

Strong, Donald S. *Bibliography of Birmingham, Alabama, 1872-1972.* Tuscaloosa: University of Alabama Press, 1956.

Synan, Vinson. *The Holiness-Pentecostal Movement in the United States.* Grand Rapids: William B. Eerdmans Publishing Company, 1971.

Townsend, Willa A. and others. ed. *Gospel Pearls*. Nashville: Sunday School Publishing Board, National Baptist Convention, 1921.

Tucker, David M. *Black Pastors and Leaders: Memphis, Tennessee, 1918-1972*. Memphis: Memphis State University Press, 1975.

Walker, Clarence. *A Rock in a Weary Land: The African Methodist Episcopal Church During the Civil War and Reconstruction*. Baton Rouge: Louisiana State University Press, 1982.

Walker, James H. Jr. *Roupes Valley: A History of the Pioneer Settlement of Roupes Valley which is located in Tuscaloosa and Jefferson Counties, Alabama*. Bessemer: Montezuma Press, 1871.

Walker, R.H. Jr. *The Trumpet Blast*. Washington, D.C.: R. H. Walker, Jr., Publisher, 1902.

Walker, Wyatt T. *"Somebody's Calling My Name" Black Music and Social Change* New York: W. W. Norton and Company, 1971.

Walls, William Jr. *The African Methodist Episcopal Zion Church*. Charlotte: AME Publishing House, 1974.

Washington, Booker T. *The Negro in Business*. Boston: Hertel, Jenkins and Company, 1907.

West, Anson. *History of Methodism in Alabama*. Spartanburg: The Reprint Company, Publisher, 1938.

Wheeler, Edward L. *Uplifting the Race: The Black Minister in the New South, 1865-1902*. New York: University Press of America, 1982.

White, Marjorie Longenecker. *The Birmingham District: An Industrial History and Guide*. Birmingham: Birmingham Historical Society, 1981.

Wilson, Mabel Ponder, Youngblood, Woodyerd, and Busby, Rosa Lee. Compilers. *Some Early Alabama Churches*. Birmingham: Parchment Press, 1973.

Wood, Clement. *Nigger: A Novel*. New York: E.P. Dutton and Company, 1922.

Index

Adam, 10
Adams, Oscar, 84, 91, 104
African American Business Leaders, 91-92
African American Masonic Leaders, 91
African American Newspapers, 58-59, 66, 74
African Methodist Episcopal Church (AME), 25, 29-30, 39
African Methodist Episcopal Zion Church (AME Zion), 25, 40-41
Alabama Christian Movement for Human Rights
   bus integration, 156
   choir, 153
   city park integration, 153
   founding, 141-142
   gospel music, 153-154
   hiring of policeman, 155-156
   inner circle, 148
   limited gains, 160
   laymen, 152-153
   membership, 155
   militant, 155 opposition to, 146, 160-161
   park integration, 158
   similarity to a church, 152-155
   school integration, 157-158
   strategy, 155
   ushers, 154
   voting registration, 158-159
   weekly meetings, 154
   women, 154
Alabama Federation of Colored Civic Leagues, 125
Alabama Penny Savings Bank, 41, 61-65
Alabama Women's Clubs, 56, 84, 91
Alford, R. L., 132, 133, 145
Allen Chapel AME Church, 32
Allen Christian Endeavor Society, 85
Allen Temple AME Church, 33
Alstork, F.W., 92
Apostolic Overcoming Holy Church of God, 117
Atmore, William, 94
Avondale School, 59
Baptist Church, 24-25, 37-39, 79-80
Baptist Education Association, 73
Baptist Young People's Union (BYPU), 85
Becton, Wilson Evangelist, 84
Benefit societies, 74-75

Bessemer churches, 33
Bethel AME Church, 29
Bethel AME Zion Church, 25
Bethel Baptist Church, 32, 104
Bethlehem Methodist Church, 10
Billups, Charles, 149
Birmingham Baptist College, 71, 95, 100, 130, 145, 146
Birmingham Baptist Ministers' Conference, 82, 84, 128, 129, 134, 135, 138, 142, 146, 160
Birmingham churches
    adjustment to urban life, 48
    democratic spirit, 83
    education, 67-72
    meeting places, 83
    moral character, 50-54
    press, 56-57
    protest, 74-75
    professional classes, 85-87
    refuge, 50
    self-esteem, 49-50, 81-82
    schools, 57
    social life, 49
    Sunday worship, 41-45, 81
    talent development, 82
    youth activities, 85-86
    welfare, 72-73
Birmingham pastors
    attempt to build hospital, 130
    business leaders, 56
    criticism by communists, 104
    economic freedom, 131
    as editors, 56-57
    growing militancy, 123-27-129, 131-140
    leaders, 55, 57, 77
    officers of NAACP, 129
    opposition to communism, 103-104
    opposition to black relocation, 137-138
    personal courage, 134
    preaching, 44-45, 49-50, 128
    preservers of institutions, 129-130
    presidents of NAACP, 139
    protest leaders, 74, 132-132-133
    supporters of NAACP, 139-140
    supporters of voting rights, 133
Birmingham Reporter, 84, 92, 97, 103
Birmingham World, 126, 137, 143, 147, 151
Black Belt Churches, 21-22
Booker T. Washington Insurance Company, 94, 131, 142
Boothe, Charles Octavius, 47, 71
Broad Street Baptist Church, 37-38, 41, 72
Brooks, C.W., 69
Brownville Methodist Church, 27
Brown, William Wells, 7

Index

Brown v. Board of Education, 142,
Bryant Chapel AME Church, 30
Cahawba Baptist Church, 9-10
Camp Meetings, 4-5
Canaan Baptist Church (white), 4, 9, 13, 14
Canaan Baptist Church (black), 14, 16, 22, 33
Canepa, John Father, 49
Capers, Charles, 5
Caste system, 23
Central Alabama Institute and College, 70, 95-96
Central Baptist Minister's Conference, 134
Chanting preaching, 44, 81
Church of God in Christ, 116-117
Churches of early migrants, 27-35
Civil Rights Act of 1964, 141, 161
Civil War in Jones Valley, 11-12
Clinton, George Bishop, 40
Coffee, Thomas, 32
Colored Methodist Episcopal Church, 26, 71-72
Communism in Birmingham, 102-105, 125
Conner, Eugene (Bull), 142-143, 160, 161
Cross, John, 161
Daniel Payne College, 72, 79, 130-131, 159
Davis, P.D., 85
Depression, 101-102
Diffay, J.O., 41

Discrimination, 123-124, 141, 142
Disfranchisement, 55-56, 79, 138
Doyle, H.S., 58, 74
Eason, James, 53-54, 104
Easonian Baptist Seminary, 146
Edmonds, Henry, 104
Ephesus Seventh Day Adventist Church, 28
Elyton Iron Works Mission, 5
First Baptist Church, Brighton, 34
First Baptist Church, East Bessemer, 29
First Baptist Church, Ensley, 33
First Baptist Church, Graymont, 28
First Baptist Church, Kingston, 27
First Baptist Church, Powderly, 14
First Baptist Church, Pratt City, 27
First Baptist Church, Woodlawn 80, 82
First Methodist, Tarrant, 4
First Congregational Church, 84, 88-89
Fisher, Charles L., 41, 52-53, 59, 90-91, 92
Forten, Charlotte, 6
Founding of Birmingham, 19-20
Fourteenth Street Baptist Church, 33

Fraternal groups in
    Birmingham, 58
Freedmen's Aid Society, 70
Gaines Chapel AME Church,
    28
Gaines, Wesley, 39, 68
Gardner, Edward, 148-149
Gaston, Arthur, G., 91, 94,
    131, 147
Genovese, Eugene, 6
Goodgame, John, Jr., 128-
    129, 130
Goodgame, John W.,
    Sr. Birmingham Baptist
    College, 71
    Birth and early life, 96-
    97
    Builder, 97
    Community leader, 98
    Education,73, 99-100
    Friendship with whites,
    98
    Moral character, 99
    Opposition to
    communism, 104
    Self-help philosophy, 98
Gospel music, 105-107
Grace, Bayliss E., 11
Green, J.J., 71
Greek Orthodox Church, 48
Green Liberty Baptist Church,
    32
Harmony Street Baptist
    Church, 80, 93
Hawkins, Williamson, 3
Holcombe, Hosea, 10
Holiness Church, 27, 113-119
Hood, James Bishop, 51
Hudson, B.H., 60, 88
Hudson, B.H., Mrs., 62
Hudson, Hosea, 102-104

Interdenominational
    Ministerial Alliance, 75, 134
Jackson, Andrew, 3
Jackson, Emory, 126, 132,
    143, 147, 151
Jackson Street Baptist
    Church, 46, 80
Jefferson County Baptist
    Association, 38
Jefferson County Betterment
    League, 152
Jefferson County Progresssive
    Democratic Council, 122
Jerusalem Baptist Church, 33
Job, 10-11
Johnson, Charles, 5
Johnson Chapel AME Zion
    Church, 25
Jones Valley, 3- 5, 12, 17
Jones Valley Methodist
    Circuit, 10
Jordon, T.L., 57, 74
Kendrick, M.G., 32
King, Martin Luther, Jr., 141,
    142, 160, 161, 162
Kingston school, 57
Ku Klux Klan, 78, 131, 132
Ladd, Hewitt, 6
Lane, T.L., 145
Latham, Sam, 5, 15
Lauderdale, W.L. 41, 56
Lily Grove Baptist Church, 80
Lively Hope Baptist Church,
    82
Lomax Hannon College, 72
Macedonia Baptist Church,
    Ensley, 33, 73
Magnolia AME Church, 29
Mason Chapel Methodist, 29,
    71
Mason, Charles, H., 117

Index

Mays, Benjamin, 80-82, 149
Methodist Episcopal Church, 26, 71-72
Methodist Minister's Alliance, 134
Metropolitan AME Zion Church, 31, 83, 89, 92
Metropolitan Baptist Church, 38
Metropolitan CME Church, Ensley, 33
Migration of African Americans, 20-21,77, 79
Miles College, 70-71, 72, 96, 131, 159, 160
Miller Memorial Presbyterian Church, 69, 122
Missionary society meeting, 46
Mitchell, G.W., 30, 33, 56
Mixon, Winfred, 30, 39-40, 74
Mt. Pleasant Methodist Church, 26
Mt. Zion Baptist Church, Ishkooda, 33
Morning Star Methodist Church, 26
Mims, William Jemison, 6, 11, 12, 14
Mt. Calvary Baptist Church, Leeds, 15
Mt. Hebron Baptist Church, Leeds, 9
Mt. Hebron Baptist Church, North Birmingham, 82
Mt. Joy, 5, 15, 16
Mt. Pilgrim Baptist Association, 16, 38-39, 82, 85, 94
Mt. Pilgrim Women's Convention, 74
Mt. Pilgrim Baptist Church, 14, 16
Mt. Pleasant Baptist Church, Leeds, 16
Mt. Vernon Baptist Church, 16
Mt. Zion Baptist Church, Ishkooda, 14
Mt. Zion Baptist Church, Rising, 82
Mudd, Willliam Judge, 12
National Association for the Advancement of Colored People, 78, 23-124,126-127, 128, 139-140, 144-146, 162
National Negro Banker's Association, 66
National Negro Business League, 62, 65
New Bethlehem Baptist Church, 28
New Hope Baptist Church, 27
New Salem Baptist Church, Bessemer, 27
New Salem Baptist Church, Muscoda, 29
New Zion Baptist Church, Bessemer, 33, 73
Nicholson, James, 80
Oak Grove Baptist Church, Brighton, 34, 59, 73
Olmstead, Frederick, 6
Owen, W. C., 57
Parker, Arthur, H., 62-63, 90
Parker (Industrial) High School, 57, 62
Payne, Daniel, 7, 71, 127

Pentecostal Church, 27, 113-120
Pettiford, William R.
    birth and early life, 58
    branches of Penny Bank, 64
    builds Sixteenth Street Baptist Church, 41
    Christian family life, 52
    establishes Christian Aid Society, 73
    friendship with Booker T. Washington, 58-59, 74
    failure of Penny Bank, 64-65
    founder of Alabama Penny Bank, 60-61
    founder of Parker High School, 60
    founder of Representative Council, 59-60
    homeownership, 63
    pastor, 59, 90
    president of National Negro Banker's Association, 64
    president of Alabama Penny Bank, 61-65
    protest, 74
Pettiford, William, R., Mrs., 71-72
Petty's Chapel AME Zion Church, 25
Phillips, Herbert, J., 60
Pilgrim Rest Baptist Church, 10
Pleasant Hill Methodist Church, 10
Pollard, Robert, T., 74
Porter, John, 146, 156

Prejudice against blacks, 23-24
Protestant Episcopal Diocese, 69
Pruitt, G. E., 145
Quartet singing, 107-113
Ragland, F.C., 93
Randolph, George, 138
Ravizee, Shelton, H., 94-95
Reese, Carlton, 153
Riddick, C.S., 38
Reconstruction in Jones Valley, 12
Riley, W. H., 5
Rogers, L. J., 151
Roman Catholic Church, 48-49, 128
Ruhama Baptist Church, 9, 14, 15
St. James AME, 27, 59
St. James Baptist Church, 82
St. James Methodist, Warrior, 27
St. John AME, 32, 40-41, 57, 69
St. John Baptist Church, Pratt City, 42
St. John Episcopal, 10
St. Mark AME, Brighton, 30
St. Mark's Academy, 69
St. Mark Episcopal Church, 87
St. Paul CME Church, 14, 26
St. Paul Methodist, 26
St. Phillips Street Baptist Church, 13
Salem Baptist Church, 9
Sardis Baptist Church, 57, 145
Sears, M., 104-105

Index

Segregation, 55, 56, 79, 141, 142,
Shady Grove Baptist Church, 15
Shaw, Benjamin, J., Bishop, 129, 130, 133
Shiloh Baptist, 41, 48, 56, 69, 73-74
Shores, Arthur Attorney, 127, 145
Shortridge, W. E., 143, 152, 153
Shuttlesworth, Fred
   autocratic leadership, 143
   birth and early life, 147
   charismatic leadership, 147, 157
   coming to Birmingham, 147
   divine compulsion, 147
   forms Interdenominational Ministerial Association, 138
   house bombed, 148
   invites King to Birmingham, 160
   organizes ACMHR, 144-146
   petitions for African American policeman, 138
   work in NAACP, 144-145
Sixteenth Street Baptist Church, 31-32, 41, 58, 60, 83, 85, 89, 92
Sixth Street Peace Baptist Church, 80
Sixth Ave Baptist Church, 32, 82, 83, 84
Slavery in Jones Valley, 3-4
Slave Preachers, 10-11, 15-16
Slave Religion, 6-9
Smith, Nelson, Jr., 145, 150-151
South Elyton Baptist Church, 38
Southern Negro Improvement Association, 135-136
Southern Christian Leadership Conference, 159
Spirituals, 8
Spiritualist Church, 115-116
Splits in Baptist Churches, 80
Sturdivant, Elder M. C., 28
Tabernacle Baptist Church, 32, 133
Temperance, 51
Thomas Elementary School, 57
Thirgood CME Church, 26-27, 83, 89
Trinity Baptist Church, 38, 93
Truss, John, 10
Tuggle Institute, 57, 68
Turner, Henry McNeal, 30-31, 39, 51
Twenty-Third Street Baptist Church, 52
Ullman, Samuel, 62
Union Baptist Church, 15
Union churches, 30
United Mine Workers of America, 125
Van Hoose, James, A., 87
Waldrop, A.J., 15

Walker, Thomas W., 41, 43
 birth and early life, 65
 businesses established, 66-67
 established Union Central Relief Association, 67
 influenced by Booker T. Washington, 65
 ordained by Pettiford, 65
 pastor of First Baptist, Brighton, 66
 pastor of Shiloh Baptist Church, 47-48, 66
 pastor of Sixth Avenue Baptist Church, 66
 preaching, 43-44, 66
Ware, James L., 132, 133, 135, 137, 146, 157
Ware, William, 15-16
Washington, Booker T., 58-59, 62, 76
Welch, Isaiah, 52
Wilson, James General, 12
Woods, Abraham, Jr., 149
Woods, Calvin, 150
Woodward AME, 30
Women in churches, 45-46, 73-74

For Product Safety Concerns and Information please contact our EU
representative GPSR@taylorandfrancis.com
Taylor & Francis Verlag GmbH, Kaufingerstraße 24, 80331 München, Germany

www.ingramcontent.com/pod-product-compliance
Lightning Source LLC
Chambersburg PA
CBHW071828300426
44116CB00009B/1482